International Money

International Money

Theory, Evidence and Institutions

Paul Hallwood and Ronald MacDonald
with contributions from Robert Shaw

Basil Blackwell

First published 1986

Basil Blackwell Ltd
108 Cowley Road, Oxford OX4 1JF, UK

Basil Blackwell Inc.
432 Park Avenue South, Suite 1503,
New York, NY 10016, USA

British Library Cataloguing in Publication Data
Hallwood, Paul
International money: theory, evidence and
institutions.
1. International finance
I. Title II. MacDonald, Ronald III. Shaw,
Robert, *1936–*
332.4'5 HG3881
ISBN 0-631-14445-5
ISBN 0-631-14446-3 Pbk.

Library of Congress Cataloging in Publication Data
Hallwood, Paul.
International money.

Bibliography: p.
Includes index.
1. International finance. I. MacDonald, Ronald.
II. Shaw, Robert, 1936 May 2– . III. Title.
HG3881.H255 1986   332.4'5   86-6171
ISBN 0-631-14445-5
ISBN 0-631-14446-3 (pbk.)

Typeset by Unicus Graphics Ltd, Horsham
Printed in Great Britain by T. J. Press, Padstow

Contents

1 Introduction

The field of international monetary economics has become an especially dynamic discipline during the last fifteen years or so as major institutional changes and theoretical developments have followed upon one another. At the institutional level, gold has been demonetized and the major industrial countries have abandoned the adjustable peg exchange rate system; whilst at the theoretical level attention has switched away from the theory of the balance of payments to finding a robust theory of exchange rate determination. This is hardly surprising as the causes and consequences of exchange rate movements are of concern to many groups – governments, bankers and private asset holders besides international economists.

David Hume and Gustav Cassel did provide widely held theories of the balance of payments and the exchange rate but their theories with their modern developments have been found to be deficient in certain respects. Cassel's theory of purchasing power parity (ppp) simply does not seem to explain the actual behaviour of exchange rates since they were floated in the early 1970s; and Hume's theories, which culminated in the monetary approach to the balance of payments, are deficient when adapted to explain the determination of exchange rates. The main problem with the ppp is that it is exclusively a current account explanation of the exchange rate which does not seem to explain exchange rate movements very well. On the other hand, the monetary views of the exchange rate tend to concentrate overmuch on the capital account and to ignore both the large menu of assets which are now internationally transferable and the feed-back effects of current account imbalances on asset holders' wealth.

In chapters 4–8 these points, mentioned only in the barest outline here, are developed at a level suitable to senior undergraduate and postgraduate students. They are preceded by a short chapter on balance of payments theory developed between *circa* 1930 and 1960 as well as referring to Hume's eighteenth-century original version of the monetary approach to the balance of payments. Chapter 4 looks at purchasing power parity and its deficiencies and subsequent chapters explain the modern monetary, asset and portfolio approaches to the exchange rate. Chapter 8 assesses the econometric evidence on the efficiency of currency markets. The final section of this Introduction provides a perspective preview of these chapters on international monetary theory.

Institutional developments precipitated much of this theoretical frenzy for until 1971 and again briefly during part of 1972–3 the major industrial countries pegged their exchange rates to gold and so created the so-called parity grid exchange rate system. The institutional setting for this was the international conference held in the Mount Washington Hotel at Bretton Woods, New Hampshire, in 1944. Following the unhappy experience with floating exchange rates during the 1930s gold was resurrected as the commodity base of the international monetary system. A good deal of the 1960s was spent by leading economists and the IMF trying to find a substitute for gold. It was eventually agreed to create the Special Drawing Right (SDR) account in 1967 as an IMF operated 'paper gold' replacement. So far, though, the SDR has not even approached the level of importance which had been planned for it and international liquidity is still largely augmented, as it was in the 1960s, through US balance of payments deficits. But, in briefest outline, what are the main events during the last decade and a half of international monetary history?

'Shocks' and Instability

The period 1970–3 is most interesting as it marks the breakdown of the Bretton Woods international monetary system: i.e. the demonetization of gold and move to floating exchange rates. By 1970 the US was virtually freed from the obligation to supply gold to either the private market or to central banks at $35 per oz and pursued a policy of benign neglect towards its balance of payments. In fact in 1970 the US ran a balance of payments deficit of $10 billion compared to a surplus of almost $3 billion in 1969. The deficit was wholly due to a large capital outflow from the US to European countries and this outflow persisted through to 1973. The net outflow of dollars through the balance of payments increased the monetary base in the rest of the world (ROW) since, for example, European countries were forced to monetize their capital inflows in an attempt to prevent their currencies from rising. The increases in the ROW's money supply for the period 1970–3 suggests that they were unsuccessful in sterilizing the effects of the reserve inflows on their monetary base. For example, the ROW's money supply increased by 21 per cent per year between 1970 and 1972, having averaged about ten per cent in the years preceding 1970. By the third quarter of 1971 the exchange rate realignments that took place with the dissolution of the Bretton Woods system led to a US balance of payments surplus and a reduction in the ROW's monetary growth by the end of 1973 to 5.4 per cent. By 1973 and 1974 the effects of the expansion of the world money supply was to raise the ROW's inflation rate to eight per cent and 12 per cent respectively.

The crucial question about the 1970–73 world monetary expansion is: what was its source? On the face of it one would be tempted to infer that it was excess growth of the US money supply spilling through the balance of payments into the rest of the world as in the monetary approach to the balance of payments discussed in chapter 5. It has been argued that excessive monetary growth in the US was a consequence of attempts to finance the Vietnam War via monetized budget deficits. However, a closer look at the figures reveals that during this period, the US money supply increased at a lower rate than the ROW's. How then do we reconcile the low US money supply growth with the rapid growth in international liquidity during the period?

Heller (1976) has argued that during the 1960s the perceived strength of the US dollar induced non-US private entities, particularly commercial bankers, to accumulate large dollar balances. But by the late-1960s such investors, worried by the accelerating inflation in the US and a belief that the dollar was overvalued, began to switch from dollars to other currencies. For example, during the period end-1969 to end-1971 liquid US liabilities to private foreigners fell from $28 billion to $15 billion and furthermore deposits at US banks owned by foreign commercial banks fell from $19 billion to $7.3 billion. There is, moreover, some evidence to suggest that there was a decreased demand for dollars in the US (i.e. by individuals and corporations in anticipation of the devaluations which occurred in 1971 and 1973). Hence the net capital outflow from the US during 1970 to 1973 resulted not from excessive US monetary growth but rather from a substitution of other currencies for dollars.

The outflow of dollars, the collapse of the international monetary system and accelerating world inflation led many countries to adopt floating exchange rates. This was partly because international capital flows had become so enormous as to overwhelm a nation's foreign exchange reserves and partly, proponents of floating exchange rates argued, so that countries could insulate their own domestic monetary conditions from external monetary shocks. It has been pointed out that the dispersion of national inflation rates amongst the seven leading industrial countries was higher in the fourteen or so years after 1971 than it had been in the previous decade of pegged exchange rates. Yet this difference was not great and there is a striking fact: the correlation of real GDP rates of growth amongst industrial countries which had been low in the 1960s became high in the 1970s (de Grauwe, 1983). Why was this?

The answer seems to lie with the impact of three major shocks to the international economic and financial system during the 1970s which affected all countries at the same time. Chronologically, the first was the flood of dollars into foreign exchange reserves, referred to above, which set off monetary expansion and stimulated economic activity around the world. The 1971–3 world economic boom was unusual both for the large number of countries which participated in it and for the speed of its acceleration from cyclical trough to following peak (Cooper and Lawrence, 1975). The second shock was the fourfold rise in oil prices in 1973 which added to world inflation and sent the industrial oil importing countries and the non-oil less developed countries (ldcs) into balance of payments deficit. The oil shock was repeated in 1979–80. On the first occasion the industrial countries attempted to prevent deflation of real economic activity by running larger fiscal deficits and the non-oil less developed countries stepped up the rate of their international borrowing. While, after 1979–80, many of the industrial countries responded with a policy of monetary tightness in an effort to curtail inflation and the less developed oil importers soon ran into a debt crisis which provoked the adoption of severely deflationary policies.

What then of the case for flexible exchange rates which had been so strongly argued in many quarters in the 1960s? (See, e.g. Friedman, 1953 and Johnson, 1970).

The case for flexible exchange rates was usually made with reference to the supposed independence that that regime gave to domestic economic management, particularly control over the money supply. With a flexible exchange rate the objectives of full employment, economic growth and price stability could be pursued without the authorities being constrained by the balance of payments consequences of their actions. The exchange rate would take the strain. Indeed, it has been argued that the pegged but adjustable exchange rate system (supplemented by conditional liquidity managed by the IMF) created at Bretton Woods itself increased the scope for domestic economic management in comparison with the fixed exchange rate gold standard system of 1870–1914 (Cooper, 1982). But do the facts bear out the argument that progression to floating exchange rates would improve economic and financial stability in each of the member countries of the international financial system?

The evidence for the UK, the US and Germany – shown in table 1.1 – is by no means supportive of this proposition, in fact the opposite is often true. It is not being argued here, though, that floating exchange rates were themselves responsible for the increased instability. It is more likely that the causality was the other way around. Thus, exchange rate instability has not necessarily been excessive if it has been caused by volatility in the fundamentals which drive exchange rates – the money supply and real income, for example. These issues are discussed at length in chapters 6 and 7 on, respectively, the monetary and portfolio approaches to the exchange rate and in chapter 8 on the efficiency of foreign exchange markets. It is, however, difficult if not impossible to know for sure what the effect of floating exchange rates has been as a rerun of the 1970s and 1980s with fixed exchange rates is not possible!

The international financial system of the 1950s and 1960s still had gold as its nominal commodity base and, as in the period of the nineteenth century gold standard, inflation rates were contained below a relatively low ceiling. In all three cases shown in table 1.1 inflation was much higher in the 1972–84 period than it had been before the change over to managed floating. From a monetarist perspective the reason for this is clear: money growth was also sharply higher in the UK and the US (not in Germany though – floating the Deutschmark in 1973 had to some extent relieved German monetary aggregates from the distorting effects of periodic surges in currency inflow). Higher inflation might not have mattered too much except that the variability of inflation in each country also sharply increased after 1971 – almost tripling in the UK and US and doubling in Germany. If more unstable inflation is also less predictable inflation, microeconomic efficiency will have suffered as changes in relative prices became less predictable. A decline in real GNP growth did occur after 1971 but this cannot have been entirely due to microeconomic factors, rather lower pressure of aggregate demand relative to that experienced in the 1960s was the dominant factor. This was caused partly by and partly as a disinflationary reaction to the shocks suffered by the world economy in the 1970s.

It is entirely to be expected that the move to floating rates would correspond with the increased exchange rate variability of 1972–84 compared with 1960–71 (see tables 1.1 and 1.2); and, although

Table 1.1 Growth and Instability 1960–71 and 1972–84

	UK		US		Germany	
	1960–71	1972–84	1960–71	1972–84	1960–71	1972–84
Average annual inflation (%)[a]	4.15	11.47	2.64	7.27	2.58	4.39
Variability of the annual price index[b]	0.15	0.43	0.11	0.30	0.09	0.17
Average annual % growth in real GNP[c]	2.86	1.30	4.10	2.50	4.10	2.00
Average annual growth in money %[d]	4.10	12.40	4.47	14.02	7.63	6.66
Variability of annual average money stock[b]	0.16	0.52	0.16	0.26	0.26	0.24
Variability of annual average exchange rate[b,e]	0.07	0.17	–	–	0.05	0.15
Variability of annual average reserves[b,f]	1.29	0.53	0.57	0.69	0.64	0.27
Variability of annual average interest rates[b,g]	0.21	0.23	0.32	0.34	0.40	0.40

Source: IMF, *International Financial Statistics*, Yearbook 1985.

Notes: [a] Consumer price index
[b] Coefficient of variation
[c] Measured in 1980 prices, exponential time trend
[d] M1, exponential time trend
[e] $ per £ and DM per $
[f] Total reserves excluding gold
[g] Treasury Bill rates in UK and US, call money rates in Germany

exchange rates continued to be managed, that the variability of foreign exchange reserves would decline relative to 1960–71 when countries were allowing very little variation in their exchange rates.

What is perhaps more surprising is that there was no great change in the variability of interest rates: a floating exchange rate regime is supposed to increase monetary independence and so allow countries to fine tune independent monetary policies. Interest rate variability

Table 1.2 Mean Absolute Monthly Percentage Changes in Prices and Exchange Rates (June 1973 to February 1979)

	Wholesale Price Index (WPI)	Cost of Living Index (COL)	Spot exchange rate against the dollar	COL/COL$_{US}$
US	0.009	0.007	–	–
UK	0.014	0.012	0.020	0.007
France	0.011	0.008	0.020	0.004
Germany	0.004	0.004	0.024	0.004

Source: Frenkel and Musa (1980).

Note: Monthly data are used in this table as the annual data used in table 1.1 masks a lot of the within-year variability that is more clearly shown in the monthly data.

could, on these grounds, be expected to have increased. That this was not especially marked might, of course, have been due to a country maintaining similar policies on interest rates pre- and post-1971. But this is probably not the main reason for the similar interest rate variability experience of the two periods. (It might be noted that quarterly data, rather than the annual data upon which table 1.1 is based, shows a larger, 40 per cent, increase in interest rate instability in the US and the UK and an actual fall in Germany, but these changes are still not great when compared with the much larger changes in the variability of the consumer price index, money, exchange rates and foreign exchange reserves).

More fundamentally, it is now widely believed that the arguments that floating exchange rates must increase monetary independence were bogus. For example, the early proponents of floating exchange rates placed almost total emphasis on the current account in their view of the determination of the exchange rate. The dominant feature, however, of the international monetary system of the 1970s and 1980s has been the huge outstanding pool of international capital responsive to small interest differentials between financial centres. In their effects on the exchange rate, such capital movements swamp day-to-day current account transactions. As we shall see in later chapters, a high degree of capital mobility has fundamental implications for the determination of a floating exchange rate and for the insulation properties of such a rate.

The supposed monetary independence of floating exchange rates may be questioned from a different but related perspective. Thus, 'there is no such thing as independence so long as governments have inflation, real wage and employment objectives' (Dornbusch, 1983). That is, so long as governments adopt explicit, or even implicit, exchange rate targets, changes in monetary conditions still get transmitted from one country to another and, given the fact that governments do pursue domestic macroeconomic targets, cannot be locked out (or locked in). This is especially true of the international monetary system as it now stands with one large economy – the USA – dominating the level of interest rates throughout the system. For example, monetary tightness in the first half of the 1980s led to dollar appreciation which induced European industrial countries, fearing inflationary effects, also to pursue monetary tightness. The earlier experience of the second half of the 1970s also supports this view of monetary policy dependence in the international economy. Expansionary monetary policy and lower interest rates in America led to dollar depreciation and enhanced American competitiveness; this was countered by expansionary monetary policy and lower interest rates in Europe so as to regain some of the competitive edge lost to America (de Grauwe, 1983).

The main difference between the 1960s and the later period is that in the 1960s synchronized changes in monetary conditions were achieved through changes in the foreign exchange reserve component of domestic money supply, as is explained by the monetary approach to the balance of payments, while since 1971, synchronization has been brought about by countries being induced to follow similar policies with regard to changes in the domestic component of local money supply.

However, the 'monetary-conditions-dependence' view should not be overstated. Countries do retain discretion over the choice of macroeconomic objectives and, therefore, over their explicit or implicit exchange rate targets. The election of a new government in the UK in 1979 is one such case. The new government raised the priority of reducing the rate of inflation and so adopted a policy of increased monetary tightness and accepted sharp exchange rate appreciation. The extent of sterling's appreciation might have been greater than the authorities had expected (or wanted), the exchange rate following a time path that accords well with the exchange rate 'overshooting' hypothesis – see chapter 6.

The Following Chapters

Chapter 2 gives a brief insight into traditional exchange rate theory. According to the 'traditional' paradigm that exchange rate is determined by the supply and demand flow for foreign currency, and exchange rate stability requires the fulfilment of the Marshall–Lerner condition. The traditional covered interest parity theory of the forward exchange rate, similarly set in a flow-variables context, is also explainedin chapter 2. Keynesian, or income-expenditure, theories which were developed in the two decades following the publication of *The General Theory* in 1936 are then briefly outlined and are seen as stepping stones towards the modern monetary and asset stock-adjustment theories of the balance of payments and exchange rate determination.

Before looking at these, however, we assess the problems of macroeconomic management in an open economy in chapter 3. After all, one of the main benefits of improving our understanding of the exchange rate mechanism is to enhance the efficacy of economic management. The plank upon which this chapter is based is the Mundell–Fleming model developed in the early 1960s and later transformed to account for modern theoretical developments in, for instance, the theory of rational expectations.

The traditional balance of payments theory considered in chapter 2 contrasts sharply with the Monetary Approach to the Balance of Payments (MABP) which is discussed in chapter 5. Proponents of the MABP argue that the balance of payments is a monetary phenomenon and should be analysed using familiar monetary tools; namely, the demand for and supply of money. One of the key feature of the MABP is its implications for economic policy: for example, a devaluation can at best only have a transitory effect on the balance of payments and the effects of domestic credit expansion on the domestic economy will be purely transitory because of offsetting balance of payments movements. The econometric evidence on such policy conclusions is also presented in chapter 5, as is the evidence on the determination of the world inflation rate.

In chapter 4 the hypothesis that exchange rates are determined by relative national price levels – purchasing power parity (ppp) – is discussed and shown to be questionable on both theoretical and empirical grounds. One particular feature of the recent behaviour of prices *vis à vis* exchange rates is that the former have exhibited less variability than the latter, as table 1.2 shows. Thus short-run, monthly, movements in exchange rates seem to bear little relationship to national inflation rates.

How do we explain the above volatility of exchange rates? A number of researchers have argued that the exchange rate is more akin to prices of assets, such as bonds and stocks, than the prices of commodities such as those included in the WPI and COL indices in table 1.2. Viewing the exchange rate as an asset price leads to statements such as: 'Exchange rates are determined in asset markets which are conceptually different to the markets for ordinary goods and thus require analysis using tools different to the standard kit of demand and supply analysis.' The tools of the asset approach to the exchange rate are considered in chapters 6, 7 and 8.

In chapter 6 the concept of the exchange rate as an asset price is discussed and three particular versions, which concentrate on the demand for and supply of money, are considered: namely, the flex-price monetary approach, the fix-price monetary approach and the currency substitution approach. These monetary models give insights into the issue of exchange rate volatility. The flex-price monetary model highlights the crucial role that expectations play in determining the exchange rate. Thus, if, for example, agents expect less monetary growth in the future this may move the current exchange rate by a greater amount than is justified by the current money supply. The sticky-price monetary model, due to Dornbusch (1976) gives a story of exchange rate volatility in terms of asymmetric adjustment speeds in goods and asset markets. The currency substitution model, which focuses on the desire by agents to hold a portfolio of currencies in a regime of floating exchange rates, shows that exchange rate volatility may reflect agents switching between different currencies. The policy implications of the monetary-asset models are also stressed in chapter 6.

The portfolio balance approach to the determination of the exchange rate is considered in chapter 7. This model falls within the asset class of models, but it differs from the monetary models considered in chapter 6 in that it includes a broader menu of assets in the determination of the exchange rate. The portfolio model can usefully be used to analyse policy changes, particularly of a fiscal nature, which are not amenable to discussion in the monetary model. The portfolio model can also be used to give answers as to why exchange rates may be volatile and also give an interesting adjustment mechanism for the exchange rate from short-run to long-run equilibrium.

Further implications of the exchange rate as an asset price are considered in chapter 8. In particular, the implications of the efficient markets hypothesis for the forward exchange rate are discussed and empirical evidence presented. Furthermore, it is shown that the bulk of exchange rate changes should be unanticipated and respond to new information about such factors as money supplies and income. Other explanations of exchange rate volatility which rely on an essentially 'non-rational' view of foreign exchange market participants are also given in chapter 8.

However, developments in international monetary theory do not have an abstract life all of their own; rather they have grown out of the changing international monetary system, the features of which theory itself tries to explain. Thus chapter 9 on international monetary arrangements briefly describes the evolution of the international monetary system since the Second World War. Attention is paid to the Bretton Woods system, its origin, objectives and mode of operation. The roles of gold, the IMF and international economic management are pointed out. But the Bretton Woods system was to turn into a kind of 'dollar standard', with the US dollar and American financial stability at the centre of the international monetary system rather than gold and the IMF as had been planned at Bretton Woods in 1944. The problems encountered by the international monetary system from the late 1960s onwards are viewed as being problems of a 'dollar standard on the booze'. The important question of the optimal amount of international liquidity is also considered in this chapter.

One of the most prominent features of international finance in the last two decades or so is the enhanced mobility of money between financial centres. This feature has brought both benefits – providing a mechanism for financing planned current account deficits for example, and costs – rendering independent national monetary management more difficult. Chapter 10 on the Eurocurrency market explains the function of Eurobanking and its economic significance. The Eurobanks are seen as being akin to non-bank financial intermediaries which have little or no power to create money but are an efficient means for intermediating credit between ultimate depositors and borrowers.

While Third World countries were once seen as peripheral to the international monetary system this is hardly true today. Chapter 11 considers the relationship between the IMF and the Third World, paying particular attention to the rationale behind the IMF's payments adjustment policies and the structuralist school's criticisms of these policies. After considering some empirical evidence conclusions are drawn that are generally supportive of the IMF's stance which gives priority to medium-term adjustment over medium- and long-term financing.

Chapter 12 on international debt explains that the origin of the international debt crisis, which came to a head in 1982, lies with the reliance that many Third World countries place on financing rather than the adjustment of payments deficits. For the non-oil less developed countries the shock of higher oil prices contributed in a major way to the deterioration of their balance of payments positions.

Additionally, some of these countries as well as the heavily populated oil exporting countries allowed large budget and external payments deficits to undermine their credit-worthiness in international credit markets.

The final chapter of the book assesses a response by a group of developed countries to the deteriorating international monetary environment: this is the establishment of the European Monetary System in 1979. In an effort to create the monetary stability that has been lacking in the wider international monetary system, several West European countries clubbed together to manage exchange rates and components of their international liquidity. The political motivation, institutional characteristics and economic aspects of the EMS are given consideration.

2 Basic Exchange Rate Concepts and Some Early Balance of Payments Analysis

In section 1 of this chapter the concepts of spot and forward exchange rates are defined and the market clearing processes by which they are determined explained. Section 2 reviews the main strands of international monetary theory which predate the modern monetary and asset approaches to the balance of payments and exchange rate determination. This is done so that the reader may have a perspective within which to understand and assess the recent contributions to the literature.

SECTION 1 EXCHANGE RATES

The Spot Exchange Rate

The spot exchange rate, S, is the domestic currency price of a unit of foreign exchange for immediate (within three days) delivery. The forward rate, F, is for the purchase or sale of foreign currency at some future date, usually a standard contract period – 30, 60 or 90 days ahead. Spot and forward rates are determined daily in the foreign exchange markets, which are formed by banks in various countries in instantaneous communication with each other. Spatial arbitrage maintains a uniform exchange rate between any two currencies (transactions costs apart) throughout the world.

The factors behind the supply of foreign currency are the items which appear on the credit side of the balance of payments (exports of goods and services, inflows of foreign capital and the running down of official reserves) and those behind the demand for foreign currency are the items on the debit side of the balance of payments (imports of goods and services, overseas investment and additions to

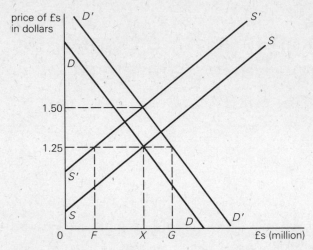

Figure 2.1   Supply and demand for foreign currency

official reserves. Determination of the sterling/dollar exchange rate is shown in figure 2.1. This is what may be called *the balance of payments view of the exchange rate* as it is flows through the balance of payments accounts which determine a country's exchange rate.

If *DD* and *SS* are respectively the demand and supply schedules for pounds, the equilibrium price would be $1.25 and the equilibrium quantity £x million. If tastes were to change in both countries in favour of British goods the demand and supply schedules in figure 2.1 would move to new positions. With the new schedules *S'S'* and *D'D'* the new equilibrium price of pounds will be higher at $1.50 per pound – sterling will have appreciated and the dollar depreciated.

If the UK wanted to maintain a fixed exchange rate then to prevent appreciation from the parity of $1.25, in the face of such a change the Bank of England would be required to buy dollars, adding them to the official reserves, in exchange for FG pounds – the amount by which demand exceeds supply of pounds at the price of $1.25. To maintain a system of fixed exchange rates in all circumstances the monetary authorities would have to be prepared to buy or sell foreign exchange in unlimited amounts which they cannot do.

On usual assumptions, and assuming other things equal, the exchange rate will be positively related to domestic real income and negatively with the domestic rate of interest. That is, a rise in real income will shift *DD* upwards so causing the exchange rate to depreciate while a rise in the domestic interest rate will cause capital to flow into the country (*DD* and *SS* can both shift downwards) so that the exchange rate appreciates. These results are in sharp contrast with those derived from the *monetary approach to the exchange rate* where a rise in income causes currency appreciation and a rise in the domestic rate of interest depreciation (see chapter 6).

Under a regime of floating rates the degree of exchange rate variability largely depends upon the stability of short-term currency flows through the capital account. Sharp fluctuations in these would be reflected in exchange rates. An important question therefore is would capital flows be stabilizing or destabilizing of the exchange rate? Misinformed speculation or speculation with elastic price expectations would cause the exchange rate to fluctuate more violently than otherwise and this could be damaging for a number of reasons: domestic price levels would be destabilized, the volume of world trade might be reduced due to the increased uncertainty, and real resources would be tied up in risk-reduction facilities such as currency forward, future and option markets.

However, early proponents of floating exchange rates such as Friedman (1953) claimed that speculation would normally serve to stabilize a country's exchange rate since, for the speculators as a group, destabilizing speculation would be unprofitable. In the long run only profitable speculators could survive so that currency speculation was expected to contribute to the stabilization of currency markets. Anyway, despite the misgivings of economists such as Baumol (1957) on the supposed unprofitability of destabilizing speculation, this was the dominant view for 20 years or more amongst economists who generally supported the case for floating exchange rates.

The Forward Exchange Rate

Three groups of participants use the forward exchange market: traders, arbitrageurs and speculators. An international trader of goods or services seeks to divest risks by hedging assets or liabilities denominated in foreign currencies. An arbitrageur seeks a riskless profit from the configuration of interest rates and spot and forward exchange rates. Speculators accept risks, taking open positions in forward exchange in anticipation of exchange rate changes.

The hedger might be an exporter due to be paid in a foreign currency in 60 days. The forward market can be used to sell this foreign currency for domestic currency in 60 days at an exchange rate fixed *now*. Receipts denominated in domestic currency become fixed in value. The position is 'closed', for the hedger has both a foreign currency asset, the foreign currency due in 60 days, matched by a foreign currency liability, the obligation to deliver the foreign currency in fulfilment of the forward contract also in 60 days.

Speculation in forward currency involves lower transaction costs than in spot currency as the opportunity cost of funds is limited to the 10 per cent margin required by the brokerage house. As an example of speculation in forward currency, suppose that the 60 day forward rate for the dollar was £0.80 and that a speculator held the expectation that spot sterling in 60 days would depreciate to £0.85 per dollar. The speculator could contract to buy dollars forward. If correct then the dollars received when the forward contract matures can be sold at a profit of £0.05 per dollar. The speculator's position is 'open' as there is no corresponding asset to set against the liability to buy dollars. (Such an asset could, in the case of a British trader, be 'goods received' from an American exporter whose sterling value will have increased). If the expectation had turned out to be incorrect a loss would have been incurred.

The nature of arbitrage can be explained using the theory of covered interest parity. The theory states that the premium on forward exchange, expressed as a percentage of the spot exchange rate, is equal to the difference in interest rates between a given pair of currency centres.

Arbitrageurs' portfolios are in equilibrium when

$$1 + i^{US} = \frac{1}{S}(1 + i^{UK})F \tag{2.1}$$

That is, equilibrium occurs when the return on one-dollar invested in the US at, say, a 90 day interest rate of i^{US}, is equal to the return on one-dollar, converted into sterling at the spot exchange rate, S, and 'covered' by a forward sale of £$(1 + i^{UK})$ at the 90 day forward rate, F.

Defining p as the forward premium $(F-S)/S$, and by simple manipulation[1] of equation (2.1)

$$p = i^{US} - i^{UK} \tag{2.2}$$

Thus, if $i^{US} > i^{UK}$, forward sterling is at a premium.

The covered interest differential (CD) is defined as

$$CD = (i^{US} - i^{UK}) - p \tag{2.3}$$

which is obtained by rearranging equation 2.2. If $CD > 0$ funds will flow from the UK to the US. Arbitrageurs' profit from investing at the higher interest rate (assuming $i^{US} > i^{UK}$) will be greater than the cost of forward cover (p). When $CD = 0$, arbitrageurs asset portfolios are in equilibrium, and when $CD < 0$ funds will flow to the UK.

Arbitrage funds might flow from a high to a low interest rate country if the cost of this is more than offset by a forward discount on the recipient country's currency. This configuration can arise when the high interest rate country's spot exchange rate is expected to depreciate and is brought about by speculators taking open positions selling that currency on the forward market, so sending it to a forward discount.

Uncovered Interest Parity

Assuming perfect capital mobility but that arbitrageurs are risk neutral, so that they do not use the forward market for cover, there exists the relationship of uncovered interest parity, which must hold at any moment in time. In place of the forward rate of the currency, arbitageurs use the expected future spot rate, S^e. Equilibrium requires that if the interest rate in the US is lower than that in the UK, there must be a premium on the expected future spot rate for the dollar to offset the US interest rate disadvantage, so that a given sum of money will yield the same return in either country. The premium (p) is $\dot{S}^e/S$ where $\dot{S}^e$ is the expected change in the spot exchange rate. But given equation 2.2:

$$\dot{S}^e = (i^{US} - i^{UK})S \qquad (2.4)$$

That is, the expected proportionate appreciation of the dollar is equal to the difference in nominal interest rates (i.e. remember that given the definition of S a reduction is an appreciation).

In reality the forward rate can depart from the *covered* interest parity rate because arbitrageurs are not alone in using the forward market, in particular there are hedgers and speculators. To simplify the analysis traders are assumed always to hedge and that international trade is always balanced so that hedgers' supply and demand for forward exchange are always balanced.

The equilibrium forward exchange rate is then determined by arbitrageurs and speculators as is shown in figure 2.2.

If A is the current exchange rate and with US interest rates above UK interest rates the covered interest arbitrage forward exchange rate for sterling will be at a premium at B with the percentage premium being AB/OA. At this forward exchange rate the increment to an arbitrageur's income from investing at US interest rates rather than the lower British rate is exactly offset by the premium cost of

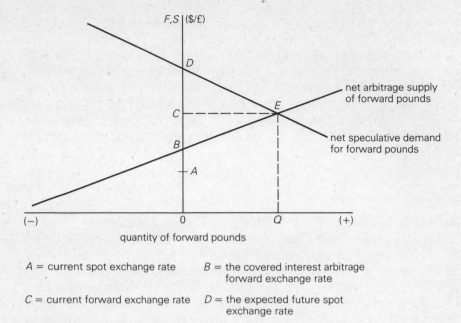

A = current spot exchange rate   B = the covered interest arbitrage
                                      forward exchange rate

C = current forward exchange rate   D = the expected future spot
                                        exchange rate

Figure 2.2   Determining the forward exchange rate

purchasing forward pounds. The net demand for forward pounds will be zero. If the forward rate were to be less than *OB* there would be a net demand for forward pounds as the profit from higher American interest rates is not completely offset by the cost of forward cover. Conversely, if the forward rate was more expensive than *B*, arbitrageurs would supply forward pounds. Thus the net arbitrage supply curve of forward pound slopes upwards from left to right.

Speculators form a view of what they expect the spot rate to be at a relevant future date, e.g. 90 days on if considering the 90 days forward market. For example, *D* may be the expected future spot exchange rate – a depreciation relative to the current spot rate at *A*. If *D* happened to be the current spot exchange rate there would be neither a net supply of nor a demand for forward pounds for speculative purposes. If the forward rate is below the expected future spot rate (*B* is 'below' *D*) speculators expect sterling to appreciate and will create a net demand for forward pounds. If the current spot rate was above *D*, so that sterling depreciation was expected, speculators would contract now to sell sterling forward – in the left quadrant of figure 2.2. Thus the net speculative demand curve will slope down from left to right.

The intersection of the two schedules at E in figure 2.2 establishes the equilibrium forward rate C with arbitrageurs supplying OQ forward pounds to meet the speculators' demand at this price. In this example arbitrageurs would be moving funds to the lower interest rate centre, the UK, and covering themselves forward by supplying pounds, with the forward premium on the pound being such as to more than offset the lower interest rate.

The upward slope of the arbitrage supply curve could arise because arbitrage funds are obtained at rising opportunity cost or because the risks in foreign investment (e.g. sovereign default) are greater than in home investment, or because it leads to imbalance in arbitrageurs' portfolios. If no such problems were faced by arbitrageurs in the availability or allocation of funds the arbitrageurs' supply curve would be perfectly elastic at the covered interest parity rate, B, and would determine the forward rate, with speculators determining the volume of foreign currency exchanged by the two groups. But if the net speculative demand for foreign exchange were infinitely elastic (i.e. with no budget constraint and risk neutrality) and that of arbitrageurs was not, then the former would determine the forward market rate. In reality both parties are likely to have some influence, that party having greater influence whose schedule is more elastic.

The question now arises as to why interest rates differ? One answer is that in a world of capital mobility only nominal interest rates can differ, since the real return must be equalized everywhere. A higher nominal rate of interest will, for an asset of a given risk class, merely compensate for a higher rate of inflation, and relative rates of inflation according to monetary analysis are determined by the relative rates of monetary growth. Hence, in this view, what ultimately happens to the forward rate depends on the rates of monetary growth in the two countries. It is but a short step from analysis of this nature to a new view of the exchange rate which emerged in the 1960s from work by the monetarist school – see chapters 5 and 6. The lineage is much older than this, however, going back to David Hume in the eighteenth century.

SECTION 2 THE BALANCE OF PAYMENTS (by Robert Shaw)

The Balance of Payments

Hume's *monetary explanation* of the adjustment process which would ensure balance in international payments had two components: the price-specie-flow mechanism and the quantity theory of money.

If for reasons of a general rise in prices a country had a deficit in international payments, because cheaper foreign goods supplanted home-produced goods, this would lead to an outflow of specie (i.e. money), which would reduce the quantity of money in the deficit country and increase it in the surplus countries. The changes in the quantities of money according to the quantity theory would reduce prices in the deficit country and raise them elsewhere, with the exchange rates between countries being fixed. The deficit country, in Hume's words, would have 'the advantage of cheapness of labour and commodities', which would encourage exports and discourage imports until equilibrium in the form of 'money nearly proportional to the art and industry of each nation' was restored. Hume effectively assumed a stable demand for money function.

This approach had its critics, e.g. Ricardo, who felt that there was likely to be a role for changes in income as well as changes in price. Empirical studies (e.g. Angell, 1926) also suggested that the mechanism seemed to work too quickly and too well for the specie flows were small, and prices in deficit and surplus countries did not move strongly in opposite directions as the theory suggested they should. Despite the unease with the analysis, it remained orthodox doctrine until it was supplanted by two new bodies of theory: the elasticities approach which rests on relative price changes but ignores money and income-expenditure models developed from Keynes' *General Theory*. The monetary explanation was, though, to resurface and acquired an important position in balance of payments analysis.

The Elasticities Approach

For the equilibrium mechanism to work as Hume suggested, the market for foreign exchange had to be stable as it is in figure 2.1: this required the investigation of the conditions under which the price elasticities of supply and demand for a country's exports and imports would ensure that the relative reduction in a country's prices would lead to an improvement in its balance of payments position. In a situation of high elasticities of supply of commodities the requirement is that the sum of the domestic elasticity of demand for imports plus the foreign elasticity of demand for the country's exports should exceed unity. This is not a particularly stringent requirement given the observed price elasticities of demand for most goods (see Houthakker and Magee, 1969). This condition is known as the *Marshall–Lerner condition*, since the condition was discovered at least twice. (Marshall, 1923 and Lerner, 1944; see also Robinson, 1937 and Haberler, 1949.)

Consider a devaluation by the home country in a two-country, two-good model on Marshall–Lerner assumptions, i.e. of high price elasticities of supply: assumed here to be infinite. The goods are 'exports', sent abroad by the home country, and 'imports' bought abroad and consumed in the home country. The situation of equilibrium in the import and export good markets is illustrated in figure 2.3. The rectangular hyperbola has the property that the areas of revenue/expenditure for all points on its are equal. The initial supply and demand schedules for exports and imports respectively are drawn so that they intersect on the hyperbola, thus ensuring that the balance of payments (on goods account) is in balance, the initial equilibria being at A for imports and B for exports.

Assume that the home currency is devalued. The domestic supply price of exports will be unchanged but to foreigners they will be cheaper by the extent of the devaluation, so that the foreign demand curve – DX – will shift outwards to DX' in terms of home currency. The new equilibrium at D, to the right of RH, indicates increased export receipts. Indeed, except in the case where foreign demand is completely price inelastic, export receipts (measured in home currency) will always rise. The price of imports will remain unchanged

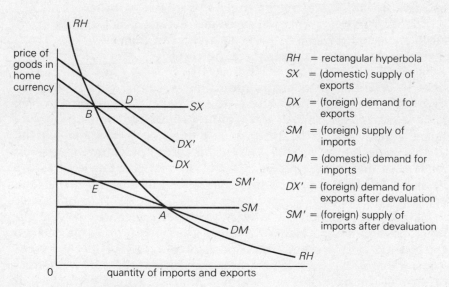

Figure 2.3   The Marshall–Lerner condition

in a world currency but will rise in home currency. In figure 2.3 the new supply curve of imports is SM' with the equilibrium at E to the left of RH, so that with this particular demand curve, total expenditure on imports falls. Starting with balance between exports and imports, the combination of demand elasticities implied by the demand curves has resulted in a devaluation of the currency leading to a surplus of receipts over payments.

Carrying out the calculations in domestic currency will, except for the case of completely inelastic foreign demand, result in export receipts rising after a devaluation, but expenditure on imports may well rise so that E would lie to the right of RH. If we imagine a map of rectangular hyperbolae the trade balance will improve if the rectangular hyperbola on which D lies is to the right of that on which E lies. It will be unchanged if D and E lie on the same hyperbola and deteriorate if E is on a hyperbola to the right of D.[2]

Moreover, assume that we again commence with points A and B and that the currency is devalued. If the foreign demand for exports were completely inelastic, an identical physical quantity would be bought at a lower price in foreign currency, which in terms of figure 2.3 would require the foreign demand curve DX to be vertical through B. Assume also that the domestic demand for imports was such that the new equilibrium E lay on RH above A. This would imply unitary price elasticity of demand for imports. In this example the payments position would be unchanged after the devaluation, because B and E are on the same hyperbola: in other words the payments position neither improves nor deteriorates when (ignoring algebraic signs) the sum of price elasticities of demand is one. Holding import demand at unitary elasticity (E on RH) but permitting some elasticity in foreign demand, so that D is on a hyperbola to the right of RH, the payments position improves: this occurs when the sums of price elasticities exceeds unity. Lastly assume zero foreign price elasticity of demand, so that the post devaluation equilibrium remains at B, but an elasticity of less than one for import demand so that E lies to the right of RH. In this case expenditure on imports rises, with export receipts unchanged, so that a deficit emerges on payments: here the sum of price elasticities of demand is less than one.

Defining E_F as the price elasticity of the foreign demand for the home country's exports and E_H the price elasticity of home demand for imports then, starting from a position of balance between expenditure on imports and receipts from exports and with high elasticities of supply, the payments position will improve, remain unchanged or deteriorate accordingly as $E_F + E_H \gtreqless 1$.[3]

The 'J' Curve

The elasticities approach ignores time in its analysis, but one of the lessons of experience has been that while exchange rates may adjust instantaneously, the prices of goods and demand change only after a lag. Thus if the country is running a payments deficit the first effect of a devaluation or depreciation of its currency may be to make the deficit larger. If imports are bought at world prices and demand is price inelastic there will be little change in foreign expenditure in response to a higher price in domestic currency. Export receipts in foreign currency on the other hand may drop unless the domestic price of exports is raised by the full extent of the devaluation. It is estimated (Cairncross and Eichengreen 1983) that over the first two years after the British devaluation of 1967 there was no net gain in export earnings, since the loss through lower export prices (in foreign currency) was only offset by an increased volume in the second year.

Devaluation and the Terms of Trade

The effect of devaluation on a country's terms of trade (measured as the ratio of an index of export prices divided by an index of import prices) cannot be settled *a priori*. The outcome depends upon the independent effects of devaluation on export and import prices. If a country faces downward sloping demand curves for its exports but is 'unimportant' in its import markets (i.e. faces perfectly elastic foreign supply curves in terms of foreign currency) devaluation will worsen the devaluing country's terms of trade. Meade (1951) has shown that the terms of trade will deteriorate if the product of home and foreign supply elasticities is greater than the product of demand elasticities. In practice it seems likely that the terms of trade will deteriorate with a devaluation because, as Michaely (1962) has shown, countries are more important in their export markets than in their import markets, i.e. countries are specialized in exports but diversified in imports.

The Foreign Trade Multiplier

Keynes' *General Theory of Employment, Interest and Money* (1936), written in response to the mass unemployment of the 1920s and 1930s, endeavoured to give a theoretical explanation for the persistence of unemployment and to propose policy measures to reduce unemployment. Keynes showed that the equilibrium level of income is that at which the autonomous expenditures (injections), such as government expenditures or physical investment, were just matched by leakages, such as savings or taxation, induced by that level of income. The ratio which income bears to injections is defined as the multiplier. When this value is known it can be applied to the level of injections to find the level of national income or to changes in injections to find changes in income. Though the analysis was originally developed for a closed economy, its implications were soon noted for an open economy and for the process of balance of payments adjustments (Paish, 1936 and Salant, 1941). Exports were seen to be injections to which the multiplier applied, and imports were leakages. Assuming that prices are stable, that there are unused resources, and that there is only one injection (exports) and one leakage (imports), a rise in exports would cause income to rise until an equal volume of imports has been induced. This mechanism would, however, be incomplete, if there were more leakages than just imports, for then a rise in exports would cause income to rise until the aggregate rise of all leakages equalled the initial rise in exports. The increased imports would be only a fraction of all leakages and, therefore, less than exports, so that the balance of payments would remain in surplus.

The elasticities approach and the Keynesian approach to balance of payments adjustment rest on very different assumptions. The former assumes, mostly implicitly, full employment and flexible prices and concentrates on the role of prices. The latter assumes unemployment and rigid prices and concentrates on income effects. The deficiency in the elasticities approach, namely its partial equilibrium nature and its neglect of income effects in particular, was exposed by models deriving from Keynesian analysis, in particular the absorption approach to the balance of payments.

The Absorption Approach

Alexander (1952) showed that the extent to which a country enjoyed a surplus, B, on its foreign trade depended on the extent to which its production, Y, exceeded its absorption (or expenditure), A. The balance of payments position can be represented as $B = Y - A$. Since output can be used or absorbed within a country for purposes of consumption or investment, A can be replaced by C (consumption) and I (investment), so that:

$$Y - A = Y - C - I \qquad (2.5)$$

and since the difference between Y and C is equal to saving:

$$B = Y - A = Y - C - I = S - I \qquad (2.6)$$

The advantage of this formulation (see Black, 1959) is that it integrates balance of payments theory with the central relationship of Keynesian analysis, that between savings and investment.

If a downward movement in relative prices (e.g. a devaluation) is to improve the payments position of a deficit country, the absorption approach has to provide a mechanism to explain how Y will rise relatively to A, or S to I. While such a relative movement may be possible with unemployed resources, since a devaluation could well raise Y or S more than A or I respectively if the marginal propensity to consume is less than one, it is difficult to find a convincing non-inflationary mechanism to effect the change at full employment, the situation usually assumed in the elasticities analysis.

Alexander suggested that the following forces may decrease absorption at full employment: a cash balance effect, an income redistribution effect, a money illusion effect and miscellaneous effects. He devoted most attention to the cash balance effect: consequent upon a devaluation the domestic prices of imports and exports will rise, so that to restore a real cash balance to its desired level it will be necessary to 'hoard' money, thereby reducing absorption. This emphasis on maintaining a real cash balance anticipates the arguments of monetarist protagonists as will be seen in chapters 5 and 6. It has been pointed out (Johnson, 1976) that the absorption approach is quite schizophrenic in its treatment of the real balance effect. It recognizes the need to rebuild real balances in the face of the price rises after a devaluation, but ignores the reduction in the money supply which is the counterpart of the deficit which caused the devaluation.

The absorption approach suggests in fact that the removal of a balance of payments deficit would normally require the simultaneous adoption of *expenditure switching* and *expenditure reducing* policies (Johnson, 1961). An expenditure switching policy, such as a devaluation, channels demand in the deficit country away from tradeable commodities, so that fewer are imported and more are made available for export, and switches demand in surplus countries towards tradeable goods. If the Marshall–Lerner condition is met these effects tend to improve the deficit country's balance of payments but at the same time raise the level of aggregate demand in the deficit country via increased net exports. If resources in this country were near full capacity use, then a domestic expenditure reducing policy, such as a tax increase, would be necessary to avoid inflation.

There were two major defects in the balance of payments analysis derived in this Keynesian tradition, defects shared also by the elasticities approach but not by the earlier Humean analysis. These were that the analysis applied only to the current account of the balance of payments and virtually ignored capital transactions, and secondly that the analysis ignored the monetary consequences of payments imbalance. The former defect can be explained in that most of the analysis was developed in a period when international capital flows were subject to severe controls. As these were relaxed in the 1960s, models (Mundell 1963, Fleming 1962) were developed to take account of international capital flows and they also showed the implications of the free flow of capital for policies to attain internal and external equilibrium (see chapter 3).

Money and the Balance of Payments

The monetary consequences of payments imbalances were stressed by Tsiang (1961) and Johnson (1961). Johnson argued that balance of payments deficits were essentially 'monetary phenomena' which could only exist because national banking systems could create money which was not internationally acceptable. While any deficit persists the domestic money supply will continue to decline. The fact that deficits did persist under the regime of fixed exchange rates was due to the sterilization of the monetary decline by governments concerned about the diminishing employment prospects caused by a deficit. It was the inappropriate monetary response which was the reason for the continuing deficit. The rediscovery of the importance of money provided a stimulus to look again at the analysis of the older monetary tradition.

The monetary analysis was initially applied to explaining the balance of payments equilibrating process in a regime of fixed exchange rates. It was essentially long-run and explained positions of equilibrium and, unlike the Keynesian and elasticities approaches, it had little to say about the dynamics of short-run adjustment, which still remains an area of controversy. The approach focuses its attention on the demand for and the supply of a stock of money with equilibrium only being possible in all markets when the stock of money in existence is willingly held.

In an open economy if the money supply is increased by the monetary authorities, actual money holdings will exceed desired money holdings for it is presumed that there is a stable demand for money function. Holders of excess balances will reduce them by moving into goods and bonds. Some of these goods and bonds will be foreign provided the currency has international acceptability, so that the process of re-establishing monetary equilibrium will involve an apparent flow balance of payments deficit, which is the counterpart of the stock adjustment to the monetary disequilibrium. This issue is taken up again in the following chapter and then at length in chapters 5 to 8.

Notes

1 By rearrangement $p + 1 = F/S$ and by substitution in 2.1

$$1 + i^{US} = (1 + i^{UK})(1 + p).$$

Solving this for p and ignoring the term pi^{UK} because of its smallness, yields equation 2.2.
2 The mathematical proof of the conditions for an improvement in the payments position is fairly tortuous. (See for example, Grubel, 1981, pp. 680-82 and Stern, 1973, pp. 128-33.)
3 Most attention has been focused on the Marshall–Lerner case of infinite supply elasticities, but the formula can be generalized to derive the conditions for trade balance improvement, when supply elasticities are less than infinite (see Stern, 1973). In figure 2.3 upwards sloping supply schedules can be introduced and conclusions derived by the method explained.

3 Macroeconomics in an Open Economy

by Robert Shaw

This chapter reviews a particular issue: the conflict between internal equilibrium and external equilibrium. By internal equilibrium economists mean a situation of full employment with a stable price level and by external equilibrium a situation of balance in foreign payments. The issue is alternatively denoted as that of internal and external balance.

The analysis is developed predominantly for the small open-economy country, which takes the prices, incomes and interest rates in the rest of the world as given. The justification for this is that few countries are large enough to influence the world economy and the marked lack of international co-operation on economic policy makes it sensible to focus attention on the individual country. The analysis is also important because it explicitly introduces international capital flows, a feature further developed in the global monetary approach to the balance of payments (see chapter 5).

The chapter begins by examining the rules of the theory of economic policy in an open economy and then considers the roles of fiscal and monetary policies in macroeconomic stabilization under fixed and flexible exchange rates on varying assumptions about capital mobility and expectations about the exchange rate.

An Early View of Economic Management

Governments of countries have many acknowledged economic goals, e.g. price stability, full employment, economic growth, balance in foreign payments and an equitable distribution of income, and one of the lessons of the theory of economic policy (see Tinbergen, 1952) is that as a general rule each policy objective requires a corresponding policy weapon or instrumental variable. If there are more policy goals than there are weapons, simultaneous attainment of all the goals can occur only by chance. The problem can be illustrated on the assumption of two goals, namely full employment and balance on foreign trade, in figure 3.1 devised by Swan (1955).

A country's international competitiveness – measured on the vertical axis – is determined by the exchange rate in combination with the level of domestic prices. If the price level is fixed, then it is the exchange rate alone which determines a country's international competitiveness. Domestic real expenditure is measured on the horizontal axis.

The curve II represents combinations of international competitiveness and domestic real expenditure which would maintain full employment (i.e. internal equilibrium). At *A* for example, full employment is attained by low levels of domestic expenditure but high levels of international competitiveness: the required level of effective demand is maintained by a proportionately high level of sales of goods abroad rather than at home. At *B* on the other hand, the same level of aggregate demand is generated by large domestic expenditures to compensate for lower foreign demand which arises because the country is less competitive. The II curve, therefore, slopes downwards from left to right. The schedule *EE* represents balance on foreign payments. At low levels of domestic expenditure such as at *J*, relatively little will be spent on foreign goods so that the country does not need to be very competitive to earn the foreign exchange necessary to pay for imports. When there is a high level of

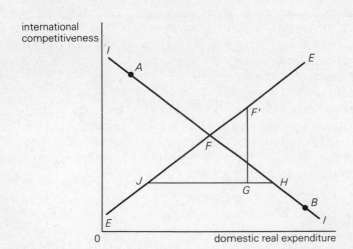

Figure 3.1   The Swan diagram of internal and external balance

expenditure as at F', the country requires to be more competitive to earn foreign exchange to pay for the greater volume of imports on which some of the expenditure goes. The external balance curve, therefore, rises from left to right. The intersection of the two curves at F represents simultaneous attainment of both internal and external balance.

Suppose that an economy with a fixed exchange rate found itself at G, where neither objective is being attained. The balance of payments is in deficit as the economy is inadequately competitive for the level of expenditure at G. The economy also suffers from unemployment as there is inadequate domestic expenditure to add on to that coming from foreign demand at the level of competitiveness corresponding to G. To achieve internal equilibrium would require an increase of domestic expenditure of GH, which would worsen the balance of payments. To restore external balance would require a reduction in domestic expenditure of GJ, which would lead to increased unemployment. One goal can be achieved only if the other is relinquished to an even greater extent.

Some economists argue that the above dilemma was faced by several countries in the 1950s and 1960s. Under the Bretton Woods system improved competitiveness by exchange rate adjustment was infrequent and wages and prices tended to be downwardly inflexible. Thus, given the stress which most countries placed on the maintenance of internal balance, international payments could only be kept in equilibrium by welfare-reducing controls on trade[1] and by deflating domestic aggregate demand. Not surprisingly, economists came to argue that full employment and free trade were only likely to be attained if exchange rates were allowed to fluctuate. Then international competitiveness should never be a problem. Countries would then have two policy weapons, variations in exchange rates and changes in expenditure levels, to attain the two goals of full employment and balance on trade.

Devaluation now makes it possible to move from G to F' – so attaining external balance. However, at F' domestic real expenditure is excessive and inflation would result. Deflationary domestic policies should, therefore, be simultaneously employed with the devaluation, allowing the economy to move directly from G to F where internal and external balance are achieved together.

A More Complete Model

One problem with the 'Swan diagram' is that it is insufficiently explicit. *IS/LM* analysis has the advantage of bringing monetary equilibrium directly into focus and, as reference to a good macro-economic text will show,[2] is entirely explicit on important 'background' elements such as the aggregate production function, the aggregate labour supply function, the propensities to import and export and the elasticity of international capital flows.

It is assumed that the student is already familiar with the derivation of the IS/LM diagram, and, therefore, only a brief description of it is given here. The IS schedule shows the combinations of rates of interest and income at which saving equals investment. At a high rate of interest there would be little investment so that income, found by multiplying investment and other autonomous expenditures by the multiplier, would be low and so, therefore, would be the savings induced by this income level. A low rate of interest would permit a larger volume of investment, a higher income and, therefore, higher savings, so that the IS curve will slope downwards from left to right. Two other 'injections' exports and government expenditure, and 'leakages' imports and taxes, both insensitive to the rate of interest, can be added to the IS schedule. Thus, the IS schedule used in this chapter shows equilibrium in the goods market in an open economy with private and governmental sectors. Formally this may be represented as:

$$Y = D \tag{3.1}$$

where

$$D = A(Y, i) + T + G, A_y > 0; A_i < 0 \tag{3.2}$$

where Y is output, D aggregate demand, A absorption, i the domestic interest rate, T the trade balance, G government expenditure and A_y and A_i the partial derivatives. Since prices are assumed constant all the variables are real. This definition of internal balance diverges from that used in figure 3.1 since it says only that the goods market is in equilibrium at each combination of interest rates and income, but only one combination would give full employment income.

The LM schedule shows the combination of interest rates and income at which the money market is in equilibrium. It is drawn on the assumption that the supply of money is fixed and that the demand for money is a negative function of the rate of interest. At low levels of income the transactions demand for money is low and, as wealth holders use surplus money to buy securities, interest rates tend to be low. At a higher level of income money demanded for transactions purposes is also higher, so that little remains for speculative purposes and interest rates rise. The LM curve, therefore, slopes upwards from left to right. Hence:

$$M^D = M(Y, i), M_y > 0; M_i < 0 \tag{3.3}$$

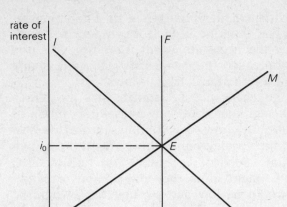

Figure 3.2   Open economy equilibrium with constrained capital flow

and

$$M^D = M = \bar{M}^S \tag{3.4}$$

with $\bar{M}^S$ the exogenously determined money supply and M^D the demand for money. Since the price level is constant, it is not necessary to deflate M by P, the price level.

The FF schedule in figure 3.2 represents zero balance on foreign payments. It is drawn initially on the assumption that the foreign payments position – in particular international capital flow – is insensitive to the domestic rate of interest: international capital movements are either zero or a given constant. With this constraint on international capital flows the payments position is determined by trade flows which in turn are determined by the country's income level and by relative prices (determined by relative national price levels and the exchange rate). For any given exchange rate (and zero or fixed volume of capital movement) there will be one income level at which foreign payments are in balance. Formally this may be represented as:

$$T = T(S, P, P^*, Y, Y^*) \tag{3.5}$$

and

$$T = \Delta K, \ \Delta K = 0 \tag{3.6}$$

where T is the trade balance, ΔK is capital inflow, S is the exchange rate, P is the domestic price level, P^* is the foreign price level and Y^* is foreign income. The above situation is schematically representative of the position of many countries in the 1940s and 1950s before the removal of controls on international capital flows.

The three schedules are drawn on the assumption of a given foreign exchange rate. If, for example, the currency were to be devaluated the FF curve would move to the right, since demand for imports at all income levels will be reduced by an increase in their relative price compared to home produced goods. The LM curve would move upwards to the left as prices would rise and the real money supply falls after a devaluation. The IS schedule would shift upwards to the right: increased net demand (exports minus imports) for domestic output, caused by the relative price change, would be added to the original IS schedule.

Full open economy equilibrium occurs at the intersection of the three schedules – at E in figure 3.2 with income level Y_0, which is taken as the full employment income level, and interest rate i_0.

If this system is subjected to a shock a new equilibrium will be established. Assuming that the rest of the world suffers from a recession, FF will move to $F'F'$ and IS to $I'S'$ in figure 3.3 as exports to the rest of the world fall. For balance in foreign payments, imports must also decline which can only occur in a system of fixed exchange rates if income declines. The new equilibrium will establish itself at G, for while the economy remains on $I'S'$ to the

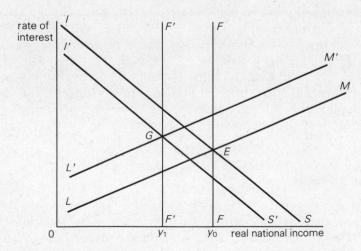

Figure 3.3   Adjustment with constrained capital flow

right of G, the balance of payments will be in deficit. Importers will be exchanging domestic currency for foreign exchange supplied from central bank reserves. As exporters will be paying a smaller quantity of foreign exchange into the reserves to obtain domestic currency, the net effect will be a reduction in the domestic money supply and a leftwards movement of LM to intersect the $I'S'$ schedule at G where equilibrium is once more established. However, internal balance in the sense of full employment may not exist if Y_1 is below the full employment level Y_0.

If for political or other reasons unemployment cannot be tolerated, then a government is likely to try one of two actions. With a fixed exchange rate a government has typically opted for a policy of monetary sterilization, i.e. one of offsetting the balance of payments effects on the domestic money supply. In terms of figure 3.3, this would mean maintaining the LM schedule at its original position by replacing, probably through open market operations, the money stock lost through reserve decumulation. Such a policy can only be temporary, for while the economy is located to the right of $F'F'$, the balance of payments will continue in deficit. The whole process could be repeated, but since a country's holdings of foreign exchange (or its ability to obtain overseas credit) is finite, a shortage of reserves must in the end thwart the procedure. It ought to be clear that the foreign payments deficit persists only because of the government's monetary stance.

The other action open to the government is to devalue the currency. This would cause FF to remain at its original position, as the devaluation will maintain external balance. The IS schedule should also remain in its original position because net exports are unchanged. The LM curve would move temporarily to the left as devaluation raises the domestic price level. However, LM would then intersect IS to the left of FF, implying a balance of payments surplus. This surplus would, in turn, lead to an increase in domestic money supply and eventually return LM to its original position. In the longer term, therefore, the devaluation will have insulated the domestic economy from the 'shock' of economic depression in the rest of the world.

An Amendment to the Model

The liberalization measures introduced to international transactions at the end of the 1950s applied first to goods and services but were gradually extended to the capital account. At the same time the development of new international capital markets, those in Eurocurrencies in particular (see chapter 10), led to the greater integration of national financial markets and to greater elasticity of shortrun international capital movements in response to interest rate differentials. Economists, especially Mundell (1963) and Fleming (1962), were quick to see that these changes raised new issues for economic analysis and for economic policy.

Allowing for the free flow of capital between countries in response to interest rate differentials requires amendment of the *FF* schedule used in figures 3.2 and 3.3. From being vertical when there are no capital flows, it will tend towards the horizontal, depending upon the interest elasticity of international capital flows. The more elastic the supply of capital, i.e. the more domestic and foreign assets are perfect substitutes for each other, the more horizontal will be the schedule. The *FF* schedule now shows the combination of interest rates and income at which the foreign exchange market balance is zero. Intuitively, as income rises, the balance of payments tends to worsen on current account as more imports are absorbed. To offset this, the rate of interest must rise to attract a compensating capital inflow so that *FF* will slope upwards to the right. *FF* is drawn flatter than *LM*.[3] The equation for the capital flow given above must be amended to

$$\Delta K = k(i - i^* - 100 \dot{S}^e / S) \tag{3.7}$$

where with perfect capital mobility k approaches infinity and with static expectations $\dot{S}^e = 0$, i^* is the foreign interest rate and $\dot{S}^e$ is the expected change in the spot exchange rate.

In figure 3.4 it is assumed that the country maintains a fixed exchange rate and that equilibrium for the system is given at point E with income Y_1 and interest rate i_1. Full employment income is Y_2 corresponding to point G on the *FF* schedule. What domestic policy must now do is to cause the *IS* and *LM* schedules to intersect *FF* at G. This requires a fiscal stimulus to *IS* to send it to $I'S'$ and an increase in the money supply to shift the *LM* schedule rightwards to $L'M'$. Internal balance is attained at Y_2 and external balance is maintained on *FF* at G. While the higher income at Y_2 worsens the balance of payments on trade account the rise in the interest rate to i_2 improves it by an equal amount on capital account. Indeed, if the monetary authorities adopted a passive monetary policy, fiscal action itself would, because of the feedback through the balance of payments, attain G and Y_2. An expansive fiscal policy with a passive monetary stance would send the economy to H, but at H the balance of payments would be in surplus with the exchange rate tending to

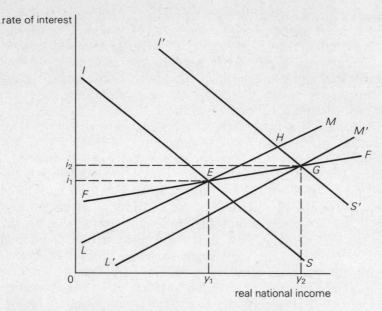

Figure 3.4   Equilibrium with capital mobility

rise. To prevent this the monetary authorities would have to buy foreign exchange with domestic currency, so increasing domestic money supply. *LM* would shift to *L'M'* with internal/external equilibrium at *G*.

The Relative Effectiveness of Monetary and Fiscal Policy Under Fixed and Flexible Exchange Rates

Taking the case of perfect capital mobility between countries, where capital is perfectly interest elastic, it can be shown that monetary and fiscal policies vary in their relative effectiveness according to the exchange rate regime. Initially it is assumed that the country is small in relation to the world economy so that the domestic interest rate is determined by the foreign rate, and there is no expectation of a change in the exchange rate. Consider first a fixed exchange rate.

In figure 3.5, because of the assumption of a perfectly elastic supply of capital, the *FF* schedule is drawn horizontal and the initial equilibrium of the system is at *E* with income level Y_0. It is assumed that the government wishes to raise the income level to Y_1.

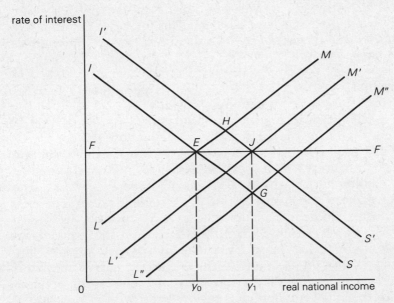

Figure 3.5   Equilibrium with a fixed exchange rate and perfect capital mobility

Consider first monetary policy where the monetary authorities raise the quantity of money by a open market purchase of securities. The LM schedule moves to $L''M''$ which would give a closed economy equilibrium at G. In an open economy, however, such a move can be no more than incipient, for a reduction in the domestic interest rate below the foreign would lead to an immediate capital outflow, which would put downward pressure on the exchange rate. To maintain the fixed parity the monetary authorities have to buy back domestic currency with foreign exchange from the reserves. The domestic money supply is reduced and the system returns to E and Y_0. The policy has been quite unsuccessful. In effect the central bank has swapped domestic assets (the purchase of securities) for foreign assets (the sale of foreign exchange). But the domestic money supply has remained unchanged.

Consider now expansionary fiscal policy, defined as an increase in government expenditure financed by the issue of debt. This raises the IS schedule to $I'S'$ with intersection with LM at H below income level Y_1. The balance of payments is in surplus at H because of the capital inflow induced by the incipient higher rate of interest at H. There is pressure on the exchange rate to appreciate and, to keep the currency at its parity, the monetary authorities must supply domestic currency to purchase foreign exchange. This increases the domestic money supply and moves LM rightwards to $L'M'$ with equilibrium at J and the target level of income Y_1.

Thus in a small open economy with a fixed exchange rate and perfect capital mobility, monetary policy is powerless to increase income, while fiscal policy is extremely effective.

Under flexible exchange rates this result is reversed. Recall that IS and LM are drawn for a given exchange rate, but with perfect capital mobility in a small economy FF is fixed at the level of the world rate of interest. In figure 3.6 with fiscal expansion IS shifts to $I'S'$ and an apparent equilibrium appears at G at the target income level Y_1. The balance of payments is in surplus and the exchange rate appreciates. The depressing influence of this causes $I'S'$ to drift leftwards. Though LM may have moved rightwards, because the transactions demand for money has fallen by virtue of cheaper imports, any equilibrium at the intersection of these shifting curves above FF implies the appreciation of the currency and downward pressure on IS, until the initial equilibrium is restored at E with income Y_0.

A monetary expansion on the other hand would be more effective. An open market purchase of securities would increase the money

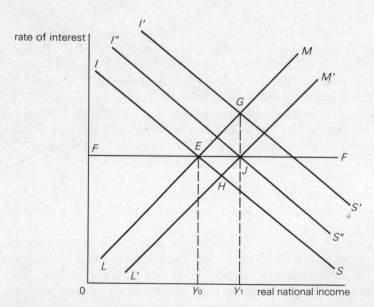

Figure 3.6   Equilibrium with a flexible exchange rate and perfect capital mobility

stock and permit LM to move to $L'M'$ with an apparent equilibrium at H. Since this is below FF, foreign payments are in deficit and the exchange rate tends to depreciate. This causes IS to move rightwards to $I''S''$. The higher price level following the depreciation may have some minor effects on $L'M'$, but ignoring these the ultimate outcome will be a move to J.

Thus, with a flexible exchange rate the conclusion is reached that monetary policy is a powerful tool for income and employment stabilisation while fiscal policy is ineffective.

Formally these Mundell-Fleming results may be stated as follows:

$$\frac{dY}{dG} > \frac{dY}{dM} \text{ for a fixed exchange rate} \tag{3.8}$$

$$\frac{dY}{dM} > \frac{dY}{dG} \text{ for a flexible exchange rate} \tag{3.9}$$

$$\frac{dY}{dM} \text{ (flexible rate)} > \frac{dY}{dM} \text{ (fixed rate)} \tag{3.10}$$

and

$$\frac{dY}{dG} \text{ (fixed rate)} > \frac{dY}{dG} \text{ (flexible rate)} \tag{3.11}$$

where M represents money supply and G government expenditures.

The Principle of Effective Market Classification and the Assignment Problem

Mundell (1962) proposed that the Tinbergen rule which required one independent policy instrument for each policy target should be complemented by what he called the *principle of effective market classification*, which concerns the pairing of instruments and targets. He argued that policies should be paired with the objectives on which they have most influence. Failure to observe this rule would, he believed, lead to a cyclical approach to equilibrium or to instability. In terms of the analysis above, in the case of a small country in a fixed exchange rate regime and perfect capital mobility, fiscal policy should be paired with the goal of internal equilibrium.

While the principle of effective market classification is still relevant, one of the corollaries of the analysis above is that it is not possible to allocate one policy instrument unequivocally to one policy target, since the effectiveness of a policy instrument varies according to the exchange rate regime in which it operates. While it is correct to pair fiscal policy and internal equilibrium under a fixed exchange rate, the pairing is inappropriate under a flexible exchange rate. This dilemma associated with the correctness of pairing is called the *assignment problem*: it is not possible to assign one instrument in all cases to one target.

The Large Country Case

The conclusions of this analysis have to be modified in the case of a large open economy such as the United States, for even with a fixed exchange rate US monetary policy can have some domestic effectiveness. A rise in US money supply reduces the rate of interest in the US and leads to a monetary outflow of a size significant to the rest of the world, whose money supply is increased and rate of interest reduced. Thus the increase in money supply in the US reduces rates of interest throughout the world and expands output in both the US and abroad. In terms of figure 3.5 the US has the power via monetary expansion to lower the *FF* schedule, so that equilibrium is possible on *IS* to the south-east of *E*. Monetary policy is no longer ineffective in a fixed exchange rate regime, when the country is large.

The conclusion that a flexible exchange rate renders a fiscal expansion impotent also needs to be amended. The initial effect of such an expansion in the US would cause a rise in the US interest rate and an inflow of capital from abroad. The size of this flow in relation to foreign capital markets would raise interest rates abroad. The *FF* schedule in figure 3.6 would rise producing a new equilibrium northeast of *E*, so that in the case of a large country not all of the expansionary effects of a fiscal stimulus would flow abroad but would be shared between the large country and the rest of the world.

On the other hand the effectiveness of the correctly paired instruments and targets, fiscal policy for fixed exchange rate and monetary policy for flexible exchange rate, is diminished. A fiscal expansion with a fixed rate will pull up interest rates both in the US and abroad and induce a smaller capital inflow, and consequent increase in the money supply, than is the case with a small country, so that the expansion would be less proportionately for the US than for a small country. In addition the rest of the world may suffer a fall in income as a result of the rise in interest rates, unless the US takes from it an extra quantity of imports, which offsets this.

In the case of a monetary expansion with a flexible rate the rate of interest will decline leading to a monetary outflow. This will reduce interest rates abroad and cause a downward movement of *FF* in figure 3.6. The payments deficit for the US would be reduced with a lower required depreciation of the exchange rate. *IS* will move less far to the right than *I"S"* in figure 3.6 and the expansion of income will be less.

In short, the results differ for a large country in that it is a price-maker and not a price-taker with regard to the interest rate. As fiscal policy and monetary policy affect interest rates under both exchange rate regimes, they are both effective to some degree under both regimes.

Qualifications to the Analysis

The analysis of the small country case has been subject to several qualifications. These include the empirical question of whether modern political systems can use fiscal policy with the speed and flexibility assumed in the analysis and whether the validity of the analysis is not impaired by the neglect of the supply side of the economy, for it is implicitly assumed that demand creates its own supply. There is also the neglect of the effect of exchange rate changes on the domestic price level.

Other qualifications, which are examined below and more fully in later chapters, have extended the analysis by considering the assumptions of less than perfect capital mobility, of different speeds of operation in goods and asset markets, of expectations that the exchange rate may change, of the possibility that capital flows may represent situations of portfolio adjustment and finally of wealth effects.

Imperfect Capital Mobility Perfect capital mobility requires that domestic and foreign assets be perfect substitutes and that adjustment be instantaneous. Empirical investigations (e.g. Kouri and Porter, 1974) suggest that neither condition is met. In terms of figures 3.5 and 3.6 the *FF* schedule for imperfect capital mobility will now have a positive slope, which may be greater or less than that of *LM*. The relative slopes are of no significance for a monetary expansion which will induce a payments deficit under both fixed and flexible rates. The relative slopes do, however, matter for fiscal policy. Consider the case in figure 3.7 of a fiscal expansion with a fixed exchange rate, where *FF* is steeper than *LM*.

A fiscal expansion would move the economy from *E* to *F* with a payments deficit. To maintain the exchange rate domestic currency must be bought with reserves so that *LM* would drift leftwards with an eventual equilibrium for the system at *G*. The rise in income is less

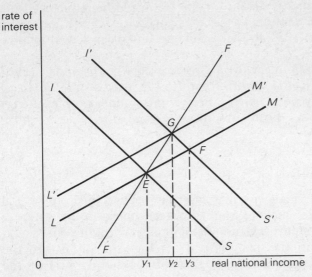

Figure 3.7   Fiscal expansion with a fixed exchange rate and imperfect capital mobility

than it would be if *FF* were shallower than *LM* and less, of course, than in the case of perfect capital mobility. The more effective instrument with a fixed rate has lost some of its effectiveness.

Indeed this is but one instance of the general conclusion which emerges, namely that imperfect capital mobility reduces the effectiveness of the effective instrument and the ineffectiveness of the ineffective instrument. Effectiveness and ineffectiveness both have their origins in balance of payments effects with perfect capital mobility. Imperfect capital mobility constrains these effects; thus with a fixed exchange rate not all of a domestic monetary expansion would leak abroad, while not all of increase in money supply necessary to validate a fiscal policy expansion would flow in.

The Speed of Adjustment in Markets It is assumed in the analysis above that a currency depreciation will improve the trade account and provide a stimulus to domestic output, i.e. that the Marshall–Lerner conditions are fulfilled. Empirical evidence (Artus and Young, 1979) throws doubt on this. While for 14 industrial countries the average value for the sum of short-run price elasticities of demand for imports and exports just exceeds one, for nine of the countries it is below this value. Even in the longer term of up to four years the figure is still below one for four countries.

While quantities (of goods) respond to price changes only with a lag, capital flows respond promptly to interest rate differentials and the implications of these different speeds of adjustment have been considered. Niehans (1975) has analysed the case where the Marshall–Lerner conditions are not met and where an increase in the money supply with a flexible exchange rate leads to a decline in, rather than expansion of, output. This can occur as follows. A monetary expansion reduces the domestic rate of interest, causes a capital outflow and a depreciation of a the exchange rate. Because of the non-fulfilment of the Marshall–Lerner conditions the balance of trade does not improve and aggregate demand within the economy falls as more is spent on buying the same volume of imports. The failure of the trade account to improve can lead to further depreciation of the exchange rate and another decline in domestic demand as higher priced imports absorb home demand. The demand spiral can only be halted by an assumption about the future equilibrium value of the exchange rate, which Niehans calls the 'permanent' rate, namely that capital will flow back into the country to benefit from an anticipated future appreciation of the domestic currency and this capital flow will restore the balance of payments position. Under these circumstances monetary policy will fail to have the expansion effects predicted by the original analysis.

Expectations and the Exchange Rate With a fixed exchange rate it may be reasonable to expect no change in the future rate, but it would be strange to expect no change in the future value of a flexible exchange rate. A flexible rate system will contain both a spot and a forward rate and their existence has implications for the analysis. A domestic monetary expansion leading to an incipient lower domestic interest rate will cause a capital outflow and a depreciation of the spot rate. If, however, lenders cover themselves in the forward market by selling foreign currency forward, the forward rate for the domestic country will show an appreciation, and this will reduce the net covered advantage of lending abroad. Equilibrium requires that money invested should everywhere have the same yield, but the yield from overseas investment has two components, namely the interest on the asset plus any loss or gain in converting foreign currency back into domestic currency. The equilibrium condition is that the covered interest differential is zero, as is shown in chapter 2, equation 2.3.

Two consequences follow from this. First, not all of a monetary expansion will leak out of the country as the spot and forward rates diverge to offset the interest rate differential and secondly it is now possible for domestic and world rates of interest to diverge. The expansion in domestic output through the change in the exchange rate will be less, since it will have depreciated less than it would have done in the absence of a forward market, but there will be a second stimulus from a lower interest rate, absent when there is no forward market.

Similar reasoning can be used to extend the argument to expectations about the future spot rate. The case normally considered is that of regressive expectations, i.e. of an elasticity of expectations of less than unity. A monetary expansion leads to a reduction in domestic interest rates and a rapid outflow of capital, which causes the exchange rate to depreciate. Some of this depreciation is, however, expected to be reversed as, for example, the current account improves over time in response to changed relative prices. People who lend overseas earn a higher interest rate but suffer an offsetting capital loss on converting foreign currency back into domestic currency. The domestic interest rate can be untied from the world rate to the extent of this expected future appreciation of the domestic currency.

In figure 3.8, the monetary expansion moves LM to $L'M'$ and the economy from E to G. The domestic rate of interest is below the world rate, capital flows out and the exchange rate depreciates. In response to the depreciation IS moves to $I'S'$. The expectation of a partial future reversal of the depreciation permits the domestic

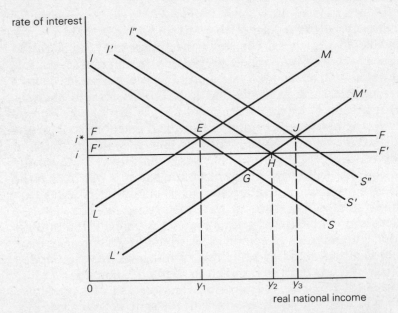

Figure 3.8 Monetary expansion with a flexible exchange rate and regressive expectations

interest rate to remain below the world rate by the extent of the future appreciation of the currency, so that an equilibrium such as H is possible, which can be compared with the Mundell–Fleming equilibrium of J. Income has risen less at H because the interest rate stimulus is less than the loss of balance of trade stimulus because of the reduced currency depreciation.

Dornbusch (1976) has argued that the assumption of regressive expectations even makes it possible for the trade balance to deteriorate after a monetary expansion and exchange rate depreciation, when the Marshall–Lerner conditions are met. Two forces operate on the trade balance. The exchange rate depreciation increases output and, if the propensity to spend is less than unity, the trade balance will improve. The lower interest rate made possible by regressive expectations will on the other hand increase aggregate spending, induce more imports and worsen the trade balance. If the latter effect is dominant, a capital inflow will be required to cover the deficit. In the longer run, however, unitary elasticity of expectations is assumed to hold with respect to the exchange rate, so that there would be no role for the interest rate effect.

The Nature of Capital Flows The nature of international capital flows has also been subject to scrutiny and it is suggested that most of the capital which responds to interest rate differentials between countries is likely to be part of a stock of 'hot' money rather than a flow of savings. If a country raises its interest rate, capital will flow from the rest of the world, as portfolios are adjusted to take account of the changed structure of interest rates. When this has been completed capital flows will cease. To maintain a constant capital flow in such circumstances would require a continually increasing interest rate differential between the country and the rest of the world. This is unlikely to be consistent with internal equilibrium.

Wealth Effects The analysis has been concerned only with flow equilibria and has not pursued the effect of flows on stocks. It is a matter of indifference whether external balance is achieved by acquiring foreign currency (to buy imports of goods or securities) through the export off goods or the import of capital. The latter option is clearly not viable in the long term since no country can continue to amass foreign debt.

The influence of wealth has also been subject to a more sophisticated analysis. If a country runs a current account surplus it acquires claims on foreign nationals; that is, it acquires overseas assets, which increase domestic wealth. Wealth, it is argued, will have a positive effect on aggregate demand and on the demand for money, so that a term for wealth should be included in a fuller specification of equations 3.2 and 3.3 above.

If a country experiences a monetary expansion under a flexible exchange rate and this results in a depreciation of its currency and a subsequent trade surplus, the country will acquire overseas assets. This increase in wealth will raise both aggregate demand, which will tend to reverse the trade surplus, and the demand for money, which will put upward pressure on the interest rate and cause a capital inflow and exchange rate appreciation, which should further diminish the trade surplus. A debtor country would be subject to reverse effects.

The empirical magnitude of the wealth effect may not be significant, but it does indicate that the earlier analysis is incomplete. Such wealth effects are discussed more fully in chapter 7 where the portfolio balance approach to the exchange rate is discussed.

The Significance of the Qualifications The qualifications carry the following significance for the original analysis.

(1) The effectiveness of the effective policy instrument and the ineffectiveness of the ineffective are both overstated. This follows from the analysis when allowance is made for imperfect capital mobility or for expectations about future exchange rates.
(2) The analysis is applicable only in the fairly short term. The nature of capital flows and the effects of wealth in the long term indicate that apparent equilibria cannot be sustained through time.
(3) There is the real possibility that an economy may react in an unstable manner in the short run, if certain crucial relationships e.g. the Marshall–Lerner do not hold.

Notes

1 For a detailed discussion of the major results in this area see W. M. Corden, *Trade Policy and Economic Welfare*, Oxford University Press 1974.
2 See for example R. Dornbusch and S. Fisher, *Macroeconomics*, McGraw-Hill 1984 or R. Levacic and A. Rebmann, *Macroeconomics* (2nd edition), Macmillan 1982.
3 The slope of *FF* is the ratio of the responsiveness of the trade balance to income to the responsiveness of capital inflow to the rate of interest, while

LM is the ratio of the responsiveness of money demand to income to the responsiveness of money demand to the rate of interest. Because it is assumed that foreign assets are perfect substitutes for domestic assets, the influence of this term, K_i, will dominate the other three so that FF has a shallower slope than LM,

i.e. $\dfrac{M_y^{\mathrm{D}}}{M_i^{\mathrm{D}}} > \dfrac{T_y}{K_i}$.

4 Purchasing Power Parity: Theory and Evidence

Since purchasing power parity (ppp) underlies much of the modern literature on the balance of payments and exchange rate determination (to be discussed in chapters 5–8) and also since it has been viewed as a theory of exchange rate determination in its own right, attention is turned in this chapter to an exposition of the concept and a review of the relevant empirical evidence.

The concept of ppp is generally attributable to Cassel, who formulated the approach in the 1920s. Cassel's theory essentially represents a synthesis of the work of the nineteenth-century economists, Ricardo, Wheatley and Thornton.[1] Put in its most general terms, the ppp doctrine suggests that we should be able to buy the same bundle of goods in *any* country for the same amount of currency, (or, put slightly differently, people value currencies for what they buy). At first glance this may seem a rather odd proposition. It can, however, be illustrated by making the distinction between *absolute* and *relative* purchasing power parity which is turned to in the following section. After discussing the basic ppp doctrine the chapter moves on in section 2 to consider what ppp has to say about the expected change in the exchange rate: this is labelled 'inter-temporal *ppp*'. In section 3 it is demonstrated that ppp should be regarded as a long-run rather than a short-run concept. Criticisms of the ppp concept are considered in section 4 and, finally, in section 5 the empirical validity of ppp is examined.

SECTION 1 THE ABSOLUTE AND RELATIVE PURCHASING POWER PARITY CONCEPTS

'Law of One Price'

Let us consider two countries, the UK and the US, where both countries produce only goods which are tradeable, that the goods produced by each country are homogeneous (i.e. a washing machine produced in the UK is identical to a unit produced in the US), there are no impediments to international trade, such as tariff barriers and transaction costs, there are no capital flows, the economies are operating at a full employment level and *the price system 'works'*. Given these, albeit heroic assumptions, an important arbitrage condition, the law of one price, must hold:

$$P^{i,\text{UK}} = P^{i,\text{US}} \cdot S \qquad \text{for all } i = 1, \ldots n \qquad (4.1)$$

Thus, the price of good i in the UK (in terms of pounds sterling), say washing machines, must equal the price of an identical washing machine in the US (in US dollars) times the spot exchange rate, S (where the exchange rate is defined as the home currency price of a unit of foreign exchange). Given these assumptions, if equation 4.1 does not hold then it would be profitable for arbitrageurs to trade.

For example if $P^{i,\text{UK}}$ is for some reason greater than the quotient of $P^{i,\text{US}} \cdot S$ it would be profitable for economic agents in the US to buy good i in the US and transport it to the UK and sell it at the higher price. Equally it would be profitable for speculators in the UK to convert funds into dollars and buy good 'i' in the US and ship it to the UK. This process of arbitrage will continue until it is no longer profitable; i.e. the equality 4.1 is again restored. Transaction costs would modify this result in the sense that they create a 'neutral band' within which it is unprofitable to engage in arbitrage. Thus in the presence of transaction costs equation 4.1 would not hold exactly.

How does the adjustment in the above example take place? If the exchange rate is fixed or pegged, then the price of i will rise in the US and fall in the UK as the commodity is arbitraged to the UK to restore equality 4.1. If the exchange rate is perfectly flexible then the pressure to convert sterling into dollars, in order for the British to obtain the cheaper US good, will cause the pound to depreciate (S rise). Thus, the prices of good i will stay fixed both in the US and the UK and equation 4.1 will be restored by an exchange rate change rather than price level adjustment. Hence under a system of fixed exchange rates ppp can be used to explain the change in reserves caused by changes in the international exchange of commodities and under a system of flexible exchange rates it determines the exchange rate.

Absolute ppp

By rearranging equation 4.1 and summing all prices (using the same weights in constructing each countries' price level) the absolute version of ppp is obtained:

$$S = \sum_{i=1}^{n} P^{i,\text{UK}} \bigg/ \sum_{i=1}^{n} P^{i,\text{US}} \tag{4.2}$$

Hence if $P^{i,\text{UK}} = £50$ and $P^{i,\text{US}} = \$100$ then the pound/dollar exchange rate will be $2 per £1 or 50 pence per dollar.

Relative ppp

The absolute version of ppp relates an exchange rate to the absolute price level of all $i = 1 \ldots n$ goods in the two countries. In a period of relatively stable prices, exchange rates would not be expected to change very much. However, in a period of rapid inflation, such as the experience of the 1970s, it is likely that relative national price levels would be changing a lot and, therefore, so would the exchange rate. The question is: by how much should an exchange rate change? In practice equation 4.2 is not a particularly useful construct because different countries use different price index weights to calculate price levels, an issue which is discussed in more detail later. As a matter of practicality the relative *ppp* theory is used to overcome this problem. Thus, even if countries use different price weighting schemes, as long as the weights remain constant over time, changes in relative *price levels* will be reflected in the relative *price indices*. Thus:

$$S_t/S_b = P_t/P_b \tag{4.3}$$

where the subscript b represents the base period and t represents, say, the current period:

$$P_b = \left(\sum_{i=1}^{n} P_i, \text{UK} \bigg/ \sum_{i=1}^{n} P_i, \text{US} \right)_b \tag{4.4}$$

$$P_t = \left(\sum_{i=1}^{n} P_i, \text{UK} \bigg/ \sum_{i=1}^{n} P_i, \text{US} \right)_t \tag{4.5}$$

Thus the relative version of ppp simply states that if relative prices double in the UK between the base period and time t the exchange rate will change by an equal opposite percentage, i.e. it will depreciate by 50 per cent.

SECTION 2 INTERTEMPORAL PURCHASING POWER PARITY

In chapter 2 it was indicated that the balance of payments consisted of a current and capital account, and that they must sum to zero with a flexible exchange rate. So far the discussion of ppp has concentrated on current account items i.e. trade in commodities. The ppp concept has, however, an important bearing on the international exchange of capital account items.

Consider two countries (the UK and US) where absolute ppp as in equations 4.1 and 4.2 is assumed to hold, each country issues a bond which represents titles to the country's capital stock, and the bonds offer the investor real rates of interest, r^{UK} and r^{US}. Thus, in the absence of risk, transaction costs and other impediments to the exchange of bonds, the *real* rate of interest in the UK should equal the real interest rate in the US.

$$r^{UK} = r^{US} \tag{4.6}$$

If for any reason $r^{UK} > r^{US}$, there would be an incentive for capital to flow from the US to the UK and this would continue until equality was again restored. But, in practice, capital is often observed moving from a country with high *nominal* interest rates to one with lower *nominal* interest rates; this phenomenon was also mentioned in connection with covered interest arbitrage in chapter 2. This apparent paradox may be resolved by introducing the familiar relationship between nominal interest rates, real interest rates and expected inflation: the so called *Fisher relationship*. The Fisher relationship in the example for the UK and US is captured by equations:

$$i^{UK} = r^{UK} + \dot{p}^{e,UK} \tag{4.7}$$

$$i^{US} = r^{US} + \dot{p}^{e,US} \tag{4.8}$$

where i represents the nominal interest rate and $\dot{p}^e$ is the expected change in the price index ($\dot{p}^e = \ln(p^e/p)$). Equations 4.7 and 4.8 state simply that investors are prepared to hold bonds only if they are compensated for expected inflation (i.e. they are interested in maintaining the real purchasing power of their investment). Thus if the international exchange of bonds equalizes real interest rates, r^{UK} and r^{US}, nominal interest rate differentials will be determined by differential rates of inflation

$$i^{UK} - i^{US} = \dot{p}^{e,UK} - \dot{p}^{e,US} \tag{4.9}$$

Equation 4.9 can be used to explain why a high nominal interest rate country may export capital. If the UK, for example, has greater expected inflation than the US, its nominal interest rate will be greater than the nominal interest rate in the US but if, in the absence of capital flows, the US has a higher real rate of interest, capital will flow from the UK to the US. Equation 4.9 may also be used to explain the expected change in the exchange rate.

It has been demonstrated above that absolute ppp determines the current exchange rate (equation 4.2) but it may also be used to determine the expected exchange rate in any period. Thus the expected exchange rate in any period will be given by:

$$S^e = \frac{P^{e,\text{UK}}}{P^{e,\text{US}}} \tag{4.10}$$

using this expression and 4.2 the expected change in the exchange rate can be derived:

$$S^e/S = \frac{P^{e,\text{UK}}/P^{e,\text{US}}}{P^{\text{UK}}/P^{\text{US}}} = \frac{P^{e,\text{UK}}/P^{\text{UK}}}{P^{e,\text{US}}/P^{\text{US}}} \tag{4.11}$$

and taking natural logarithms yields:

$$\dot{s}^e = \dot{p}^{e,\text{UK}} - \dot{p}^{e,\text{US}} \tag{4.12}$$

This simply says that if the expected inflation rate rises in the UK relative to the US the exchange rate will be expected to depreciate. By substituting equation 4.12 into the expression for the nominal interest differential, equation 4.9, the following is obtained:

$$\dot{s}^e = i^{\text{UK}} - i^{\text{US}} \tag{4.13}$$

which is the so-called *Fisher open or uncovered interest parity condition*. Notice further that if the forward exchange rate is equal to the expected future spot rate the forward premium could be substituted for $\dot{s}^e$ in equation 4.13.

The ppp concept seems to be a very appealing construct for the determination of the exchange rate, not least because of its inherent simplicity. There are, however, a number of complications that have to be considered: does ppp hold continuously? What happens if the assumption that all goods are traded is relaxed, so introducing non-traded goods? And which price indices should be used in the computation of ppp? Attention is now focussed on a discussion of these issues.

SECTION 3 PPP, A LONG-RUN OR SHORT-RUN CONCEPT?

In the definition of ppp, given by equation 4.2, it was noted that in the absence of transaction costs this relationship will hold continuously. However, as the reader will have noted, the conditions necessary for equation 4.2 to hold are extreme and, as Officer (1976) has argued, remove any operational content from the theory. In the form in which ppp has been described it is a tautology: the exchange rate can only deviate from ppp if commodity arbitrage is imperfect.

The obvious problem with the derivation of ppp in equation 4.2 is that it has been assumed that all goods are internationally traded. This is clearly an unrealistic characteristic of the real world: all countries produce outputs, e.g. personal services, which are not internationally traded but enter the computation of price indices. The essential reason why such goods are not traded is that they have to be consumed at the point of purchase and thus there are normally very high transaction costs facing a foreign resident wishing to purchase a domestic service (consider, for example, the case of a US resident wishing to purchase a UK haircut). As Yeager (1958) points out, the dividing line between traded and non-traded goods is fuzzy and continually changing. Proponents of ppp, such as Cassel, would argue that a realistic definition of ppp should include both traded and non-traded goods. Furthermore, this is not regarded as creating any problems in the computation of ppp because the prices of traded and non-traded goods are linked by a variety of mechanisms, i.e. some traded goods serve as inputs into non-traded goods and vice versa; traded and non-traded goods may be produced by common factors of production; and by direct or indirect substitutability in consumption.[2] The issue of traded/non-traded goods will be returned to below where it will be argued that it *can* create problems for the computation of ppp (one such mechanism will be illustrated in Section 4 under 'Biased productivity growth').

Relaxing the assumption that all goods are traded makes ppp more realistic, so it must be asked whether it is also realistic to assume that the concept holds continuously. In fact few proponents of ppp would argue for a strict acceptance of ppp at all points in time. Rather, ppp is seen as determining the exchange rate in the long run and a variety of other factors may influence the exchange rate in conditions of disequilibrium. Thus assume that the 'long-run' or equilibrium exchange rate, $\bar{S}$, between the US and UK is determined by absolute ppp.

$$\bar{S} = P^{UK}/P^{US} \tag{4.14}$$

but in the short run the actual exchange rate, S, may diverge from the long-run rate due to the influence of other factors.

$$S = g(\bar{S}, X_i, \ldots X_n) \tag{4.15}$$

where $X_i \ldots n$ represents the potential influences on the short run exchange rate. What are these influences?

Basically the ppp doctrine captured by equations 4.2 and 4.3 asserts that currencies are demanded for transaction purposes, i.e. current account transactions. But capital account items are an important component of the balance of payments and may even dominate current account transactions. Although in defining inter-temporal ppp capital account items have been introduced, notice that in equilibrium it is implicitly assumed that the reason agents hold bonds is to finance expected future transactions (i.e. they are a hedge against expected inflation). Away from equilibrium – i.e. if for some reason $r^{US} > r^{UK}$ – long-term capital will flow from the UK to the US pushing S away from $\bar{S}$. The latter could also occur if speculators expect the pound to depreciate and move *short-term* capital funds from the UK to the US.

Other reasons why S may deviate from $\bar{S}$ have been gathered from the writings of Cassel by Officer (1976) and they are:

(1) Trading restrictions, such as tariffs and quotas on imports, imposed by a country but not by its trading partners, which may result in a fall in the value of the currency relative to ppp.
(2) Changes in consumers' preferences away from the home country's goods towards the foreign country's goods, which may lead to an exchange rate depreciation not predicted by ppp.
(3) Government intervention in the foreign exchange market.
(4) A natural resource discovery such as that of North Sea oil in the UK.
(5) Productivity changes generally (the chapter returns to the effects of productivity growth on ppp below).

SECTION 4   CRITICISMS OF PURCHASING POWER PARITY

In the previous section a number of factors were mentioned that may limit the relevance of ppp in the short run. There is, however, a further set of issues which question the efficacy of ppp in both the short and long run. The first issue covers the actual price index used; the second relates to the problem that biased productivity levels or growth imparts into a ppp calculation in the presence of non-traded goods; the third concerns the choice of a base period for relative ppp.

The Price Index Issue

The choice of an appropriate price index in a ppp calculation is the source of much controversy in the literature on ppp. The difficulty with using such a measure, however, is that different countries weight goods differently and this will impart a bias into the calculation of ppp. Furthermore, Keynes has argued that even if countries weight traded goods in an identical manner a purchasing power parity based purely on traded goods is nothing more than a tautology; i.e. ppp for traded goods prices only (assuming commodity arbitrage) simply states that the price of a commodity must be the same elsewhere when converted into a common currency. This has led to some economists advocating a price index based purely on *non-traded* goods since this is the only index that avoids the tautological element introduced into a price index when traded goods are the sole or part component. Proponents of a non-traded goods index argue for the use of wage levels (i.e. labour is the least traded commodity) rather than price levels (see Officer (1976) for a further discussion). Other proponents of ppp such as Cassel, argue for the use of a general price index, such as the retail price index or GDP deflator, on the grounds that it better reflects purchasing power and inflation. But this broader measure is also open to the criticism that different countries will use different weighting schemes, thus introducing a bias into the calculation of ppp.

Aside from the issue of the appropriate weights to be used in a price index, a problem arises when comparing developed and less developed countries using a ppp exchange rate calculated from general price indices rather than from purely traded prices. This problem, labelled here the Balassa–Samuelson thesis, depends on the supposition that traded goods prices determine the equilibrium exchange rate, that developed and less developed countries have different productivity levels and that both countries produce non-traded goods. The existence of non-traded goods may also create other problems in the calculation of ppp if the income elasticity of demand for non-traded goods is greater than one and if there are transport costs. We shall consider each of these issues in turn.

Biased Productivity Growth: The Balassa–Samuelson Thesis

An American visiting, say, Mexico will notice that locally supplied services – or non-traded items generally – are inexpensive compared to back home. Looking a little further, provided that the pesos had been bought at a free market clearing exchange rate, no such marked differences would arise with the prices of internationally traded goods. The American might conjecture, therefore, that the pesos bought with US dollars provided such good value that, maybe, the dollar was overvalued.

This same question arises when currency conversions are made at market exchange rates to compare national *per capita* income levels. An American, for example, cannot imagine how the average citizen of a less developed country can live on just a few hundred dollars per year. Just a little thought, though, prompts the question: perhaps the *per capita* income conversions were made at the wrong exchange rates? Could it be that for some reason the local currencies are under-valued against the dollar?

The matter that needs to be settled is this: is it possible that ppp exchange rates calculated using general price measures systematically undervalue currencies of less developed countries relative to those of developed countries?

Consider again a two country model, in which the US and Mexico produce non-traded goods in addition to traded goods. Assume that there are two elements in the cost of producing traded and non-traded goods – wages, W, and labour productivity, $\emptyset$, (output per worker). Furthermore, there is assumed to be a positive relationship between prices and wages and an inverse relationship between productivity and prices. In addition, wages are equalized within a country – between the traded and non-traded goods sectors – but may differ across countries. These assumptions lead to the following relationships:

$$P^{\mathrm{M}}_{NT} = \frac{W^{\mathrm{M}}_{NT}}{\emptyset^{\mathrm{M}}_{NT}}, \ P^{\mathrm{M}}_{T} = \frac{W^{\mathrm{M}}_{T}}{\emptyset^{\mathrm{M}}_{T}} \quad \text{and} \quad P^{\mathrm{US}}_{NT} = \frac{W^{\mathrm{US}}_{NT}}{\emptyset^{\mathrm{US}}_{NT}}, \ P^{\mathrm{US}}_{T} = \frac{W^{\mathrm{US}}_{T}}{\emptyset^{\mathrm{US}}_{T}} \quad (4.16)$$

$$W^{\mathrm{M}}_{T} = W^{\mathrm{M}}_{NT} \quad \text{and} \quad W^{\mathrm{US}}_{T} = W^{\mathrm{US}}_{NT} \quad (4.17)$$

where the subscript T denotes traded and NT represents non-traded goods. It is assumed that competition in the labour market in each country enforces the identities (4.17).

Now, the equilibrium exchange rate is determined by the relative domestic prices of traded goods, and it is these which determine the position of the foreign currency supply and demand curves in the basic exchange rate determination figure, for example, figure 2.1. Thus:

$$S = \frac{P_T^{\mathrm{M}}}{P_T^{\mathrm{US}}} \tag{4.18}$$

Next, the relative prices of traded and non-traded goods in each country are given by the relative productivity of labour in the traded and non-traded goods sectors (π^{M} and π^{US}):

$$\frac{P_{NT}^{\mathrm{M}}}{P_T^{\mathrm{M}}} = \pi^{\mathrm{M}} \quad \text{and} \quad \frac{P_{NT}^{\mathrm{US}}}{P_T^{\mathrm{US}}} = \pi^{\mathrm{US}} \tag{4.19}[3]$$

Balassa (1964) and others have argued that countries with high *per capita* incomes typically have high productivity. This high productivity is, however, not evenly distributed between traded and non-traded goods. Rather, it is argued that the traded goods sector will be more productive than the non-traded goods sector. (While the manufacturing sector may have vastly superior labour productivity, it is hard to imagine that this could also be true of, say, barbers and cobblers). Thus in terms of this one-factor, two country model, if $\emptyset_T^{\mathrm{US}} > \emptyset_T^{\mathrm{M}}$ the internal price ratio of non-traded to traded goods in the US will be greater than the corresponding Mexican ratio, i.e. $\pi^{\mathrm{US}} > \pi^{\mathrm{M}}$.

It is now possible to answer the questions posed at the beginning of this section: is the dollar over-valued against the Mexican peso? Conversely, is the peso undervalued relative to the dollar?

Remember that the equilibrium exchange rate is determined by the relative prices of traded goods only – equation (4.18), but that non-traded goods also enter into the calculation of national price levels. Furthermore, relative to traded goods' prices, American non-traded goods are more expensive than Mexican ($\pi^{\mathrm{US}} > \pi^{\mathrm{M}}$) e.g. the dollar price of services is higher in the US than in Mexico. Hence, the American price level – inclusive of non-traded goods – is higher than is allowed for by the exchange rate conversion at the market clearing exchange rate – the ppp exchange rate over values the dollar. Thus the American's conjecture was correct. Furthermore, when the argument is extended to relative ppp it implies that changes in productivity growth over time will impart a bias into the predicted exchange rate changes.

The second conclusion which follows from this reasoning is that the correct way to compare *per capita* incomes is not through exchange rate conversion for, as has been shown, the market clearing exchange rate is not the ppp exchange rate. Rather, *per capita* incomes should be compared at ppp. The commodity and service items which appear in the US price index should be calculated at Mexican peso prices, as Kravis (1978) has done, or the items in the Mexican price index at US dollar prices. If the former, the value of Mexican non-traded goods will be raised to the American level. And in the second case, the price of American non-traded goods would be reduced to the Mexican level. Either way, Mexico's *per capita* income will rise relative to the USA's.

Thus, in conducting ppp calculations for developed *vis-à-vis* less developed countries, care has to be taken in the choice of an appropriate price index. However, when comparing countries at a similar level of development, such as France and West Germany, the use of a general price index rather than a traded goods price index would not be expected to impart a productivity bias.

The Demand Side and Non-traded Goods

The existence of non-traded goods may allow a demand side bias to be introduced into the calculation of ppp. For example, Genberg (1978) has suggested that if the income elasticity of demand for non-traded goods is greater than one, and assuming unbiased productivity growth, then the relative price of non-traded goods will rise as income rises. This relative price change will be reinforced if, as seems likely, the share of government expenditure devoted to non-traded goods is greater than the share of private expenditure, and if income is redistributed to the government over time.

Differential Transportation Costs

In section 1 it was mentioned how transaction costs modified ppp in a world with only traded goods. Do transaction costs make any difference when non-traded goods are introduced? It only makes a difference for the absolute ppp case if there are differential transport costs between the two countries which is the fundamental reason for making a distinction between the two sectors. With differential transportation costs between the US and UK it was shown that the relative price of traded to non-traded goods will differ in the two countries and this will impart a bias into the calculation of absolute ppp when a broadly based price index is used (i.e. the sterling price of the non-traded good will differ in the home and foreign country).

As might be expected, relative ppp will hold even with differential costs between traded and non-traded goods, as long as the relationship remains constant over time. However, if the relative price of traded to non-traded goods changes over time, due to increased transportation costs (or if $\emptyset^{UK}$ changes relative to $\emptyset^{US}$), then relative ppp will of course also be violated.

Notice that the important implicit assumption underlying the productivity bias and demand side arguments is that non-traded goods are *not* relevant for the determination of the exchange rate.

SECTION 5 THE EMPIRICAL VALIDITY OF PPP

This section considers some of the empirical evidence which tests the validity of ppp when exchange rates are flexible (the existence of ppp under fixed exchange rates is considered in chapter 5).

Figures 4.1–4.3 present the relationship between nominal and real exchange rates for a selection of currencies (the real exchange rate is defined as P/P^*S). On strict ppp grounds (i.e. the relationship presented in section 1) it is expected that the real exchange rate is independent of the nominal exchange rate. If, however, factors such as those described in section 2 have an independent effect on the

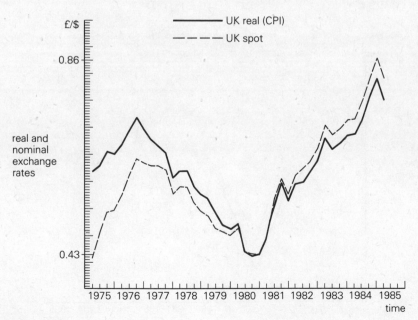

Figure 4.1

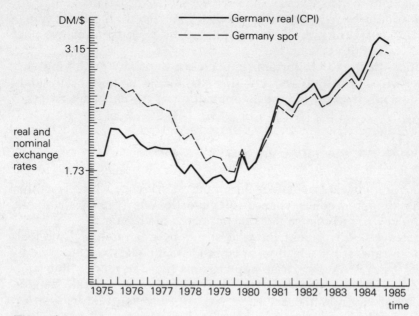

Figure 4.2

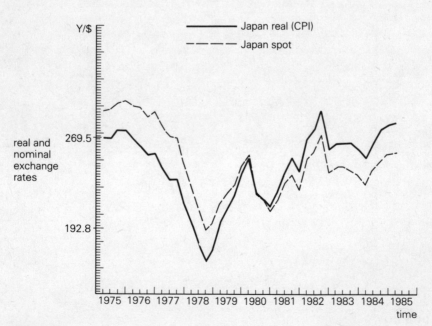

Figure 4.3

exchange rate, pushing it away from its ppp rate, it is expected that nominal exchange rate changes will result in real exchange rate changes. Which view does the evidence support? In figure 4.1 the logarithm of the UK pound–US dollar nominal and real exchange rate is presented where the latter has been calculated using consumer price indices. It is clear that for the period considered, nominal and real exchange rates move closely together. Thus the nominal appreciation of the sterling rate from mid-1976 to the end of the 1970s is seen to be also a real appreciation and the nominal depreciation of the exchange rate thereafter is seen to be also a real depreciation. (This pattern also holds when wholesale price indices are used, instead of CPIs.) Notice that the close correlation between real and nominal exchange rates is borne out by the other dollar bilateral exchange rates considered – see figures 4.2 and 4.3. The broad conclusion from this evidence would be that attention needs to be focussed on the factors which push the nominal exchange rate away from its ppp value (this in fact is the topic of chapters 6 and 7).

One of the crucial assumptions underlying the derivation of the law of one price defined in section 1 was that traded goods are homogeneous. That is to say, a UK-produced unit of any good is identical to a US-produced unit. The empirical evidence strongly suggests, however, that with the exception of agricultural commodities, goods entering international trade are not close substitutes. For example, Isard (1977) takes the most disaggregated groupings of manufactured goods for which US, German and Japanese prices are readily available (wholesale and export prices) and finds that for the period 1970–5 the law of one price fails to hold. Thus it is impossible to construct aggregate price indices, such as in equation 4.2 above, which would be expected to obey the law of one price.

Frenkel (1978, 1981) presents regression estimates of absolute and relative ppp based on a selection of aggregate price indices for the inter-war and recent experience with floating exchange rates. The equations estimated are of the form,

Absolute ppp:

$$\ln S_t = \alpha + \beta \ln P_t - \beta^* \ln P_t \qquad (4.20)$$

Relative ppp:

$$\ln \Delta S_t = \beta \ln \Delta P_t - \beta^* \ln \Delta P_t \qquad (4.21)$$

where it is expected that $\beta = \beta^* = 1$ and the constant is equal to zero if ppp holds. Estimates are presented for equations (4.20) and (4.21) for the dollar–pound, franc–dollar and franc–pound exchange rates using the ratio of material price indices, the ratio of food price indices and the ratio of wholesale price indices for the period February 1921–May 1925. Frenkel's results are highly supportive of the ppp hypothesis in both the absolute and relative versions. Thus in the majority of cases the hypothesis that $\beta = \beta^* = 1$ cannot be rejected at usual significance levels. In the relative ppp case the inclusion of a constant term is shown to be statistically insiginficant.

However, when equations (4.20) and (4.21) are estimated by Frenkel (1981) using data (wholesale and cost of living indices) from the recent floating exchange rate experience for the dollar–pound, dollar–French franc and dollar–Deutschmark exchange rates, it is shown that ppp in both its relative and absolute versions is not supported by the data. Similar results to Frenkel's are reported by Krugman (1978) for the inter-war and recent floating experience: ppp seems to hold reasonably well for the inter-war period, but the relationship is not empirically supported by the 1970s data. Krugman concludes: 'There is some evidence then that there is more to exchange rates than ppp. This evidence is that the deviations of exchange rates from ppp are large, fairly persistent, and seem to be larger in countries with unstable monetary policy'. (This point is picked up in chapters 6, 7 and 8.)[4]

Concluding Comments

This chapter has summarized the ppp hypothesis in both its absolute and relative versions. Purchasing power parity is probably at its most useful as a description of the long-run exchange rate, when short-run relative price effects have worked themselves out, or when inflationary forces dominate real changes. But does ppp in fact provide a theory of the exchange rate or is it rather a theory of the determination of prices? That is to say which way does causation run? From prices to exchange rates as proponents of ppp would argue, or from exchange rate changes to price changes? This issue is still unclear and it is probably correct to say that both the exchange rate and prices are endogenous variables and are determined simultaneously (see, for example, Yeager 1958).

The most glaring failure of ppp, which is obliquely referred to in figures 4.1–4.3, is that the theory as outlined fails to explain the large volatility of exchange rates that have been such a prominent feature of the recent floating experience. It is this phenomenon which we attempt to explain in succeeding chapters.

Notes

1 For a discussion of the historical development of ppp see Frenkel (1978) and Myhran (1976).
2 See Yeager (1958).
3 Equation 4.19 is derived for the US as follows:

$$P_{NT}^{US} = \frac{W_{NT}^{US}}{\emptyset_{NT}^{US}}$$

and

$$P_T^{US} = \frac{W_T^{US}}{\emptyset_T^{US}}$$

But

$$W_T^{US} = W_{NT}^{US},$$

therefore,

$$P_{NT}^{US} \times \emptyset_{NT}^{US} = P_T^{US} \times \emptyset_T^{US}$$

and

$$\frac{P_{NT}^{US}}{P_T^{US}} = \frac{\emptyset_T^{US}}{\emptyset_{NT}^{US}} = \pi^{US}$$

The ratio π^M is derived similarly for Mexico.

4 Further evidence on the failure of ppp to hold during the recent float may be gleaned from table 1.2. Thus exchange rates and prices for the countries quoted are not closely correlated.

5 The Monetary Approach to the Balance of Payments

The monetary approach to the balance of payments (MABP) argues, in contrast to Keynesian theory, that the balance of payments is a monetary phenomenon and not a real phenomenon, and should be analysed using the familiar tools of monetary analysis, namely, the demand for and supply of money. Thus, it is argued that any disequilibrium in the balance of payments is a reflection of disequilibrium in money markets. In its most extreme version, the MABP has a number of important and iconoclastic conclusions:

(1) It implies that a devaluation, in contrast to the models outlined in chapter 2, can have only a transitory impact on the balance of payments.
(2) A growing country will run a balance of payments surplus (this is in contrast to the Keynesian model where economic growth leads to a balance of payments deficit).
(3) A country can only run a balance of payments deficit until it runs out of foreign exchange reserves.
(4) Import quotas, tariffs, exchange restrictions and other interferences to international trade can have only, at best, a transitory effect on the balance of payments.
(5) With pegged exchange rates a country cannot run an independent monetary policy.
(6) A rise in the domestic rate of interest will result in a balance of payments deficit.

Why then does the MABP focus attention on the money market as the relevant market for the analysis of balance of payments issues, and how are the above important conclusions derived? It is the purpose of this chapter to explain why a view of the balance of payments different to those presented in chapter 2 is required, and the implications of this monetary view of the balance of payments for economic policy are spelled out. The outline of the remainder of this chapter is as follows.

In section 1 some familiar identities are presented to show that in an *ex post* accounting sense the MABP should give similar answers to balance of payments issues as the elasticities and absorption approaches. Since this is so, it is shown why proponents of the MABP say it is a preferable means of analysing balance of payments issues to the alternatives. In section 2 a simple MABP model is outlined to illustrate the impact of devaluation and domestic credit expansion under fixed exchange rates. Some policy conclusions stemming from this model are then discussed. In the final two sections there is an assessment of the empirical evidence on two of the most crucial policy implications of the MABP namely: the conclusion that under a system of pegged exchange rates a country cannot pursue an independent monetary policy and also the view that with fixed exchange rates inflation is an international monetary phenomenon.

SECTION 1 WHAT'S SO DIFFERENT ABOUT THE MONETARY APPROACH?

In this section some simple and familiar identities are presented in order to illustrate the relationship between the elasticities, absorption and monetary approaches to the balance of payments. As will be seen, in an *ex post* general equilibrium sense these models are perfectly compatible and reconcilable and thus the question that naturally arises is why is it useful to analyse the balance of payments as a monetary phenomenon.[1]

Consider first the familiar balance sheet of the *consolidated monetary sector* (i.e. the central bank, the exchange stabilization authorities and all other issuers of money are lumped together).

Assets	Liabilities
D	M
F	

where M is the stock of money, F is the foreign backed component of M, D is the domestic assets of the banking system (i.e. all other assets net of all other liabilities of the consolidated banking system). Thus the banking (*ex post*) identity is:

$$M = F + D \qquad (5.1)$$

and taking first differences of 5.1 and rearranging:

$$\Delta F = \Delta M - \Delta D \tag{5.2}$$

where clearly ΔF is the change in reserves, ΔD is the change in the domestic component of the money supply or domestic credit expansion and ΔM is the change in the money stock which in the MABP literature is the flow demand for money, or hoarding. Now it is known that with a fixed exchange rate system, the change in reserves is equal to the sum of the current and capital accounts of the balance of payments, i.e.:

$$\Delta F = B + K \tag{5.3}$$

where B represents the current account balance (a flow) and K is the capital account balance (also assumed to be a flow). Thus if both the current and capital accounts are in deficit the country must be losing reserves. Equation 5.2 explains why: for the country to be losing reserves domestic credit expansion must exceed hoarding. Thus to control a balance of payments deficit domestic credit expansion has to be controlled relative to the flow demand for money. Alternatively, if ΔM is greater than ΔD then there is an excess flow demand for money which in an open economy can be satisfied by the public swopping bonds and goods for reserves; i.e. the country will run a balance of payments surplus.

The identities 5.1–5.3 are those relevant to MABP. It is now shown that the monetary approach identities should, in an *ex post* accounting sense, give the same result for the change in reserves as the elasticities and absorption approaches.

From national income accounting it is known that *ex post*:

$$Y = A + B \tag{5.4}$$

where A represents aggregate absorption and B represents the trade balance (exports minus imports – other current account and the capital account items are ignored for simplicity). The elasticities approach utilizes the relationship:

$$B = X - M \tag{5.5}$$

and assuming that the Marshall–Lerner condition holds, then, as has been shown in chapter 2, a devaluation leads to an improvement in the balance of trade. The absorption approach, on the other hand, draws attention to the fact that the balance of trade can only be improved if income is increased relative to absorption (and, as we have seen, a country may require a combination of expenditure-switching (devaluation) and expenditure-reducing policies):

$$B = Y - A \tag{5.6}$$

Using 5.2, 5.3 (assuming for simplicity $K = 0$), 5.4, 5.5 and 5.6, and taking all variables as *ex post* identities then:

$$\Delta F = B = X - M = Y - A = \Delta M - \Delta D \tag{5.7}$$

Thus, in an *ex post* sense the three approaches are equivalent. But as Whitman (1975) notes, perhaps identities are not very meaningful; one has to look behind the identities in order to see how variables are defined and what the implicit assumptions are underlying the approaches in order to give the above reconciliation. Nevertheless, the identity 5.7 does highlight the fact that if the three different approaches are potentially reconcilable, why do proponents of the MABP favour using equation 5.2 rather than 5.5 or 5.6? A quotation from Johnson (1977) should help to highlight the differences:

... the monetary approach should in principle give an answer [to balance of payments questions] no different from that provided by a correct analysis in terms of the other accounts. The main reason for preferring the monetary approach is that less direct alternative approaches have almost invariably attempted to explain the behaviour of the markets they concern themselves with, by analytical constructs in which the role of money in influencing behaviour, and the connection between these other markets and the money markets, are neglected as being 'of the second order of smalls', which may be a legitimate procedure for many economic problems, but cannot be so for an analysis which aims to explain and predict behaviour in the money market.

This quotation can be illustrated in the following way. Consider a closed economy in which there are goods, bonds and money. The overall aggregate budget constraint of such an economy must imply that the sum of the excess demands equals zero. Thus:

$$ED_g + ED_b + ED_m = 0 \tag{5.8}$$

where ED represents an excess demand and the subscripts g, b and m represent goods, bonds and money respectively. In a fully employed economy closed to international trade in goods and assets, excess demand will be eliminated by changes in prices but in an open economy such excess demands will be reflected in different net international flows in the balance of payments accounts. Clearly, if the country is small, in the sense of accepting world goods and bond prices as given, excess demands will be reflected solely in international flows. However if, on the other hand, the country is not small but has some influence on world prices it can be expected that excess demand will be eliminated by both price changes and international flows). The balance of payments flows will be constrained by:

$$(X_g - M_g) + (X_b - M_b) + (X_m - M_m) = 0 \qquad (5.9)$$

where X and M represent exports and imports, respectively. Thus the three accounts, the current, capital and money must sum to zero.

The budget constraint implies that if two of the markets are in equilibrium so too must the third market be. Thus an analysis of the balance of payments could concentrate on the current and capital accounts and ignore the money account. With the elasticities approach, with no capital account, attention is concentrated on the current account and the money market is ignored. *But this will be valid only if the crucial nature of the money market is ignored.* Thus money is a *stock* concept and the demand for money is a demand for a *stock*, not for a continuing flow of money.

The money identity, 5.1, shows that in an open economy residents of that country can have an influence on the total quantity of money via their ability to convert domestic money into foreign goods and securities or conversely turn domestic goods and securities into domestic money backed by foreign exchange reserves. The important point is that although stock disequilibrium in the money market will have as its counterpart a flow disequilibrium in, say, the goods market, such flows will only continue until stock equilibrium has been restored in the money market. But it is usual in non-monetary approaches to the balance of payments to have, say, goods flows depending only on prices and income, ignoring the underlying stock adjustment in money markets. We could of course 'rectify' the traditional balance of payments model by incorporating a stock adjustment mechanism directly into the relevant functions. But proponents of the monetary approach would argue that it is more straightforward to concentrate directly on the underlying disequilibrium in the money market. A direct consequence of analysing the balance of payments as a monetary phenomena is that it is clearly seen to be a stock phenomenon and not a flow phenomenon.

Attention is now turned to an elaboration of some of the concepts discussed in this section in the context of a simple model of an open economy operating a fixed exchange rate.

SECTION 2 THE GLOBAL MONETARIST MODEL

The essential feature of the MABP is that balance of payments disequilibrium should be viewed as reflecting disequilibrium in the money market. To illustrate the MABP consider, as a starting point, a version of the monetary approach which is to be found in the writings of a variety of its proponents, what Whitman (1975) has termed the 'Global Monetary Approach to the Balance of Payments' (GMABP). The global monetary model is attractive because of its inherent simplicity and also because it gives unambiguous analytical results and leads to strong policy conclusions. The 'monetarist' element of the GMABP refers to the emphasis on the supply and demand for money as the relevant tools for analysing balance of payments disequilibrium and the global element of GMABP refers to assumptions pertaining to the integration of the world economy. An example of the integration of the world economy referred to may be given in terms of commodity markets. Global monetarism assumes that commodities produced in different countries are perfect substitutes and thus, in the absence of trade barriers, arbitrage will ensure that the law of one price holds (see chapter 4 on purchasing power parity).

Let us now turn to a simple model[2] which highlights the global monetarist view of the world and consider first the monetary assertions underlying the GMABP. For simplicity the capital account is ignored: concentration is only on current account transactions. The introduction of a capital account would only complicate the analysis without helping to elucidate the salient issues of the monetary approach.

The model consists of two countries, each producing a single commodity, and the commodities are assumed to be perfect substitutes. Each country has a 'Cambridge' money demand function of the form:

$$L = kP\bar{y} \tag{5.10}$$

$$L^* = k^*P^*\bar{y}^* \tag{5.10a}$$

where L is desired nominal money balances, k is the 'Cambridge k' and represents the desired ratio of nominal money holdings to nominal income, P represents the money price of goods (or the price level) and $\bar{y}$ represents the exogenously determined full employment level of real output. Henceforth terms with an asterisk denote foreign variables. The homogeneity of money in prices, as depicted in equation 5.10, reflects an absence of money illusion and the (long-run) neutrality of money; furthermore, wages and prices are assumed to be perfectly flexible. Although equation 5.10 gives the long-run stationary state effects of, say, an excess supply of money on the price level, in the short-run money market adjustment is assumed *not* to be instantaneous. Instead, as was discussed in the previous section, individuals in an open economy can alter the money stock via the balance of payments. The flow demand for money, which is normally classed as hoarding, is denoted here as equation 5.11.

$$H = \alpha(L - M) = H(P, M) \tag{5.11}$$

$$H^* = \alpha^*(L^* - M^*) = H^*(P^*, M^*) \tag{5.11a}$$

where H and H^* represents hoarding in the domestic and foreign countries respectively and α and α^* are the domestic and foreign rates of adjustment. Equations 5.11 and 5.11a simply state that each individual believes that actual cash holdings at current prices can be adjusted by hoarding or dishoarding, i.e. by spending less or more than income respectively. Given the assumptions about the stock demand for money function – equations 5.10 or 5.10a, it follows that a rise in the price level raises hoarding since it creates a stock excess demand for money, while an increase in the nominal quantity of money reduces hoarding since it creates a stock excess supply.

Next the consolidated banking equation, noted in the previous section, is assumed to hold in each country:

$$M = F + \bar{D} \tag{5.1a}$$

$$M^* = F^* + \bar{D}^* \tag{5.1b}$$

where the domestic component of the money supply is assumed for the time being to be exogenous and is denoted as $\bar{D}$. Given the latter assumption the balance of payments feedback into the domestic money supply is defined by equation 5.12.

$$H = \Delta M = \Delta F = B \tag{5.12}$$

which states that for an exogenously determined domestic component of the money supply, $\bar{D}$, the money supply change is equal to the change in reserves which equals the trade balance surplus/deficit. Since a simple two country model is being used here any hoarding/dishoarding in the home country will have its mirror image in dishoarding/hoarding in the foreign country and a corresponding change in F^* and M^*, i.e.

$$H = \Delta M = \Delta F = B = -SB^* = -SH^* = -S\Delta F^* = -S\Delta M^* \tag{5.13}$$

where S, it will be recalled, is the exchange rate. Thus under fixed exchange rates the national money supply is *endogenous* rather than a policy instrument. This is in marked contrast to the assumptions, often implicit, underlying the Keynesian view of the balance of payments – viz. that the monetary authorities sterilise the impact on the domestic money supply of international reserve flows ensuing from payments imbalance.

Desired nominal expenditure in each country, Z, Z^*, is assumed to be a function of nominal income and the flow demand for money or hoarding.

$$Z = P\bar{Y} - H \tag{5.14}$$

$$Z^* = P^*\bar{Y}^* - H^* \tag{5.14a}$$

Thus equation 5.14 is in contrast to simple Keynesian models of the balance of payments, which not only ignore modelling the money supply implications of balance of payments changes, but also ignore the effects of monetary repercussions on expenditure. But although the MABP resolves this problem of the Keynesian approach it does, as Whitman (1975) notes, retain and intensify another inconsistency, viz. it combines long-run full equilibrium assumptions on the demand side with the essentially short-run assumption of the stationary state on the output side (i.e. income is exogenously given at the full employment level). Notice too that the expenditure functions in equation 5.14 imply a marginal propensity to spend out of income which is less than unity in the short run (because of the H term) but which is equal to one in the long run when money market disequilibria have worked themselves out.

The global aspect of the GMABP is reflected by equation:

$$P = SP^* \tag{5.15}$$

The law of one price holds in this one commodity world and this clearly *precludes* the terms of trade issues which are so crucial to the elasticities approach.

Thus there are three strands to the global monetarist view of the world. First, it is assumed that there is perfect commodity arbitrage and thus ppp holds continuously (equation 5.15) – this is the global element of the GMABP. The monetarist element of the GMABP is reflected in equation 5.10: the effect of an increase of M on P is proportional. The third strand, which may be interpreted as the monetary approach to the balance of payments element, is that with pegged exchange rates, the domestic money supply becomes endogenous, rather than an exogenous, variable (this is reflected in equations 5.1 and 5.13, that the excess demand for money plays a key role in the functioning of all markets in the economy (equation 5.14) and that such excess demand is a disequilibrium phenomenon (equations 5.10 and 5.11).

The simple model described by equations 5.11–5.15 is illustrated in figure 5.1. The schedules H and $-S_0 H^*$, drawn for given nominal

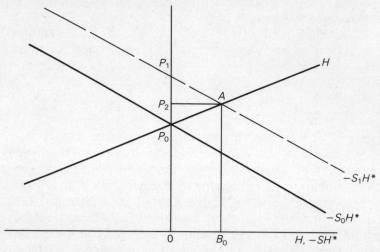

Figure 5.1   Devaluation and the price level in a two country GMABP model

M, M^* and S_0, represent the domestic and foreign rates of hoarding and dishoarding respectively as a function of the domestic price of goods, P. The domestic hoarding schedule will be upward sloping (i.e. $\partial H/\partial P > 0$) because an increase in the home price level, for a given nominal quantity of money, M, will lead to a desire by the residents of the country to restore the real value of their cash balances, i.e. H increases in equation 5.11. This can only be achieved with a given M, by a decline in expenditure/absorption relative to income (equation 5.14) and an improvement in the balance of payments (i.e. a current account surplus) and thus the F component of the money supply will increase. The same reasoning gives the foreign rate of *dis*hoarding as a negative function of P^3.

In figure 5.1, notice that at the equilibrium price P_0 there is neither hoarding nor dishoarding and this implies that the balance of payments must be in equilibrium, that is $B = 0$. This is therefore a position of long-run equilibrium and such an equilibrium requires that each country holds the desired quantity of real balances and that the arbitrage condition is satisfied.

Short-run Dynamics

Devaluation

It is known that in the short-run stock equilibrium need not obtain. Instead an alternative short-run definition of equilibrium is used, defined as a position where world income equals world expenditure, or equivalently, where the domestic rate of hoarding is equal to the foreign rate of dishoarding, viz.:

$$H = -S_0 H^*$$

The case of an exchange rate devaluation is illustrated in figure 5.1. The effect of a devaluation is to shift the foreign hoarding schedule upwards, the domestic hoarding schedule remaining unchanged. Such a short-run equilibrium is depicted in figure 5.1 at A. At this point the residents of the home country have a positive rate of hoarding, that is, they have an excess demand for money which, for a given domestic component of the money base, D, can only be achieved by running a current account surplus, B_0. But the balance of payments surplus at the equilibrium B_0 must imply, via equation 5.13 that M is changing and this via equation 5.11 implies that over time hoarding will be falling at home and rising in the foreign country. Such forces will drive the H and $-S_0 H^*$ schedules leftwards and this process will continue until they again intersect between P_0 and P_1 and at this point the system will have returned to equilibrium with $Z = PY$ and desired nominal money balances equal to actual money balances.

However, the devaluation will not have a proportionate effect on the domestic price level (i.e. both countries have some influence on the 'world' price level – the average of the sum of domestic and foreign prices). If domestic price was to remain fixed at P_0 after the devaluation, foreign dishoarding would exceed domestic hoarding and, with a world excess demand for goods, prices would rise in the rest of the world (i.e. the foreign country). Alternatively, if foreign price P^* is fixed, domestic price P will, via equation 5.15, rise in proportion to the devaluation. However, given that neither P nor P^* need be fixed, world excess demand will lead to price increases in both countries. In figure 5.1, equilibrium requires an increase in the domestic price level equal to $(P_2 - P_0)/P_0$. This is less than proportionate to the devaluation which would require an increase of $(P_1 - P_0)/P_0$. The price changes are distributed across both countries depending upon the relative slopes of the hoarding schedules. If the foreign dishoarding schedule had been horizontal (the home country is small in the sense that domestic prices are determined by foreign prices – equation 5.15) then domestic prices will rise proportionately with the devaluation.

Domestic Credit Expansion

Until now it has been assumed that the domestic component of the money supply, D, is determined exogenously. This assumption is now relaxed and the effect is considered of a once-and-for-all increase in the domestic money supply brought about by an increase in D. For unchanged prices this implies, via equation 5.10, that individuals have excess money balances and this, through equation 5.11, will result in dishoarding in the home country and a balance of payments deficit as individuals attempt to offload the excess money balances by buying goods (and securities if the capital account is modelled). The initial effect of the expansion of D for the two country case is illustrated in figure 5.2.

The increase in the domestic component of the money stock leads to a leftward shift in the hoarding schedule to H_1. The domestic price level rises to P_2 but, with full employment, there is still an excess demand for goods and thus at point A the country is running a balance of payments deficit and (via equation 5.13) losing reserves. The latter effect will push the hoarding schedule H_1 rightwards over time. The foreign country will be gaining reserves and experiencing an increased money supply. Thus, through equation 5.11a it will begin dishoarding which will shift the $-S_0H^*$ schedule rightwards. Stock disequilibrium will persist until the two schedules again intersect between P_1 and P_0, say at P_2. This is the only point consistent with full stock equilibrium.

The actual distribution of the increase in D on the home and foreign countries' money supplies and price levels can be seen to be a function of the *size* of the respective countries (see e.g. Swoboda,

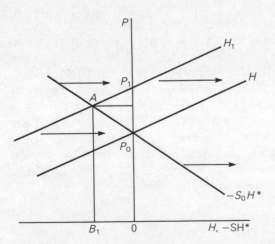

Figure 5.2 Domestic credit expansion in a two country GMABP model

1976). By substituting equation 5.10 into equation 5.15, assuming that S is constant and differentiating logarithmically

$$d \log M + d \log k + d \log Y^* - d \log M^*$$
$$- d \log k^* - d \log Y = 0 \qquad (5.16)$$

Since in the MABP model Y and k are assumed constant 5.16 can be simplified to:

$$d \log M = d \log M^* \qquad (5.17)$$

Thus the increase in the world money supply is distributed in proportion to existing money stocks, the latter being related to the size of the countries (it will be exactly related if from equations 5.10 and 5.10a $k = k^*$). This may be illustrated by means of an example. Suppose that the home country initially has a money stock of £10 million and that the foreign country has a money stock of £90 million. The home country now increases its money supply by £1 million and this will lead to an increase of its money supply in full equilibrium of £0.1 million and in the foreign country's money supply of £0.9 million. Thus a 10 per cent increase in the domestic money supply has only led to a one per cent increase in prices. There is then, as David Hume had argued in the eighteenth century, a natural distribution of the world's money supply.

The Policy Implications of the MABP

At the outset of this chapter some of the implications of regarding the balance of payments as a monetary phenomenon were listed. These implications are now discussed in a little more detail in the light of the discussion in the previous sections.

Since balance of payments surpluses and deficits are reflections of monetary disequilibrium, there is no need to have a government balance of payments policy, since, as was shown, such payments imbalances are transitory and will automatically correct themselves. A deficit country may be able to sustain its deficit by sterilizing the effects of the deficit on the domestic money supply (i.e. increase D as F falls); however, since reserves are finite such a policy must eventually come to an end. Equally a surplus country may try to sterilize the effects of its surplus on the money supply but in the longer term it will eventually exhaust its stock of domestic credit assets.

Second, under a system of pegged exchange rates monetary policy has a very limited role to play. For the small country a change in the domestic component of the money supply leads to an off-setting movement in reserves: domestic credit policy can only alter the composition of the backing to the money stock. If, however, the global component of the GMABP is relaxed by allowing monetary variables to affect real variables in the short run and by assuming imperfect substitutability of goods and assets in different countries (see Dornbusch 1973) it can be demonstrated that a change in the domestic backed component of the money supply will have real effects in the short run even under fixed exchange rates. However, the requirements of long-run stock equilibrium and the impossibility of a country adopting a continuous sterilization policy (the 'monetary' component of the GMABP) will ensure that for a small country an increase in D will lead to an exactly offsetting decrease in F: the *reserve offset coefficient* is equal to unity. When countries are not small the monetary component of the GMABP will ensure a proportional effect of money on prices in the long run.

A corollary of the last point is that *under a system of fixed exchange rates, inflation is a world monetary phenomenon* and cannot be controlled by a national monetary policy. The only way a country can pursue an inflation rate different to the rest of the world is by relinquishing the commitment to intervene in the foreign exchange market at a fixed price; the exchange rate must be allowed to float freely. (As will be shown in the next chapter it may well be impossible for countries even with floating exchange rates to pursue independent monetary policies).

The third policy implication of the GMABP model is that devaluation has only a transitory effect on the balance of payments. Thus, and as was demonstrated in previous sub-sections, devaluation has an effect on the balance of payments only to the extent that it alters the demand for money relative to its supply. Nevertheless, the period of transition during which devaluation has an effect, may be an important one for the policy makers allowing them, say, to achieve an increase in the country's reserves or increase the domestic component of the money base (perhaps as a response to a budget deficit) without having a deterioration in the balance of payments. If, however, all markets adjust instantaneously following a shock then devaluation cannot have an impact even in the short run.

Fourthly, it has been demonstrated that if the global elements of the GMABP are relaxed, the monetary approach does still predict that monetary/exchange rate policy can have 'real' effects in the short run although such effects will be vitiated in the long run (see also the Polak model in chapter 11). But some commentators (notably Kaldor, 1970), by questioning the monetary component of the GMABP, have attacked the long-run ineffectiveness of the policy described above. For example, the crucial lynchpin relationship in the monetary approach is equation 5.10 which predicts that prices are homogeneous of degree one in money. This prediction, however, is based on the assumption that k, the inverse of the velocity of money, is constant and at least a stable function of a few key variables. Diehard Keynesians, taking their lead from, for example, the Radcliffe Report (1957), would presumably question this assertion by arguing that the velocity of money is highly unstable and thus concentrating on the monetary consequences of the balance of payments is erroneous. Johnson (1977), however, has countered this by arguing that as long as k is not completely unstable, we are justified in treating the balance of payments as a monetary phenomenon.

Rabin and Yeager (1982), although accepting that a well defined and stable demand for money function may exist, argue that not all changes in the supply of money are desired or intended changes as suggested by the monetary approach. For example, the role of money as a medium of exchange necessitates it being used as a buffer stock and this may lead to unintended falls or rises in money balances. 'Money balances are pools into and out of which receipts and payments are made and so serve as buffers against short-term fluctuations in the timing and sizes of receipts and payments: since the fluctuations are unintended, the rise or fall in money balances can be unintended too',[4] Although this point is clearly correct for an individual, it is unclear how relevant the concept would be in the aggregate.[5] For other criticisms of the monetary approach as outlined in this section, the reader is referred to Currie (1976), Coppock (1980) and Rabin and Yeager (1982).

SECTION 3 STERILIZATION AND THE RESERVE OFFSET COEFFICIENT

Empirical Framework

Although the MABP has extremely strong policy implications it must be asked how well supported empirically is the underlying theory? In this section some answers to this question are given by considering a reduced form MABP equation. The reduced form equation is derived from familiar equations introduced in this chapter and summarized here as equations 5.18 to 5.21 (the country is assumed to be small and goods and assets are assumed to be perfect substitutes).

$$L = Pk Y\alpha_y i\alpha_i \tag{5.18}$$

$$M^s = F + D \tag{5.19}$$

$$M^s = L \tag{5.20}$$

$$P . kY\alpha_y i\alpha_i = F + D \tag{5.21}$$

where equation 5.18 is a Cagan-style money demand equation which posits that the demand for money balances depends upon real income, the interest rate (i.e. this is a generalization, with the inclusion of an interest rate, of the money demand equation considered in the previous section) and is homogeneous of degree one in prices; equation 5.19 is the money supply identity; equations 5.20 and 5.21 represent conditions of equilibrium in money markets where demand is equal to supply.

On taking logarithmic changes of the money market equilibrium condition:

$$\Delta \log P + \alpha_y \, \Delta \log Y - \alpha_i \Delta \log i =$$
$$[F/(F + D)]\Delta \log F + [D/(F + D)]\Delta \log D \tag{5.22}$$

By solving for $[F/(F + D)]\Delta \log F$, which we shall rename r, the following is obtained:

$$r = \Delta \log P + \alpha_y \, \Delta \log Y - \alpha_i \Delta \log i - d \tag{5.23}$$

where

$$d = [D/(F + D)]\Delta \log D$$

Notice that two interesting predictions of the monetary approach, not addressed hitherto, can be illustrated with equation 5.23. It suggests that an increase in the home interest rate results in a balance of payments deficit (since it is a small country the interest rate increase will only be incipient). This is in contrast to a more traditional view of the effects of interest rates on the balance of payments (i.e. the Mundell–Fleming model described in chapter 3) where an increase in the domestic interest rate leads to a capital inflow and a surplus on the balance of payments. This apparent paradox may be explained in the following way. In the monetary approach, an increase in the domestic interest rate, caused perhaps by changed inflationary expectations, will lead to a reduced demand for money as people substitute from money to bonds and perhaps goods (if they do expect inflation). For a small open economy at full employment and facing given foreign prices and interest rates, this reduction in the demand for money will be reflected in an excess demand for foreign exchange reserves: a balance of payments deficit. The second point that emerges from 5.23 is that if the economy is growing over time (i.e. $\Delta \log Y > 0$) it will *ceteris paribus* possibly run a balance of payments surplus. This is because income growth in this model increases the demand for money and for a given rate of domestic credit expansion, can only be satisfied via the foreign exchange market.

Equation 5.23 can be written in a form suitable for econometric investigation as:

$$r = \beta_0 + \beta_1 \Delta \log P + \beta_2 \Delta \log Y + \beta_3 \Delta \log i + \beta_5 d + u_t \qquad (5.24)$$

where it is expected that if the MABP is correct, β_1 to equal unity, β_2 and β_3 to take values similar to those estimated in conventional money demand equations (say 1 and -0.01 respectively: see Laidler 1976), and β_5 to equal -1. Perhaps the most crucial value, from the point of view of the verification of the MABP, is the magnitude of the coefficient on β_5, usually referred to as the offset coefficient.

In estimating equation 5.24, researchers have assumed that Y, P, i or d are all exogenous. The exogeneity of Y is justified on the MABP grounds of long-run full employment; i and P are assumed exogenous on the grounds that the country is small in world goods and financial markets; and if it is assumed that the authorities do not sterilize the effects of reserve changes on the money supply (i.e. if F increases D is not decreased) d may be assumed exogenous. The assumed exogeneity of the right hand side variables in equation 5.24 receives more attention below.

Empirical Results

A variety of researchers have tested equation 5.24 for different countries and time periods. For example, a representative estimated equation by Bean (1976) for Japan over the period 1959–70 (quarterly data) is reported as equation 5.25:

$$r = 1.19\Delta \log P + 0.52\Delta \log Y - 0.11\Delta \log i - 0.67d \qquad (5.25)$$
$$\quad (5.38) \qquad\qquad (6.36) \qquad\qquad (1.22) \qquad\qquad (8.32)$$

$$R^2 = 0.65 \quad DW = 1.99 \quad t \text{ statistics in parenthesis.}$$

Notice first that all coefficients are correctly signed in terms of the MABP and all, apart from the coefficient on the domestic interest rate, are statistically significant at the 95 per cent level. The coefficients on P and i are close to the predicted value; however, both the income elasticity and the elasticity of the domestic component are less than the predicted values of 1 and -1, respectively. (An explanation as to why β_5 may be less than -1 is given below.)

Since other researchers' specification of an MABP reduced form equation differs slightly from equation 5.24, table 5.1 summarizes these other results for the crucial coefficient on d.

Examination of table 5.1 reveals that the MABP prediction that a change in the domestic component of the money base will be offset by an equiproportionate change in reserves finds mixed support from the empirical evidence. The studies by Connolly and Taylor, Genberg, Guittan and Zecher are all highly supportive of the proposition $\beta_5 = 1$ (in all these papers the coefficient differs insignificantly from 1); however, the results by Bean and Kouri and Porter[6] tend to cast doubt on this proposition since the coefficient on β_5 is shown to differ significantly from unity in these studies.

Table 5.1 The Offset Coefficient and the Monetary Approach to the Balance of Payments

Author	Country	Data Period	Estimation Tech.	β_5	R^2	DW
Bean (1976)	Japan	1959–70	OLS	−0.67 (8.32)	0.65	1.99
Connolly and Taylor (1976)	Various LDC's	1959–70	OLS	−0.82 (5.47)	0.65	NA
Genberg (1976)	Sweden	1951–70	TSLS	−1.11 (3.00)	NA	NA
Guittan (1976)	Spain	1955–71	OLS	−0.958 (9.65)	0.95	2.36
Kouri and Porter (1974)	Australia	1961–72	OLS	−0.47 (5.29)	0.82	1.87
Kouri and Porter (1974)	Germany	1960–70	OLS	−0.77 (18.40)	0.96	2.17
Kouri and Porter (1974)	Italy	1964–70	OLS	−0.43 (4.36)	0.66	2.55
Kouri and Porter (1974)	Netherlands	1960–70	OLS	−0.59 (7.58)	0.82	2.54
Zecher (1976)	Australia	1951–61	OLS	−0.82 (5.47)	0.65	NA

Notes: OLS means ordinary least squares;
TSLS means two stage least squares;
R^2 is the coefficient of determination;
DW is the Durbin Watson statistic; and
t ratios are in parenthesis under the β_5 coefficients.

Problems with the Empirical Implementation of the MABP Reduced Form Equation

Some of the results reported in table 5.1 tend to question the robustness of one of the key propositions of the MABP; namely, that a change in the domestic component of the money supply will result in an equiproportionate change in the foreign component. For example, Branson (1975a) has argued that the Kouri and Porter estimates of β_5 are inconsistent with the MABP. But one reason why β_5 could be biased downwards may lie in the exclusion of certain key variables in the reduced form; i.e. there is a specification error. In particular, Magee (1976) argues that the exclusion of the exchange rate change will result in a specification error. Thus when the authorities increase d, the exchange rate, under the Bretton Woods system, was free to vary within a band and this movement may absorb some of the excess supply of money leading to a less than proportionate fall in r. Darby (1983) and Laskar (1983) have argued that the downward bias in β_5 may result from the exclusion of the expected change in the exchange rate from 5.23 (i.e. speculators may expect a change in reserve to lead to an exchange rate change).

Although four of the studies reported in table 5.1 give estimates of β_5 consistent with the MABP, critics of the approach have argued that this inverse relationship may reflect the intervention policies adopted by the central bank. Thus an autonomous reserve inflow results in the central bank contracting the domestic component of the money base to stop the reserve flow affecting the money supply. Indeed, if the cause of the inflow is an excess demand for money the sterilization will lead to a magnification effect on reserves since the unsatisfied excess demand for money will continue to draw in reserves. Thus sterilization would be expected to lead to a magnification of the coefficient on d: so it would be expected to be greater than unity in absolute terms. If sterilization was an important feature of the countries' experience summarized in table 5.1, then the familiar problem of simultaneous equation bias would be imparted into OLS estimates of equation 5.24. To account for any sterilization, a researcher should estimate equation 5.24 jointly with an equation specifying the authorities' reaction function for d. Of the studies reported in table 5.1 only Genberg (1976) utilized an estimator which accounted for simultaneous equation bias (i.e. two stage least squares). The importance of failing to account for the bias imparted by sterilization in equations such as 5.24 is highlighted in a study of Obstfeld (1982) where it is shown that the coefficient β_5 falls from a significant -0.55 to a completely insignificant 0.003 once account is taken of the simultaneity bias (the country studied by Obstfeld is Germany over the period 1961–7).

The exclusion of exchange rate expectations from equation 5.23 may also lead to an over-estimate of the offset coefficient (for a discussion of the conflicting biases that exchange rate expectations may impart into equation, see Laskar, 1983). This is because a reserve outflow, say, may lead speculators to expect a devaluation of the exchange rate and this may lead to large capital outflows which in turn exacerbate the loss of reserves. Taking account of simultaneous equation bias and the potential endogeneity of exchange rate expectations, Darby (1983) and Laskar (1983) show that non-reserve countries can exert a significant degree of control over domestic money supplies: β_5 differs significantly from unity.

But simultaneous equation bias may still be present in estimates of equation 5.24 even after a researcher has accounted for the possibility of simultaneity from d to r. This is because in estimating equation 5.24 all the researchers mentioned in table 5.1 have assumed that P, Y and i are all exogenous and therefore are unaffected by the money supply. However, in the real world this is unlikely to be so. Indeed, an increase in d is likely to affect the other variables on the right hand side of equation 5.24 and impart a further simultaneous equation bias. Hence, without proper specification and estimation it is not known whether the coefficients in equation 5.24 reflect a money demand equation or simply the effects of money supply on P, Y and i. As Magee (1976) points out, since such money supply phenomena work in the same direction as the demand side influences researchers end up with ordinary least squares estimates which are biased in favour of the MABP.

SECTION 4   THE INTERNATIONAL TRANSMISSION OF INFLATION: SOME EVIDENCE

In chapter 4 some empirical evidence on whether ppp holds during periods of floating exchange rates was considered. If exchange rates are fixed, then, as equation 5.15 makes clear, ppp becomes a relationship linking national price levels and inflation rates. The MABP outlined in this chapter provides a theory of the determination of such prices and it is shown that inflation under a system of fixed exchange rates must be a world-wide phenomenon.[7] In this section an attempt is made to shed some light on this proposition by examining some evidence on the behaviour of national price levels/inflation rates during the Bretton Woods period 1945–71.

Genberg (1978) usefully splits the statistical and econometric evidence relevant to the international transmission of inflation into two categories: those dealing with the dispersion and convergence of inter-country inflation rates and those testing the ppp relationship, using regression analysis, for the Bretton Woods period. In the former category of studies Pattison (1976), Genberg (1977) and Parkin et al. (1977) compute measures of the variance of inflation across OECD countries for the Bretton Wood period and find that there are relatively small differences across countries (although the differences tend to increase after 1967). Alternative tests of the international transmission of inflation have used regression analysis to estimate equation 5.15. For example, Genberg (1977) estimates the fixed exchange rate version of 5.15 for ten European countries for the period 1955–70 (annual data):

$$p_i = a_0 + a_1 p^* + u_i \tag{5.26}$$

$$\Delta p_i = b_0 + a_1 \Delta p^* + u_i \tag{5.27}$$

where the ps are expressed in logarithms and where the subscript i denotes country i. If ppp holds, a_1 would be equal to unity and b_0 equal to zero. Genberg (1977) reports estimates of equations 5.26 and 5.27 which are consistent with such priors. However, in estimating equation 5.26 first order autocorrelation was a problem in seven out of ten countries suggesting that there may be short-run deviations from ppp (the estimated mean lag for the re-establishment of ppp was estimated at about two years; this finding is confirmed in a further study by Genberg (1978). Serial correlation was not a problem in the estimated version of equation 5.27 for eight out of ten countries, suggesting that although a country's price level may differ from its ppp level this divergence does not increase over time.

But as Genberg (1978) points out, the above tests say nothing about the reasons for divergences from ppp and what mechanisms lead to a restoration of ppp. A number of other researchers attempt to answer these issues by estimating versions of equation 5.27:

$$\Delta p = a_0 + a_1 \Delta p^e + a_2 x \tag{5.28}$$

where x is a measure of excess demand which may reflect monetary or fiscal impulses and Δp^e represents the expected inflation rate (i.e. inflationary expectations are one channel by which inflation may be transmitted internationally). Cross and Laidler (1976) and Laidler

(1976) estimate versions of equation 5.28 for a variety of European countries where the lagged rate of change of foreign price enters the estimated equations as a proxy for inflationary expectations and excess demand is proxied by lagged income. Although the estimated results show that the rate of inflation for a country with fixed exchange rates will average over time to the ROW rate, the convergence rate is slow (between two and five years depending on the country); excess demand is also shown to be statistically significant. In a survey of other researchers' studies of equation 5.28, Genberg (1978) concludes that the estimates of a_1 (where Δp^* stands in for Δp^e) are 'almost universally below unity ... [and] ... excess demand measures summarized by x are very often significant explanatory factors'.

Interestingly, in some countries it is found that world excess monetary growth is a better proxy for excess demand than the domestic money stock.

Notes

1 For a similar derivation see, for example, Mundell (1968) and Whitman (1975).
2 This model is adapted from Dornbusch (1973).
3 The slope of the two schedules may be seen in the following way. Thus on substitution of 5.10 in 5.11 we obtain $H = \alpha(kPY - M)$ which clearly shows the positive relationship between H and P. For the foreign country a similar relationship holds, namely:

$$B^* = \alpha^*(K^*P^*Y^* - M^*).$$

Since $B = -SB^*$ we may rewrite this latter expression as:

$$B = \alpha^* \left(-k^* \frac{P^*}{S} Y^* - M^* \right)$$

and thus $dB/dP < 0$.

4 Rabin and Yeager (1982) p. 5.
5 Carr and Darby (1981) present empirical evidence for a number of countries which suggests that the aggregate buffer stock concept is important.
6 Kouri and Porter (1974) estimate a reduced form capital flow equation instead of equation 5.23.
7 An alternative view of the international transmission of inflation appeals to 'special factors', such as the monopoly power of trade unions and the business sector, commodity price rises and oil price shocks. For discussions of the monetary approach/special factors view see Johnson (1977), Laidler and Parkin (1975), Laidler and Nobay (1976) and Darby and Lothian (1983).

6 The Monetary View of Exchange Rate Determination

Introduction

As was noted in chapter 2, the key issue in what we have termed the balance of payments view of the exchange rate was whether speculation would have a stabilizing impact on the exchange rate. Writing in the 1960s, advocates of flexible exchange rates strongly argued that speculation would be stabilizing and that this would tend to limit the extent of any exchange rate movements. However, as was shown in chapter 1, one of the main features of the recent float has been the extreme volatility of exchange rates relative to the recent historical past. For example McKinnon (1976) noted that 'current movements in spot exchange rates of 20 per cent quarter-to-quarter, five per cent week-to-week, or even one per cent on an hour-to-hour basis are now not unusual, although they are very large by historical standards'.

Does the extreme volatility of exchange rates during the recent float indicate a failure of speculators to act in a stabilizing fashion or is there some other explanation for the volatility which is consistent with 'well behaved' speculation? In this and the following two chapters we attempt to answer this by examining the asset approach to the exchange rate.[1] In this chapter we show why it is useful to regard the exchange rate as an asset price and outline three versions of the asset approach which have attained a considerable degree of popularity:

(1) the flex-price monetary approach to the exchange rate;
(2) the fix-price monetary approach to the exchange rate; and
(3) the currency substitution model.

These three different asset views are particularly useful because they introduce a number of concepts prominent in the asset approach which are discussed in greater detail in following chapters; however, the models introduced in this chapter do suffer from a number of deficiencies. In particular, they give little or no account of the effects of exchange rate changes on the current balance and concomitant changes in wealth, and also concentrate on a very limited menu of assets: effectively, home and foreign money supplies. In chapter 7 we rectify these deficiencies by examining asset models which incorporate current account and wealth dynamics and asset models which consider a broader range of assets than relative money supplies. Although different asset market models utilize different assumptions about asset substitutability and the role of wealth, they all share a common theoretical assumption that asset markets clear instantly.

The Asset Approach to the Exchange Rate

In order to explain the variability of exchange rates, international economists have moved away from the flow demand/supply analysis outlined in chapter 2, to the asset approach to the exchange rate (this switch in emphasis parallels the move from the elasticities and absorption approaches to the monetary approach to the balance of payments outlined in chapter 5).[2] It is argued that the exchange rate should be viewed as an asset price since it is by definition the price of one national money in terms of another (i.e. it is a relative asset price). Thus proponents of the asset approach (see, for example, Mussa 1979) argue that one should use tools normally used for the determination of other asset prices (such as stock and share prices) in analysing the determinants of exchange rates, rather than analysing the exchange rate in terms of flow demand and flow supplies.

For example, when considering an ordinary 'normal' good it is customary to think of the flow demand and supply functions as depending on essentially different variables (e.g. demand is a function of tastes, incomes and relative product prices whereas supply is a function of technology and factor prices), the price being the outcome of the intersection of the Marshallian scissors. Price changes in this analysis are caused by shifts in the demand and supply schedules, the extent of the price change being contingent on relative elasticities. By contrast the price of assets changes because the market *as a whole* changes its view of what the asset is worth; buyers and sellers are therefore motivated by the *same* factors. Thus, the price of an asset, such as a share in BP, changes because the market as a whole changes its view of what the company, to which the asset is a title, is worth. The revision of a company's worth may be due to the arrival of new information about, say, the company's profitability. 'The basic idea of the asset approach to the exchange rate is that essentially the same theory of the determination of prices of common shares is relevant to the determination of the exchange rate' (Mussa, 1979).

A number of important implications, which we briefly note here and consider in more detail in future sections and chapters, follow from viewing the exchange rate as an asset price (or, more specifically, as the relative price of national monies). First, expectations will be important in the determination of the current exchange rate. Since monies are durable, in the sense that they last for a number of periods, expectations about future exchange rates will affect the current exchange rate. Thus, if for some reason agents change their perception of the expected future exchange rate we would expect today's exchange rate to change by a similar amount otherwise there would be a (possibly) large unexploited expected return available in the foreign exchange market. Since the exchange rate is the relative price of two monies one reason why agents may alter their beliefs about the expected exchange rate could be due to a change in the money supply (or the fiscal deficit to the extent that it is financed by printing money) expected to prevail in the future. The importance of expectations in foreign exchange markets should result in a close correspondence between actual exchange rates and the markets' expected future exchange rate (this will be discussed further below and in chapter 8).

Two further implications of using a monetary framework to analyse the exchange rate have already been emphasized in the chapter on the monetary approach to the balance of payments. Thus real factors can affect the exchange rate/balance of payments, but only to the extent that they first affect the demand for money. Also, since assets are stocks, equilibrium is defined as a situation where the stock demand for money is equal to the stock supply of money. Flows of assets across the foreign exchanges can occur, but such flows are a reflection of *disequilibrium* between money demand and money supply and must eventually cease.

A final implication of regarding the exchange rate as an asset price is that such prices are usually regarded as being determined in efficient markets. An efficient asset market, following Fama (1970), is one in which market participants exploit all profitable trading opportunities and force the current price to reflect all available information. Under certain circumstances this implies that exchange rates should behave randomly: they should follow a random walk.[3] A further implication of regarding the exchange market as an efficient market is that in such a market the forward exchange rate set today is usually taken to be the market's expectation of the spot rate in some future time period. The difference between the forward rate set at time t, with maturity in $t + 1$, and the actual spot rate at $t + 1$ is the unexpected change in the exchange rate. In periods in which there is a great deal of new information about, say, the future paths of money supplies, we should not be surprised if the unexpected change in the exchange rate is large and there are correspondingly large movements in spot exchange rates.

In chapter 8 the efficient markets implications of viewing the exchange rate as an asset price will be discussed. In this chapter we concentrate on the other implications of regarding the exchange rate as an asset price: namely, the roles of money demand, money supply and expectations in the determination of the exchange rate. Consideration is initially given to the flex-price monetary approach to the exchange rate.

The Flex-price Monetary Approach to the Exchange Rate

The flex-price monetary model is in many ways an extension of the ppp view of exchange rates outlined in chapter 4; essentially it appends a theory of the determination of the price level to a ppp equation in order to explain the exchange rate. The use of ppp in a theory of the determination of the exchange rate immediately introduces a problem for, as has been shown, ppp is not well supported empirically. Nevertheless, it is useful to examine the flex-price monetary approach as a first stepping stone in the study of more complex asset models and also it offers an interesting explanation of recent exchange rate volatility.

The flex-price monetary model discussed here has the following characteristics which are common with the MABP models considered in chapter 5. First, the country is assumed to be small and is facing an exogenously determined foreign interest rate, i^*, and price level, p^*. The home country produces a single traded good which is a perfect substitute for the foreign good and thus purchasing power parity holds continuously.

$$s = p - p^* \tag{6.1}$$

where s, p and p^* are logarithmic values of the corresponding level terms. The central bank of the home country issues money, which is assumed to be non-traded and a bond which is a perfect substitute for a foreign bond. Since it is further assumed that asset holders can adjust their portfolios instantly after a disturbance, and thus capital is perfectly mobile, uncovered interest parity must also hold:

$$\dot{s}^e = i - i^* \tag{6.2}$$

this means in terms of equation 3.7 introduced in chapter 3, and repeated here, that $k = \infty$.

$$\Delta K = k(i - i^* - \dot{s}^e) \tag{6.2a}$$

$$m^D - p = \alpha_1 y - \alpha_2 i \tag{6.3}$$

where ΔK is a capital flow, m^D is the natural logarithm of money demand, p is the natural logarithm of the price level, y is the natural logarithm of the level of real national income, i is the interest rate, α_1 and α_2 are the elasticity and semi-elasticity respectively and an asterisk denotes a foreign magnitude. The money supply is assumed to be determined exogenously and money markets are in equilibrium (i.e. money demand is always equal to money supply).

$$m^D = m = m^s \tag{6.4}$$

Going back to equation 3.7 in chapter 3, notice that ΔK must equal zero in this model because the exchange rate is assumed to be perfectly flexible: ΔM must be equal to ΔD.

By substituting 6.4 into 6.3 and solving for the price level we obtain:

$$p = m - \alpha_1 y + \alpha_2 i \tag{6.5}$$

By normalizing the foreign price level to unity (and thus its logarithmic value equals zero) and substituting in 6.1 we obtain:

$$s = m - \alpha_1 y + \alpha_2 i \tag{6.6}$$

which is a standard small country flex-price monetary approach reduced form. The predictions of equation 6.6 are as follows. First, an x per cent increase in the domestic money supply leads to an x per cent increase in s (depreciation). An increase in income leads to an exchange rate appreciation. This result is in sharp contrast to the result noted in chapter 2 where an increase in income led to an exchange rate depreciation. Similarly an increase in the domestic interest rate leads to an exchange rate *depreciation* and again this is in marked contrast to the result obtained in chapter 2 where an increase in the home interest rate led to an appreciation of the exchange rate. How can these apparently conflicting results be reconciled?

The way to understand the 'puzzling' effects of y and i is to recognize that these variables only affect the exchange rate via their effect on money demand. Thus an increase in income increases the transactions demand for money and with a constant nominal money supply money market equilibrium can only be maintained if the domestic price level falls; and this in turn can only occur, given a strict ppp assumption, if the exchange rate changes. Thus the exchange rate appreciates in order to restore equality between real money demand and real money supply (i.e. the price level falls).

The positive effect of the domestic rate of interest on the exchange rate again reflects the effect of interest rates on money demand. This follows from the assumed world in which we are operating. The home country is at full employment and, furthermore, nominal interest rates are assumed to obey the Fisher parity relationship outlined in chapter 4, i.e.

$$i = r + \dot{p}^e \tag{6.7}$$

where r is the real interest rate and $\dot{p}^e$ is the expected inflation rate. Assuming the real interest rate to be constant equation 6.6 may be rewritten as:

$$s = m - \alpha_1 y + \alpha_2 \dot{p}^e \tag{6.8}$$

Thus an increase in the domestic interest rate reflects an increase in expected inflation and a reduced desire to hold real money balances. Given an exogenously fixed nominal money supply, the only way that real money balances can be altered is by a increase in the price level which is accommodated by an exchange rate depreciation.

Introducing Expectations

In the introductory remarks to this chapter it was argued that regarding the exchange rate as an asset price means that expectations about the future course of its determinants will be important for the current determination of the exchange rate. Equation 6.6 may be helpfully utilized to explain why it is possible for exchange rates to exhibit a great deal of variability relative to the *current* determinants of the exchange rate.

By substituting the uncovered interest parity term (equation 6.2) in equation 6.6, and by normalizing the foreign interest rate to have a value of zero we obtain:

$$s = m - \alpha_1 y + \alpha_2 \dot{s}^e \tag{6.9}$$

or, dating variables

$$s_t = m_t - \alpha_1 y_t + \alpha_2(s^e_{t+1} - s_t) \qquad (6.9a)$$

(where note that from 6.8 $\dot{s}^e = \dot{p}^e$). Assuming rational expectations, and thus agents know the process of exchange rate determination and its underlying stochastic structure then:

$$s^e_{t+1} = \underset{t}{E}\, s_{t+1} \qquad (6.10)$$

where E_t is the expectational operator conditional upon the information set available at period t. Clearly from the foregoing discussion, the factors that determine the expected exchange rate in the monetary model are what agents expect the money supply and income to be in the future. This may be illustrated in the following way. If equation 6.9a is rewritten as:

$$s_t = \frac{1}{1 + \alpha_2}\left[m_t - \alpha_1 y_t + \alpha_2 \underset{t}{E}\, s_{t+1}\right] \qquad (6.11)$$

then this equation may be used to find the expected value of the exchange rate in any future period $t + j$:

$$\underset{t}{E}\, s_{t+j} = \frac{1}{1 + \alpha_2}\left[\underset{t}{E}[m - \alpha_1 y]_{t+j} + \alpha_2 \underset{t}{E}\, s_{t+j+1}\right] \qquad (6.12)$$

By repeatedly substituting for $E_t s$ in (6.11) for all future time periods we obtain the rational expectations reduced form exchange rate equation:

$$s_t = \frac{1}{1 + \alpha_2}\sum_{j=0}^{\infty}\left(\frac{\alpha_2}{1 + \alpha_2}\right)^j \underset{t}{E}\,[m_{t+j} - \alpha_1 y_{t+j}] \qquad (6.13)$$

Equation 6.13 shows, in the context of a simple monetary model, with rational expectations, that the current exchange rate depends not just on current excess money supplies but also on expected future excess money supplies. The discounting factor, α_2, discounts expected future money growth into the current spot rate in a manner analogous to that in which revisions in expected future earnings are discounted into equity prices.

The effect of current changes in the money supply on the exchange rate depends crucially on what people perceive as the stochastic structure underlying the authorities money supply rule. For example, if the money supply increases by y per cent in the current period and this change is believed to be temporary then via equations 6.12 and

6.13 the expected future exchange rate would be little affected and hence the current spot exchange rate would simply reflect the current money supply change. Exchange rate expectations are likely to be regressive under such a regime. By 'regressive' is meant that, say, a current depreciation of the exchange rate generates an expectation that the exchange rate will eventually re-appreciate. If, in contrast to the above example, the y per cent increase in the money supply led to the expectation that domestic rates of monetary expansion would be y per cent higher than foreign rates for the indefinite future then the exchange rate would depreciate by far more than the current y per cent change in the money supply.

Equation 6.13 then gives an explanation for the volatility in exchange rates relative to current fundamentals, and is the correct light in which to view the issue of whether speculators have had a stabilizing or destabilizing influence on the exchange rate during the recent floating experience. Thus, it is often argued that it is regressive expectations that are stabilizing. But in the rational expectations monetary model expectations are regressive *because the underlying behaviour of the money supply makes regressive expectations appropriate.* However, it is not only regressive expectations which are stabilizing; in the context of the above model what may be regarded as destabilizing expectations may be seen as stabilizing. Thus, large movements in the current exchange rate may reflect agents' beliefs that current changes in the money supply are suggestive of higher monetary growth in the future. On this basis there is little likelihood of the exchange rate depreciation being offset by a later appreciation. Such expectations may though be regarded as 'stabilizing' because, as Mussa (1976) notes, they are the best possible prediction of future exchange rates, given the nature of monetary policy and the information available to asset holders.

The above explanation of exchange rate volatility is in terms of the underlying instability of the variables driving the exchange rate. It is interesting to note at this juncture that although Friedman argued that speculation would have a stabilizing influence on the exchange rate this was contingent on the underlying economic structure being stable. Thus '... advocacy of flexible exchange rates is *not* equivalent to advocacy of unstable exchange rates. The ultimate objective is a world in which exchange rates, while *free* to vary, are in fact highly stable. *Instability of exchange rates is a symptom of instability in the underlying economic structure*' (emphasis in last sentence added). Thus Friedman, writing in 1953, clearly anticipated the rational expectations exchange rate literature!

If the monetary model is the correct description of the exchange rate then its inherent simplicity clearly makes it an important tool for policy purposes. It implies, for example, that any change in the money supply has a proportionate effect on the exchange rate and hence on prices. Furthermore, the rational expectation version of equation 6.6 implies that monetary policy should be predictable; unpredictability in the money supply implies even greater unpredictability of the exchange rate.

But it is pertinent to question at this juncture how well supported by the empirical evidence is the flex-price monetary approach. In econometrically implementing the monetary model researchers have moved from the small country model discussed here to a two country model. This seems sensible since most exchange rates studied are bilateral rates and it is difficult to think of an exchange rate in which foreign impulses are not going to be important in the determination of that exchange rate. Foreign impulses may be introduced into our monetary approach reduced form in the following way. Rewriting equation 6.6 without the normalization of p^* to be equal to unity we obtain:

$$s = m - p^* - \alpha_1 y + \alpha_2 i \tag{6.14}$$

and assuming that p^* is determined in the same way as p, i.e.:

$$p^* = m^* - \alpha_3 y^* + \alpha_4 i^* \tag{6.15}$$

then on substituting in 6.14 and rearranging terms 6.16 is obtained, which is essentially the two country version of equation 6.6.

$$s = m - m^* - \alpha_1 y + \alpha_3 y^* + \alpha_2 i - \alpha_4 i^* \tag{6.16}$$

where home country variables have the same interpretation as above and foreign currency variables have the opposite effect on the exchange rate to home country variables.

Equation 6.16 has been econometrically estimated for a number of currencies over the recent experience with floating exchange rates. Because of the cleanness of the float of the German mark – US dollar exchange rate, in terms of the relatively low level of foreign exchange market intervention, many researchers have concentrated on this exchange rate in their tests of equation 6.16. For example, Hodrick (1978) presents the following estimated version of equation 6.16 for the US dollar – German mark exchange rate over the period April 1973 to September 1975:

$$s_t = 1.52m - 1.39m^* - 2.23y + 0.073y^* + 2.53i + 1.93i^*$$
$$\quad (0.512) \quad (0.563) \quad (0.456) \quad (0.384) \quad (1.17) \quad (0.669)$$

$$R^2 = 0.66 \quad DW = 1.61 \quad SER = 0.37$$

Standard errors in parentheses $\tag{6.17}$

Notice that, apart from the coefficient on the German interest rate, $i*$, all variables are correctly signed in terms of the flex-price monetary approach and all, apart from $y*$, are statistically significant at the 95 per cent level. Indeed Hodrick finds that the coefficients on the home and foreign money supply differ insignificantly from plus and minus unity as predicted by the approach. Other successful estimates of equation 6.16 have been presented by Bilson (1978) for the German mark–US dollar and Putnam and Woodbury (1980) for the UK pound–US dollar using data from the early experience with floating (i.e. up to approximately the end of 1977). However, the experience of estimating 6.16 for the more recent experience with floating exchange rates has not produced such successful results and we shall return to this after discussing the fix-price monetary approach.

The Fix-price Monetary Approach

In this section a version of the monetary approach to the exchange rate due to Dornbusch (1976) is discussed. This model, which we label the fix-price monetary approach shares many of the features of the model considered in the last section, but relaxes the assumption of ppp in the short run. One particularly interesting feature of this model is that it offers another example of exchange rate volatility in terms of overshooting.

The fix-price monetary model consists of an economy which is small and faces an exogenously given foreign price and interest rate. The monetary authorities issue domestic money, which is held only in the home country, and a foreign bond. Capital is assumed to be perfectly mobile; equation 6.2 is assumed to hold continuously. The country is assumed to be operating at full employment and produces a single traded good which is assumed to be an imperfect substitute, at least in the short run, for the foreign produced good. Thus although ppp is assumed to hold in the long run, in the short run deviations from ppp may be allowed and these may be considerable. Long-run ppp is described by equation 6.18 where a bar denotes a long-run, or equilibrium, value.

$$\bar{s} = \bar{p} - \bar{p}* \tag{6.18}$$

In the flex-price monetary model the expected change in the exchange rate was demonstrated to be continuously equal to the expected inflation differential. Since ppp does not hold in the short run in the fix-price monetary model an alternative representation for the expected change in the exchange rate has to be given. In the short run it is assumed that the exchange rate is expected to return to the equilibrium value, $\bar{s}$, by a constant proportion, ϕ, of the current gap:

$$\dot{s}^e = \phi(\bar{s} - s) \tag{6.19}$$

where ϕ is a parameter, which must if agents have perfect foresight be consistent with the underlying model (with perfect foresight ϕ will be a function of the model's structural parameters – see Dornbusch (1976) for a discussion).

The monetary section of the fix-price monetary model is assumed identical to the flex-price monetary model, viz. equations 6.3 and 6.4.

Since ppp may be violated in the short run, an equation to explain the evolution of the price level is required. It is assumed that the price level adjusts in proportion to excess demand. The demand function is assumed to have the form:

$$d = \beta_0 + \beta_1(s - p) + \beta_2 y - \beta_3 i \tag{6.20}$$

where d represents the logarithm of demand. This demand function is closely related to the Mundell–Fleming demand function considered in chapter 3. The $s - p$ term captures the effects of the real exchange rate on the trade balance and hence demand (i.e. if s rises relative to p demand will be switched towards home goods). The y term reflects the effect of income on expenditure magnitudes such as consumption. The i term reflects the effect of the interest rate on domestic absorption and thus an increase in i results *ceteris paribus* in a fall in aggregate demand. The β_0 term is a shift parameter which, perhaps, reflects government spending. Remembering that output is fixed at the full employment level y, then the change in the price level is given by:

$$\dot{p} = \Pi(d - y) = \Pi[\beta_0 + \beta_1(s - p) + (\beta_2 - 1)y - \beta_3 i] \tag{6.21}$$

where Π is the speed of adjustment parameter.

The workings of the above model structure may be illustrated in the following way using figure 6.1 from Dornbusch (1976).

The schedule MM represents combinations of s and p consistent with asset market equilibrium: at all points in time the money market is assumed to clear and uncovered interest parity holds continuously.[4] The schedule $\dot{p} = 0$ is the locus of s and p that are consistent with money *and* goods market equilibrium.[5]

The crucial dichotomy in the fix-price monetary model, which is implicit in the foregoing discussion is that asset markets are continuously in equilibrium (we are always on the MM schedule); however,

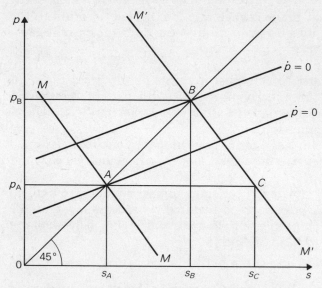

Figure 6.1   Overshooting and the fix-price model

goods market equilibrium is only a long-run feature of the model. Therefore, asset markets adjust fast relative to goods markets.

Consider now an unexpected x per cent increase in the domestic money supply from the initial equilibrium at A. It should be clear that since monetary homogeneity is a long-run property of this model (see equations 6.18 and 6.5), the exchange rate and the price level must change in proportion to the increase in the money supply increase; the new long-run equilibrium is at point B. But in the short run prices are sticky and therefore goods market equilibrium is not immediately attained and the money market is not cleared via a price increase. Instead the money market is cleared in the short run by a fall in the domestic interest rate. Unlike the situation in the Mundell–Fleming model, this is possible because $\dot{s}^e$ is not equal to zero and therefore the current exchange rate can move to allow interest rates at home and in the foreign country to diverge. In terms of figure 6.1, the exchange rate jumps from A to C in the short run. Notice that the exchange rate *overshoots* the new long-run equilibrium exchange rate, i.e. $s_C > s_B$. This follows from the uncovered interest parity equation which implies that the home interest rate can only be below the foreign rate if market participants expect the exchange rate to appreciate and the latter can only occur if the current spot rate moves by more than the long-run exchange rate.

The above overshooting of the exchange rate is captured concisely by equation 6.22.[6]

$$\frac{ds}{dm} = 1 + 1/\alpha_2 \phi \qquad (6.22)$$

Thus the extent of any exchange rate overshooting is seen to depend upon the interest response of the demand for money and the expectations coefficient. That this is so should be clear from our earlier discussion: if the interest elasticity of money demand is low, any change in the money supply will result in a relatively large change in the interest rate to restore equilibrium and therefore a relatively large change in the expected exchange rate to offset it.

For B to be a position of long-run equilibrium, there clearly has to be zero excess demand in the goods market and thus the $\dot{p} = 0$ schedule must intersect the $M'M'$ schedule at this point. But what is the adjustment process for prices from C to B? From our earlier discussion we know that at point C the exchange rate has depreciated (perhaps sharply), thus changing the terms of trade, and the domestic interest rate has fallen. Both these factors will, via equation 6.20, boost aggregate demand. Thus over time, since output is fixed at the full employment level, prices must be rising (see equation 6.21) and real money balances falling, pushing up interest rates in order to continuously maintain money market equilibrium. For the latter to be consistent with overall asset market equilibrium (i.e. equilibrium in both money and the international bond market) the exchange rate will be appreciating from the overshoot position C. Thus in this model rising interest rates are accompanied by an appreciating exchange rate.

It is important to stress that the exchange rate overshooting in the Dornbusch model is a result of the discrepancy of adjustment speeds in goods and asset markets; asset markets adjust instantly whereas goods markets adjust only slowly over time. This is in contrast to the flex-price monetary model where, as was shown, the exchange rate overshoots (or perhaps more correctly the exchange rate change is magnified) as a result of agents' expectations of the course of future exogenous variables.[7]

Many economists would argue that the fix-price monetary model offers a concise description of the real world behaviour of exchange rates. For example the monetary policies pursued by the Thatcher administration in the UK at times led to very high real interest rates in the UK relative to the US in the period 1979–81 and this did lead to a large appreciation of the nominal exchange rate. But since prices are also sticky downwards this led to a *real* exchange rate appreciation, which affected the real sector of the economy; i.e. the high real exchange rate resulted in exporters becoming uncompetitive and going out of business, with the resultant loss of output and jobs. Thus, in his evidence to the Treasury and Civil Service Committee (1980a, p. 72) Dornbusch argued

> If pursued over any period of time the high real exchange rate policy will lead to a disruption of industry; reduced investment, shutdowns, declining productivity, loss of established markets and a deterioration of the commercial position.

Thus he concluded that the high real exchange rate was a direct consequence of the high interest rate policy pursued by the UK authorities and consequently a crucial issue for the policy maker in a world of high capital mobility, sticky prices and flexible exchange rates must be how to isolate the asset sector from the real sector. Dornbusch (1980a) recommended a tax on capital inflows: 'It is quite apparent ... that both from the point of view of public finance and from the perspective of macroeconomic policy, a real interest equalisation tax is called for'. Such a policy, for periods of tight money, has been supported by Liviatan (1980). Flood and Marion (1980) have argued that the effect of the capital account on the exchange rate may be divorced from the current account by introducing a dual exchange rate system. Such a system effectively means separating current and capital account items and having an exchange rate for each account.[8]

The Hybrid Fix-flex Price Monetary Model

The fix-price monetary model is clearly deficient in one respect: it ignores inflationary expectations which are such a prominent feature of the flex-price monetary model. Thus, in periods of secular inflation (such as the 1970s) although prices are sticky in the short run, agents' expectations of inflation will be important in determining, as in the flex-price monetary approach, any short-run exchange rate overshooting. A hybrid model which combines the assumption of short-run price rigidity and also models agents' inflationary expectations has been provided by Frankel (1979a). This model draws on elements of both the fix and flex-price monetary approaches. At the heart of this model is again the uncovered interest parity equation. Only now it is modified to include inflationary expectations:

$$\dot{s}^e = \phi(\bar{s} - s) + \dot{p}^e - \dot{p}^{e*} \tag{6.23}$$

Thus in long-run equilibrium when $s = \bar{s}$ the exchange rate is expected to change at the long-run inflation differential. The long run exchange rate is determined, as in the fixed and flex-price monetary models, by ppp and monetary equilibrium. In this hybrid model the small country assumption utilized in the Dornbusch model is dropped and therefore it is necessary to consider explicitly the foreign money market as in the empirical implementation of the flex-price monetary model. Thus:

$$\bar{s} = \bar{m} - \bar{m}^* - \alpha_1(\bar{y} - \bar{y}^*) + \alpha_2(\dot{p}^e - \dot{p}^{e*}) \qquad (6.24)$$

The short run exchange rate may be derived by substituting 6.23 into 6.2 to obtain:

$$s - \bar{s} = \frac{-1}{\phi}\left[(i - \dot{p}^e) - (i^* - \dot{p}^{e*})\right] \qquad (6.25)$$

where the current exchange rate differs from its equilibrium value by a real interest differential. Consider a once-and-for-all increase in the money supply in the context of equation 6.25. In terms of the Dornbusch model (i.e. if we only have nominal interest rates) the exchange rate must overshoot its long-run equilibrium in order to maintain interest parity. But if the money supply increase causes individuals to revise their inflationary expectations upwards, equation 6.25 says that the initial exchange rate depreciation will be greater in the hybrid model.

It is possible to test econometrically whether the fix price, flex-price or hybrid model provides the better description of the exchange rate. Thus by further substitution of 6.24 into 6.25 and by assuming that current equilibrium money supplies and income levels are given by their current actual levels, we obtain the following estimatable equation:

$$s = m - m^* - \alpha_1(y - y^*) + \alpha_2(\dot{p}^e - \dot{p}^{e*})$$
$$+ \frac{1}{\phi}\left[(i - \dot{p}^e) - (i^* - \dot{p}^{e*})\right] \qquad (6.26)$$

If the fix-price monetary model is correct then in an estimated version of equation 6.26 we would expect $1/\phi$ to be negative and α_2 to be zero. In the flex-price monetary approach we would expect α_2 to be positive and $1/\phi$ to be zero. If the 'hybrid', Frankel, model is correct it is expected then that α_2 be positive and $1/\phi$ be negative.

Frankel (1979a) presents econometric estimates of equation 6.26 for the German mark–US dollar exchange rate over the period July

1974–February 1978. His 'best' equation is reported here as equation 6.27:

$$s = 1.39 + 0.97(m - m^*) - 0.52(y - y^*) + 29.40(\dot{p}^e - \dot{p}^{e*})$$
$$(0.12) \; (0.21) \qquad\qquad (0.22) \qquad\qquad (3.33)$$

$$- 5.40[(i - \dot{p}^e) - (i^* - \dot{p}^{e*})] \qquad\qquad\qquad (6.27)$$
$$(2.04)$$

where the standard errors are reported in parenthesis. In this equation notice that the coefficient for the relative money supply term is insignificantly different from unity, the coefficient on income is significantly negative and the expected inflation and real interest rate terms are both significant and have signs consistent with the hybrid view of the exchange rate.

The estimated values in equation 6.27 allow Frankel to estimate how much the mark–dollar exchange rate would have to depreciate for a once and for all increase in the US money supply of one per cent. The calculated fall in the real interest differential (i.e. the sticky-price model effect) gives a current exchange rate overshoot of 1.23 per cent. However, if the monetary expansion signals to investors a new higher target for monetary growth the initial overshooting will be greater. Frankel estimates that if agents expected inflation rate is raised by one per cent per annum, this will lead to a short-run exchange rate overshoot of 1.58 per cent. Thus ignoring the expected inflation effect biases downwardly estimates of short-run exchange rate overshooting.

Although Frankel's reduced form exchange rate equation provides an interesting representation of the monetary approach, not least because it provides estimates of exchange rate overshooting, it is important to note that attempts to estimate equations 6.26 and 6.16 for the period beyond 1978 and for other currencies have not been particularly successful.

For example, Dornbusch (1980b), Haynes and Stone (1981) and Driskell and Sheffrin (1981) argue that once equations such as 6.16 and 6.26 are estimated for the mark–dollar exchange rate for the period extending beyond 1978 the relationship breaks down.[9] A variety of rationalizations have been given for the poor performance of equations 6.16 and 6.26 for the recent floating experience. For example, Frankel (1981) argues that once wealth is included in the money demand functions which underpin 6.16 and 6.26 the monetary model continues to be well supported by the data. Dornbusch (1980b) has argued that it is perhaps surprising that any successful estimates of equation 6.16 have been reported since we know that purchasing power parity has not held during the recent floating experience (see chapter 4) and also since money demand functions, at least ones as simple as those reported in 6.6, have not been stable over the recent floating experience, it is perhaps not surprising that estimates of 6.16 and 6.26 have been unsuccessful past 1978. Finally, Driskell and Sheffrin (1981) and Haynes and Stone (1981) point to inadequacies in the way the monetary model has been econometrically implemented to explain its relatively poor performances. But perhaps empirically implementing the monetary approach in the way discussed above is somewhat misguided since we know from our earlier remarks that exchange rates, as asset prices, respond to new information; i.e. it is the unexpected component of the money supply that moves exchange rates over time. Perhaps then the empirical modelling of exchange rates in a 'news' context will offer more successful results for the monetary approach. The 'news' implementation of the monetary model is discussed in chapter 8.[10]

Currency Substitution

The specification of the monetary approach hitherto has relied on the implicit assumption that domestic residents do *not* hold foreign money; effectively the elasticity of substitution in demand between national money supplies is assumed to be zero. However, in a regime of floating exchange rates, multi-national corporations involved in trade and investment and speculators have an incentive to hold a *basket* of currencies in order to minimize the risk of revaluation effects of potential exchange rate changes on their wealth (in practice such operators will hold a portfolio of money and non-money assets; however, we shall leave inclusion of the latter in a theory of the exchange rate until the next chapter). Thus, much as in traditional portfolio theory, foreign exchange market participants have an incentive to hold a basket of currencies, the composition of the various currencies in the portfolio varying with the risk and expected rates of return of the specific currencies in the portfolio. The ability of foreign exchange market participants to substitute between different currencies has been made possible due to the lifting of exchange controls in the 1970s by most of the participating members of the floating regime. Girton and Roper (1981) were the first to use the term 'currency substitution' to describe situations where investors hold more than one currency.

In this section we examine the implications of currency substitution for the behaviour of exchange rates, the ability of central banks to adopt monetary targets and the implications it has for inflation.

Currency Substitution and the Monetary Approach

In the flex- and fix-price monetary approaches monetary services are only provided by the domestic currency (i.e. equation 6.3). However, as we have argued this is probably an unrealistic assumption; various international companies have an incentive to hold a variety of currencies and therefore monetary services may be provided by other currencies. This may be illustrated by rewriting 6.9 as

$$s = m - \Omega - \alpha_1 y + \alpha_2 \dot{s}^e \tag{6.28}$$

where Ω is the proportion of monetary services provided by domestic money. Thus an increase in Ω, by increasing the demand for domestic money results in an exchange rate appreciation.

Following King, Putnam and Wilford (1977) we assume that the share of domestic currency depends upon the expected change in the exchange rate which in turn is dependent on expected monetary growth[11], $\dot{m}^e$, and the uncertainty with which such expectations are held, represented by the variance of monetary growth, var $\dot{m}^e$. By assuming Ω has the following functional form:

$$\Omega = \beta_0 \dot{m}^e + \beta_1 \text{ var } \dot{m}^e; \beta_0 < 0, \beta_1 < 0 \tag{6.29}$$

substituting Ω in 6.28 and using the fact that $\dot{s}^e = \dot{m}^e$ 6.30 is obtained:

$$s = m - \alpha_1 y + (\alpha_2 - \beta_0)\dot{m}^e + \beta_1 \text{ var } \dot{m}^e \tag{6.30}$$

where since $\beta_0 < 0$, $\alpha_2 - \beta_0 > 0$. Thus in addition to the traditional monetary effects of m and y on the exchange rate equation 6.30 also demonstrates the effect of currency substitution on the exchange rate. The coefficient on $\dot{m}^e$ is larger than it would be in the absence of currency substitution (i.e. $\alpha_2 - \beta_0 > \alpha_2$) because of the ability of agents to substitute between domestic and foreign money, exacerbating pressure for a currency depreciation or appreciation. This effect will be reinforced if the expected variability of monetary policy var $\dot{m}^e$ changes in tandem with the expected change in m.[12]

Currency Substitution and Monetary Targetting

Until now we have discussed currency substitution in a rather abstract way, in the context of the flex-price monetary approach. But does the concept have a 'real world' applicability? A variety of central bankers would answer in the affirmative.

One notable feature of the 1970s and 1980s has been the setting of monetary targets in an attempt to control inflation (the first country to adopt monetary targets was Germany in December 1974).

However, the success of such a policy is contingent on the underlying stability of the money demand function. Although empirical studies of the money demand function suggested it was stable for the 1960s, evidence for a variety of countries for the 1970s implied that the relationship was unstable. One popular explanation for this instability has been argued to be currency substitution.

For example, the Swiss and German monetary authorities set money supply targets together of five and eight per cent respectively for the period 1977–8. The actual money supply outcome was an increase of 16.2 per cent in Switzerland and 11.4 per cent in Germany. These overshoots of the money supplies were blamed on a shift in foreign and domestic demand for financial assets based in Deutschmarks and Swiss francs (in particular a shift away from the dollar which was argued to be overvalued). Since the Swiss and German authorities were unwilling to let the exchange rate take the adjustment (i.e. this would imply, on the assumption that prices are sticky, a *real* exchange rate change) by appreciating, they intervened in the foreign exchange markets to supply Swiss francs and German marks. Since the monetary consequences of this were not sterilized increased money supplies inevitably resulted. These monetary overshoots led to the non-announcement of monetary targets by the Swiss authorities in 1979 and a more flexible target by the German authorities in 1979.

Several proposals have been made to overcome the effects of currency substitution on the ability of central banks to pursue monetary targets (see, e.g., Vaubel, 1980). The first would be to define monetary targets net of international shifts in the demand for national money and to offset all such shifts via compensatory money supply adjustment. In principle this seems a perfect solution, but in practice the issue is complicated by the difficulties of central banks knowing when and by how much net *foreign* demand for its money has changed; i.e. the observable changes in money holdings are not a reliable indicator of the extent to which money demand has changed. Thus perhaps the central bank should try to trace the shifts in money demand back to their determinants, i.e. foreign income and foreign interest rates. But it has proved difficult to estimate such parameters and in any case they are likely to change as policy changes (i.e. the Lucas 1977 critique).

An alternative method for the curtailment of the deleterious affects of currency substitution would be to move full circle from monetary targets to (nominal) exchange rate targets.[13] It is argued that this would result in international shifts in money demand being reflected instantly by exchange market pressure, the monetary authorities then adjusting the money supply to keep the exchange rate constant. One problem perhaps with this idea would seem to be the difficulty for the authorities in discerning when exchange rate movements are due to currency substitution and when they are justified by, say, real factors (for other criticisms of exchange rate targets and for a discussion of other devices for countering currency substitution see Vaubel, 1980).

Currency Substitution and Inflation: The McKinnon Hypothesis

Professor R. McKinnon has argued that currency substitution explains why countries' national monetary growth rates are not necessarily good predictors of national inflation rates. For example, in 1978 the US monetary growth was 8.2 per cent and a monetarist would presumably argue that this should have a predictable effect on inflation after 18 months to two years. However, in 1979–80 the US experienced inflation of 13 per cent which implies an appreciably higher money growth two years earlier. The monetarist proposition holds only if one compares the 'world' money supply with the 'world' inflation rate. That the latter is the relevant money concept is due to currency substitution and an important asymmetry in the international monetary standard.

In 1977–8, due to a belief that the dollar was going to depreciate, foreign exchange market participants were keen to reallocate their currency portfolios away from dollars towards European currencies. As we have seen, the Swiss and the German authorities were not prepared to let this substitution be fully reflected in the exchange rate and intervened in their foreign exchange markets, selling domestic currency for dollars. The effect of the latter was not sterilized and hence the domestic money supply rose. However, because European central banks hold their increased dollar reserves in dollar-denominated bonds their intervention has *no* effect on the US money supply (if, however, they hold their reserves as direct dollar deposit claims on the US central bank this will result in a reduction in the US base money). This asymmetrical operation of the international monetary system means that in terms of the above example, currency substitution has led to an increase in the world money supply (effectively the weighted sum of US dollars and European monies). If we compare the world money supply figure in 1977–8 with the world inflation rate in 1979–80 we find a much more satisfactory correlation. For example, the world money supply increased by 10.27 per cent and 10.98 per cent in 1977 and 1978 respectively and world inflation increased by 11.1 per cent and 13.5 per cent in 1979 and 1980 respectively. Furthermore, McKinnon argues that the world money supply is a better predictor of US inflation than US money supply. For example, in 1978 US monetary growth was 8.2 per cent and in 1979–80 US inflation averaged 13 per cent. This latter figure, it is argued, is better explained by the effect on the international business cycle of the 11 per cent world monetary growth in 1978.

McKinnon (1983) argues from the above evidence that certain money supply and intervention rules should be developed if price stability is to be achieved in the world economy. First, each country should determine, in advance of any money demand shocks, a growth path for the money supply consistent with price stability. Second, countries then agree to co-operate by pursuing *symmetric* unsterilized intervention in the event of currency substitution moving exchange rates. Thus if the Swiss franc–US dollar appreciates because of currency substitution the Swiss monetary authorities should intervene by buying dollars for Swiss francs, not sterilizing the impact of this on the Swiss money supply, and depositing the dollars with the US central bank: the monetary base would then be increased in Switzerland as much as it is decreased in the US. Assuming that money multipliers are the same in both the US and Switzerland and that the velocity is the same in both countries then this type of intervention should lead to no change in the world money supply and have no inflationary impact.

Although the McKinnon hypothesis in its various strands seems appealing it is important to note that the methodology utilized by McKinnon (1982) has been the subject of a lively debate (the reader is directed to: Ross, 1983; McKinnon and Tan, 1983; Goldstein and Haynes, 1984; Radcliffe et al., 1984; and McKinnon et al., 1984). More generally, the concept of currency substitution itself has been empirically questioned by a number of researchers (see Spinelli, 1983, for a useful summary of this evidence).

Concluding Comments

In this chapter we have outlined why it is useful to regard the exchange rate as an asset price determined in asset markets. By considering three versions of the monetary approach to the exchange rate we gave three stories to explain exchange rate volatility: agents' expectations of the future course of monetary policy; differential speeds of adjustment in goods and asset markets; and the desire by rational agents to hold a portfolio of currencies in a period of floating exchange rates.

One of the major problems with the versions of the asset approach discussed in this chapter is that they give no role to the current account in determining the exchange rate. Underlying the monetary models is an assumption of full employment and thus exchange rate changes simply have inflationary consequences. However, this is hardly a good description of the real world since exchange rate changes *do* affect the current account and this in turn will affect the flow of savings and wealth. Furthermore, the range of assets considered in the monetary approach is severely limited since non-money assets are assumed to be perfect substitutes and drop out of the analysis: attention is focused on relative excess money supplies.

In the following chapter we consider a wider version of the assets approach which rectifies some of the above deficiencies of the simple monetary approach. In particular, we consider an asset model which incorporates wealth, relaxes the assumption of perfect substitutability between non-money assets and introduces a role for the current account.

Notes

1   An asset is a means of holding wealth. Ultimately it must take a real form, but paper claims improve the liquidity or convenience of holding real assets. Money is one such financial asset as are bonds, equity etc.

2   Mussa (1979), for example, has shown that only when certain strong and unrealistic assumptions hold can the flow approach offer an explanation for exchange rage volatility.

3   See, for example, Levich (1979) for the circumstances required to hold for the exchange rate to follow a random walk. (This issue is discussed further in chapter 8.)

4   The downward sloping MM schedule may be explained in the following way: substitute equations 6.4, 6.19 and 6.2 into 6.3 to obtain:

$$p - m = -\alpha_1 y + \alpha_2 i^* + \alpha_2 \phi(\bar{s} - s) \qquad (6.1A)$$

In the long run with a stationary money supply, the current and expected exchange rate will be equal which implies, from equation 6.2, that interest rates will also be equivalent. Hence the long-run price level may be written as:

$$\bar{p} = m + \alpha_2 i^* - \alpha_1 y \qquad (6.1B)$$

and by substituting equation 6.1B into 6.1A we obtain (i.e. solve for $\alpha_2 i^*$ in 6.1B and substitute for $\alpha_2 i^*$ in 6.1A).

$$s = \bar{s} - (1/\alpha_2 \phi)(p - \bar{p}) \qquad (6.1C)$$

This equation simply states that given the condition of money market equilibrium and equalisation of yields, that if the current price level, p, rises above the equilibrium price level, $\bar{p}$, monetary equilibrium requires a higher interest rate, and via equation 6.2 the expectation of a depreciation. The latter must imply that the current exchange rate, s, falls short of the equilibrium rate, $\bar{s}$. The negative relationship between s and p is clear from 6.1C.

5 The $\dot{p} = 0$ schedule which represents jointly goods and money market equilibrium is derived in the following way. Goods market equilibrium is characterized by a situation where the excess demand for goods is equal to zero (i.e. $y = d$ and thus $\dot{p} = 0$). Thus by setting $\dot{p} = 0$ in 6.21 and on substituting the money market equilibrium condition for i we get:

$$p = [\beta_1\alpha_2(\beta_1\alpha_2 + \beta_3)]s + [\beta_3\alpha_2(\beta_1\alpha_2 + \beta_3)]m$$
$$+ [\alpha_2(\beta_1\alpha_2 + \beta_3)] [\beta_0 + (1 - \beta_2)y - \alpha_1\beta_3y/\alpha_2] \tag{6.1D}$$

which for given m and y demonstrates the positive slope of $\dot{p} = 0$ in s, p space. Further, the slope $\dot{p} = 0$ is less steep than the 45° ray for the following reason. From equilibrium, an increase in the price level results, via the $s - p$ term in equation 6.20, in a relative price change (domestic goods are more expensive *vis à vis* foreign goods) and a decrease in the real money supply and as a consequence a rise in interest rates. Both these effects in the model result in an excess supply of goods. To offset the terms of trade effect the exchange rate would have to move by the same amount as p, but since interest rates have also risen s must rise more than proportionately to the relative price change.

6 Equation 6.22 is obtained by totally differentiating equation 6.1A

$$dp - dm = -\alpha_1dy + \alpha_2di^* + \alpha_2\phi(ds - d\bar{s}) \tag{6.1E}$$

and by noting that $d\bar{s} = dm = dp$ and that y and i^* are constant.

7 Frenkel and Rodriguez (1981) have argued that the exchange rate overshooting in the fix-price model is crucially dependent on the assumption of perfect capital mobility. If capital is less than perfectly mobile the exchange rate may undershoot its new long-run equilibrium value. A further example of exchange-rate undershooting is given by Bhandhari, Driskell and Frenkel (1984). For a further discussion of the issues surrounding the overshooting/undershooting question, see MacDonald (1986).

8 For a fuller discussion of dual exchange rate systems and their practicalities, see MacDonald (1986).

9 Similar poor results from estimating equations 6.16 and 6.26 have been reported by Hacche and Townend (1981), for sterling's effective exchange rate, and Backus (1984) for the Canadian dollar–US dollar exchange rate.

10 Successful estimates of the rational expectations version of the monetary approach, equation 6.13, have been reported by Hoffman and Schlagenhauf (1983).

11 Underlying the assumption that $\dot{m}^e = \dot{s}^e$ is a further assumption that expected income growth is equal to zero. This type of assumption has been termed 'monetary super neutrality' by Artis and Currie (1981).

12 The conclusions of the currency substitution model are equally valid in the fix price monetary model.

13 For a discussion of the appropriate use of monetary and exchange rate targets see Artis and Currie (1981).

7 The Portfolio Balance Approach to the Determination of the Exchange Rate

In chapter 3 one of the main criticisms of the Mundell–Fleming model was its neglect of the stock implications of flows. In the previous two chapters the influence of stock equilibrium conditions have been emphasized: flows can only continue until full stock equilibrium is restored. However, the models considered, and this is particularly true of the flex-price monetary approach, tend to downplay or ignore any flow implications of, for example, monetary shocks: the economy moves timelessly from one long-run equilibrium to the next. The distinction between the short run and long run is blurred.

In this chapter an asset model of the determination of the exchange rate is presented in which the economy takes time to adjust to various shocks: there is therefore a split between the short- and long-run effects of such shocks. In the short run asset prices are determined by the stock requirements of asset markets, but the asset prices so determined may have consequences for real variables such as real wealth and the rate of savings over time. One important feature of the asset market model considered in this chapter is that, in contrast to the models considered hitherto, it assumes that bonds are imperfect substitutes and thus allows a role for portfolio diversification in terms of bonds between countries. Models which utilize imperfect asset substitutability and capture stock-flow interactions are termed portfolio balance models. The portfolio balance model has its origins and development in research conducted by McKinnon and Oates (1966); McKinnon (1969); Branson (1968, 1975). The portfolio model has been applied to the determination of the exchange rate by, *inter alia* Branson (1977); Isard (1978); Genberg and Kierzkowski (1979); Allen and Kenen (1978) and Dornbusch and Fischer (1980). One particular feature of such portfolio balance models is that wealth is included as a scale variable in the asset demand equations. This is in marked contrast to the asset models considered in chapter 6.

In this chapter we present a model which captures the essential features of the portfolio balance model as it has been applied to the determination of the exchange rate. Before considering the model in any detail, however, some of the issues mentioned above are discussed in a little more detail. A related topic considered in this chapter is a review of the econometric evidence on the portfolio balance model.

Whither the Current Account?

The reader who has read the previous chapter in the light of chapter 2 (balance of payments view of the exchange rate) may be forgiven for asking: what has happened to the current account? The emphasis in the monetary approach to the exchange rate is on asset markets and consequently the capital account: changes in monetary and real variables have their effects on exchange rates via asset markets. The current account may be thought of as being in the background in the different versions of the monetary approach. In the flex-price monetary approach there is nothing inconsistent with a country running a current account deficit or surplus and therefore accumulating or decumulating assets. Such imbalances are, however, due to the relevant propensities to save and invest in the respective countries (i.e. real magnitudes) and it is assumed that such factors are not influenced by exchange market developments.[1]

But how realistic is this? In the Dornbusch (1976) model, for example, the short-run exchange rate overshoots to maintain money market equilibrium. This overshoot, as was shown in the previous chapter, implies a change in the real exchange rate (i.e. ppp is violated in the short run) and thus in the terms of trade. This must, from a position of current account balance, lead to a current account imbalance and wealth must be changing. But in the Dornbusch model the change in the exchange rate has implications only for aggregate demand; the consequent wealth implications of current account imbalances have no effect on spending (via, say, a wealth effect on consumption) or on assets (i.e. if money demand is a function of wealth then a change in wealth will raise money demand). A realistic account of the dynamic adjustment from short-run asset market equilibrium to long-run equilibrium should highlight the role of the current account.

Casual empiricism also highlights a role for the current account and its effect on the exchange rate. For example, from 8 June 1977 until 1 November 1978 the dollar fell sharply against most currencies and although the US economy was suffering relatively high inflation and nominal interest rates during this period, most commentators argued that the dollar's depreciation was much more than could be explained purely on the basis of these factors. Attention was also focused on the large and growing US current account deficit as an explanation of the large depreciation (nominal and real) of the exchange rate relative to inflation rates. The absence of current account effects from the models discussed in the previous chapter make them unsuited in explaining the dollar depreciation over 1977–8.[2]

Casual empiricism also suggests that the monetary approach ignores another important factor; namely, portfolio diversification. Thus, in chapter 6 it was assumed that non-money assets (bonds) were perfect substitutes and thus had no role to play in the analysis of the determination of the exchange rate. However, a number of factors, such as differential tax risk, liquidity considerations, political risk, default risk and exchange risk suggest that non-money assets issued in different countries are unlikely to be viewed as perfect substitutes. Thus, just as international transactors are likely to hold a portfolio of currencies to minimize exchange risk (i.e. currency substitution), risk-averse international investors will wish to hold a portfolio of non-money assets, the proportion of particular assets held depending on risk/return factors. This has the implication that uncovered interest parity is not expected to hold. Indeed tests of the uncovered interest parity relationship do tend to question its validity and point towards the existence of a risk premium.[3] Thus equation 6.2 does not hold, but instead:

$$i - i^* - \dot{s}^e = \lambda \tag{7.1}$$

where λ is a risk premium (i.e. in chapter 6 it is assumed equal to zero). Thus if international investors decide that a currency has become riskier they are likely to reallocate their bond portfolios in favour of the less risky assets. This gives another explanation for the large depreciation of the dollar in 1977–8: the falling dollar meant that dollar assets were perceived to be riskier than, say German and Japanese assets, and portfolio managers were keen to switch from dollar bonds to mark and yen denominated bonds.

The above discussion has raised a number of points which are summarized. First, if ppp does not hold in the short run then exchange rate changes, caused, say, by a monetary shock, will be real changes and if the familiar Marshall–Lerner condition holds these changes may be expected to influence the current account. A current account imbalance means that the country must be accumulating or decumulating assets and wealth must be changing. As Dornbusch (1980) and Frankel (1983) have pointed out changes in wealth could be expected to influence the exchange rate in a number of ways. If consumption is a function of wealth (as posited by the life-cycle hypothesis) then income will be changing and as a corollary so too will the demand for money and the exchange rate. If the demand for money is also a function of wealth, then a change in wealth due to current account imbalance will lead to a changed demand for money and this can be expected to reinforce the exchange rate impact of the change in consumption. Wealth will also have an influence on asset market equilibrium if, as seems likely, international agents are risk averse and the riskiness of holding foreign assets implies that domestic bond holders will hold a larger proportion of domestic bonds in their portfolios than foreign investors (for the same rate of return on home and foreign bonds). Thus with imperfect asset substitutability and risk aversion, greater proportions of an increase in wealth will be held in domestic bonds and this must have asset market consequences.

Imperfect substitutability of bonds has of course a separate influence on asset markets independently of wealth effects. Thus, as was argued above, if investors decide that a particular currency has become riskier they will diversify their portfolios away from bonds denominated in that currency.

The conclusion is reached on theoretical grounds and also from casual empiricism that the current account has an important role to play in a properly specified asset market model of the determination of the exchange rate. Hence although the exchange rate is at any point in time determined so as to clear asset markets (as in the monetary approach), the range of assets relevant to the determination of the exchange rate is likely to be wider than relative money supplies and, furthermore, because the current account is a flow concept, a current account imbalance will have an affect on the stock of assets over time and thus, for the reasons noted earlier, the exchange rate. A properly specified model of the exchange rate should capture this stock-flow interaction over time.

Later in this chapter a model of exchange rate determination is examined which incorporates the effects of both current account imbalances and portfolio diversification. Before discussing this model a simple example of the stock-flow model dynamics alluded to above is explained.

The Current Account, Stock-flow Interaction and Portfolio Diversification: A Simple Example and a Basic Framework

To give a flavour of the asset model considered in later sections of this chapter a figure is presented which illustrates the essential features of this model.

Consider a simple model in which domestic residents hold two non-interest bearing assets: a home asset, H, and a foreign asset, F, denominated in foreign currency. The demand for each asset depends solely on the expected change in the exchange rate (thus we basically have a currency substitution model of the type discussed in chapter 6). In home currency terms domestic residents wealth is defined as:

$$W = H + SF \tag{7.2}$$

In figure 7.1 the FF schedule represents points of equilibrium for the stock of the foreign assets held by domestic residents. Clearly if the foreign asset market is in equilibrium so also, with two assets, must be the home asset market: FF represents overall asset market equilibrium with the stock demand for the foreign asset equal to the stock supply available to domestic residents (the factors determining the stock demand for the assets will be considered more fully below). The FF schedule is drawn downward sloping because for given values

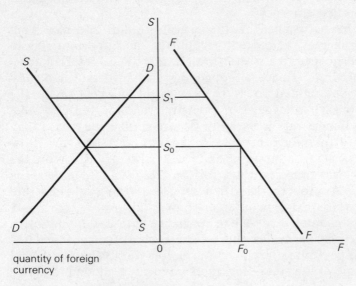

quantity of foreign currency

Figure 7.1   Stock-flow interaction

of H and the expected change in the exchange rate an increase in the stock of the foreign asset requires an appreciation in the exchange rate (i.e. from 7.2 an increase in F requires a proportional fall in S to maintain wealth constant). The left quadrant shows the flow demand and supply of foreign exchange underlying the current account of the balance of payments.

If the exchange rate is initially at S_0 with a stock of foreign assets F_0, it is clear that this is consistent with equilibrium in both the current account and asset markets. If the exchange rate now moves to S_1, and if this results in a change in the terms of trade (and if the relevant elasticities condition is satisfied), then it is evident from the left hand side of figure 7.1 that the current account must be in surplus (i.e. domestic production exceeds domestic absorption). This current account surplus, under flexible exchange rates, will have as its counterpart a capital account deficit: the country must be accumulating foreign assets over time and thus for continuous stock market, or asset market, equilibrium to be maintained the exchange rate must be falling. This appreciating exchange rate will lead to reduced competitiveness and, if the appropriate elasticities condition holds, to a reduction in exports and an increase in imports and so a reduction of the current account surplus. This process will continue until all of the current account surplus is eliminated and the equilibrium exchange rate, S_0, is reached where both stock and flow equilibrium is achieved.

The kind of dynamics underlying figure 7.1 can be illustrated schematically in figure 7.2. The outstanding asset stocks determine a vector of asset prices (of which we have only considered the exchange rate in this section) and with an appropriate transmission mechanism

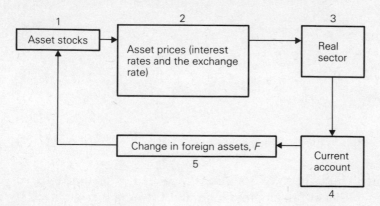

Figure 7.2   Assets, the exchange rate and the current account

they affect the real sector. The element of the real sector of particular interest here is the current account, and the outcome of 1 and 2 will have its repurcussions on the current account and this will lead to a change in the stock of foreign assets, 5, and the process 1–5 will be set in motion again untio equilibrium is reached.

This simple example gives an intuitive feel for how the current account and foreign asset interacts with the exchange rate over time. It can be given some flesh and bones by setting up a formal model which captures all of the elements introduced above. The general model outlined here is discussed in the following sections in the context of two specific time periods. The impact period is one in which only asset market adjustment is considered. Asset markets are assumed to be continually equilibrated by interest rate and exchange rate movements. However in the impact period the effect of real variables and the price level on asset stocks is ignored. The other period considered is the short run where prices and real variables are influenced by, and feedback on, as set prices. The interaction of stocks and flows in the short-run period leads eventually to a new long-run equilibrium. The generalized asset market model is as follows:

Table 7.1 The Representative Asset Market Model

$W = M + B + SF = \int \dot{q} + \int \dot{F}(\dot{S})$	(7.3)
Supply = Demand	
$M = m(i, i^* + \dot{s}^e)W; \quad m_i < 0 \quad m_{i^* + \dot{s}}e < 0$	(7.4)
$B = b(i, i^* + \dot{s}^e)W; \quad b_i > 0 \quad b_{i^* + \dot{s}e} < 0$	(7.5)
$SF = f(i, i^* + \dot{s}^e)W; \quad f_i < 0 \quad f_{i^* + \dot{s}e} > 0$	(7.6)
$m + b + f = 1$	(7.7)
$S = P^T$	(7.8)
$Y = P^T Q^T + P^N Q^N$	(7.9)
$C = Y^D + \beta(w - \bar{w}); \quad \beta > 0$	(7.10)
$Y^D = Y + i^* FS$	(7.11)
$P = P^{T,\alpha} P^{N,1-\alpha}$	(7.12)
$\dot{F} = T(S/P^N); \quad T_{S/P^N} > 0$	(7.13)

The country described by equations 7.3–7.13 is assumed to be small and operating at full employment, and thus the foreign interest rate and price level are data. Analysing a two country model would only complicate matters without shedding light on the substantive issues. Consider first the asset sector of the model.

Equations 7.3–7.7 describe the asset sector of the model, where wealth is assumed to equal the sum of domestically issued money, a domestically issued bond and a foreign bond denominated in foreign currency (thus, SF is the home currency price of the foreign bond). Notice that, in contrast to the asset models considered in the last chapter and the Mundell–Fleming model, bonds are assumed to be imperfect substitutes. Asset demand is assumed to be a function of the home and foreign interest rate, expected exchange rate appreciation and is homogeneous of degree one in wealth (this enables us to write equations 7.4–7.6 in nominal terms).[4]

For simplicity it is assumed that the asset demand equations do not depend upon income. It is further assumed that the bonds are gross substitutes, i.e. $b_i > f_i$ and $b_{(i* + \dot{s}^e)} < f_{(i* + \dot{s}^e)}$[5] and a greater proportion of any increase in domestic wealth is held in domestic bonds rather than foreign bonds. Although domestic residents can hold all three assets, foreign residents can only hold foreign bonds (and presumably foreign money which is also non-traded). The only way residents of the small country can accumulate F is by running a current account surplus (which as we shall see below equals savings).

Equation 7.7 is simply the adding up constraint: the proportion of bonds, money and foreign bonds held must add up to wealth. Asset markets are assumed to be continuously in equilibrium and thus demand equals supply in the three markets. Wealth in equation 7.3 is also written as the sum of past savings, q, and the history of capital gains and losses on the foreign asset (since the bonds are assumed to be bills, rather than consols, we ignore the revaluation effects of interest rates on wealth).

It is assumed that the small country produces a traded good, Q^T, whose price is exogenously given in the international market and for simplicity is set equal to unity (thus, equation 7.8) and a non traded good, Q^N. Total nominal income is given by equation 7.9. The supply of and demand for the traded and non-traded goods depends solely on the relative price of traded to non-traded goods P^T/P^N or S/P^N. The small country's aggregate consumption need not equal aggregate production in this model since desired and actual real wealth need not be equal: it takes time for individuals to eliminate discrepancies between the stock of wealth they hold and the stock they desire to hold. This relationship is given by equation 7.10 where consumption is assumed to be equal to disposable income plus a constant fraction of the discrepancy between desired real wealth, $\bar{w}$, (assumed constant) and actual real wealth, w, (i.e. savings). Disposable income (7.11) in turn, is equal to nominal income, Y, plus interest income from foreign bond holdings (it is assumed that interest earnings from domestic bonds are offset by a lump sum tax). The overall price level is simply a weighted average of the price of traded and non-traded goods, 7.12. The flexible exchange rate/balance of payments equilibrium condition is given as equation 7.13: the capital account, $\dot{F}$, equals the current account, $T + i^*F_s$. The trade balance, T, is assumed to depend positively on the real exchange rate (the Marshall–Lerner condition in this model). The relationship between the real exchange rate and the trade balance reflects an assumption that when the real exchange rate rises, producers have an incentive to move production from non-traded goods towards traded goods and consumers have an incentive to switch their consumption from traded goods to non-traded goods.

Notice that given the assumption of full employment, what is not consumed at home must be exported and thus savings must equal the trade balance. Substituting savings ($Y^D - C = \beta(\bar{w} - w) - i^*FS$) for T in 7.13 we obtain:

$$\dot{F} = \beta(\bar{w} - w) \tag{7.14}$$

and thus the accumulation of F over time is equal to the discrepancy between desired and actual real wealth.

Before considering the workings of the model, a little must be said about expectations. In the impact period, asset prices, the domestic interest rate, the exchange rate and the expected change in the exchange rate (remember the foreign interest rate is assumed to be exogenous), are determined by the outstanding asset stocks. But the asset system 7.4–7.6 will, on its own, be indeterminate since we have three equations, only two of which are independent, and three unknowns. Thus we need to introduce a further relationship to capture expectations. Two assumptions are common in this vintage of model: either static expectations, where $\dot{s}^e = 0$, or rational expectations where a further equation is required:

$$\dot{s}^e = \dot{s} + \epsilon_t \tag{7.15}$$

which says that the expected change in the exchange rate equals the actual change plus a white noise error. Given some expectational assumptions, the asset sector determines the spot exchange rate, S, and the domestic interest rate, i. For the time being it is assumed that expectations are static.

The workings of the model can be illustrated diagramatically in the following way: figure 7.3(A) shows combinations of the domestic rate of interest and the exchange rate that hold the demand for

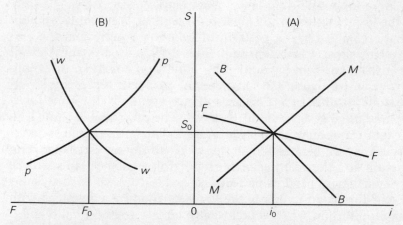

Figure 7.3   Short- and long-run asset market equilibrium

money equal to its supply (the MM schedule), the demand and supply of domestic bonds in equality (the BB schedule) and the demand and supply of foreign assets in equality (the FF schedule). An intuitive grasp of the relative slopes is quite easy. Taking money, M, and bonds, B, first, an increase in the exchange rate, S, from a position of equilibrium will, with the revaluation effect on wealth, lead to an increase in *wealth* and thus an increase in the demand for both M and B to restore portfolio equilibrium. As money demand rises – the domestic rate of interest – i must rise to maintain money market equilibrium; hence the positive MM curve in S, i space. The BB curve has a negative slope because the increased demand for bonds raises their price and depresses the equilibrium rate of interest. The negative slope of the FF schedule may be explained by a fall in i which increases the attractiveness of foreign assets leading to a rise in S. BB is steeper than FF because it is assumed that on the basis of domestic asset holders' risk preferences, domestic demand for domestic bonds is more responsive than domestic demand for foreign assets to interest rate changes. Equilibrium in figure 7.3(A) is represented by an exchange rate of S_0 and an interest rate of i_0.

Because of the wealth constraint, equation 7.3, it must be that only two of the three equations 7.4–7.6 are independent. Thus, if a given change in i or S restores equilibrium in two markets then the third market must also be in equilibrium. It is therefore possible to analyse various shocks using only two schedules.

Before considering various shocks to the model it must be determined whether the combination of S_0 and i_0 given in figure 7.3(A) is one of long-run equilibrium (since asset markets are always in equilibrium the combination i_0, S_0 must represent, at least, impact equilibrium). For S_0, i_0 to be a position of long-run equilibrium the current account must equal zero and thus desired wealth must equal actual wealth (i.e. zero savings). The condition for long-run equilibrium is given by figure 7.3(B) where the *pp* locus represents short-run portfolio balance in S, F space and has essentially the same interpretation as the *FF* schedule in Part (A). The *pp* schedule shifts leftwards when the money stock is increased. Thus, for a given stock of foreign assets an increase in M must result in an exchange rate depreciation for the maintenance of portfolio balance (this will be discussed further in a following section).

The schedule *ww* represents the locus of S and F consistent with long-run equilibrium when actual wealth equals desired wealth and it can be shown positively sloped if plausible values of trade and asset demand elasticities are chosen. Thus as S depreciates and with it the real exchange rate, the country's current account surplus grows and the associated asset accumulation must be held in foreign bonds (F). An increase in domestic money supply, M, will shift *ww* rightwards – this can be quite easily explained at the intuitive level. Recall that on *ww* actual wealth equals desired wealth and that as this is a full employment-constant income model desired wealth never alters. Now, an increase in M, through open market operations for example, is inflationary and the real value of the domestic component of wealth (held in domestic money and bonds) falls. Thus, to re-establish the equilibrium level of actual wealth the home currency value of foreign bonds held by residents must be increased, which is achieved by a rise in S (depreciation). Hence, *ww* will shift rightwards (or upwards) in F, S space. (The mathematical derivation of the *ww* schedule is presented in Genberg and Kierzkowski, 1979).

Initially equilibrium is given by the combination of S_0, F_0 and i_0. A variety of shocks are now considered which move the system from the initial equilibrium position. At first only the impact period is considered.

The Impact Period and Monetary Policy

'Helicopter' Increase in the Money Supply There may be a once-and-for-all increase in the money supply via Friedman's 'helicopter' drop, or, more realistically, through a budget deficit. Investors will now find that their portfolios have become unbalanced and will attempt to rebalance them by buying domestic bonds, B, and foreign bonds, F. With stocks of domestic and foreign bonds given in the short run,

bond market equilibrium can be maintained only by a fall in i and rise in S. Thus to maintain bond market equilibrium, at each exchange rate, the increased demand for bonds – domestic and foreign – reduces i and pushes the BB curve leftwards. Contemporaneously, the increased demand for foreign bonds, with a given i, raises the value of S to maintain equilibrium in domestic holdings of foreign fixed price bonds; this shifts the FF curve rightwards.

In terms of figure 7.4, the initial equilibrium is at L and the new, post-money-supply-shock equilibrium, is at W with a lower rate of interest and a depreciated exchange rate.

Open Market Increase in the Money Supply: Money for Bonds In contrast to the 'helicopter' money supply shock, an increase in the money supply effected by a swap of money for bonds leaves the FF schedule unchanged. This is because at an initial equilibrium of X in figure 7.5 the open market operation leaves asset holders with an excess supply of money and excess demand for bonds. In attempting to buy bonds domestic investors will have the effect of pushing the domestic interest rate down and this in turn will lead to an increased demand for foreign bonds pushing S upwards. In figure 7.5 the BB and MM schedules shift leftwards and the new equilibrium is at a point such as Y. It is interesting to note that if the domestic interest elasticity of demand for money is less than the domestic elasticity of demand for

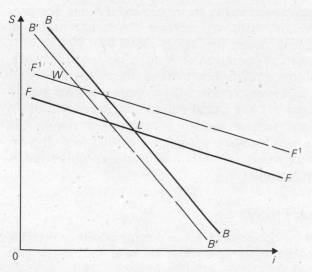

Figure 7.4   'Helicopter' increase in the money supply

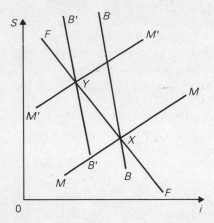

Figure 7.5   Open market increase in the money supply

foreign bonds, then the percentage change in the demand for foreign bonds will be greater than the percentage increase in the money stock. Given that there is a one-to-one relationship between S and F, this implies that the exchange rate change will be larger than the money supply change (i.e. an exchange rate overshoot which should be distinguished from the type of overshooting discussed in the previous chapter).

Open Market Increase in the Money Supply: Money for Foreign Assets The final way for the monetary authorities to increase the money supply in our models is by swopping money for foreign assets held by domestic residents. This open market operation of M for F will shift MM leftwards since at the initial equilibrium there is an excess supply of money and the rate of interest must fall for money market equilibrium to be maintained. At the initial equilibrium there will be an excess demand for the foreign asset, necessitating a rise in the exchange rate to maintain foreign asset market equilibrium: the FF schedule must shift rightwards. In figure 7.6 the initial equilibrium is at X and the new equilibrium at Y.

The Impact Period and Fiscal Policy

A budget deficit may be financed by either issuing bonds or printing money. Pure fiscal policy is usually taken to be synonymous with bond financing and that distinction is followed here.

Assuming an increase in the supply of bonds increases wealth and, for a given domestic interest rate, i, requires an increase in the ex-

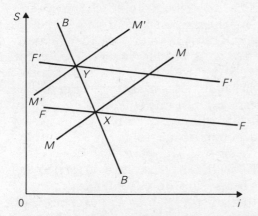

Figure 7.6 Money for foreign assets

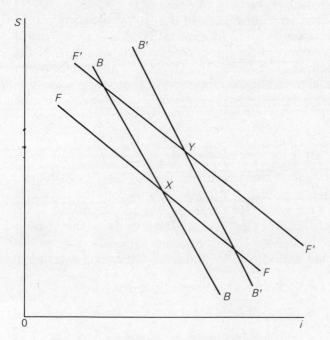

Figure 7.6a An increase in the supply of bonds

change rate S, to maintain the foreign exchange market in equilibrium as wealth holders purchase additional foreign bonds; thus, the FF schedule shifts upwards to $F'F'$ in figure 7.6a.

For a given value of the exchange rate the increased supply of domestic bonds requires an increase in the domestic interest rate to maintain bond market equilibrium: the *BB* schedule shifts rightwards and the new equilibrium is at *Y*. The increased bond supply exceeds any wealth induced increase in bond demand and the domestic interest rate is unambiguously raised. Although the new equilibrium, *Y*, in figure 7.6a shows a higher *S* the effect on the exchange rate of an increase in the stock of domestic bonds is in fact ambiguous. This is because the rise in the domestic interest rate will induce a reduced demand for foreign assets and this will tend to offset the increased demand for foreign fixed price bonds due to the wealth effect. Whether in figure 7.6a the *Y* value of *S* will be greater or less than the *X* value depends essentially on the degree to which foreign and domestic bonds are regarded as better substitutes to domestic money. If *F* and *B* are regarded as better substitutes then the exchange rate will be lower at the new equilibrium because the shift of demand from *F* to *B* as a result of the rise in *i* will be greater the closer *F* and *B* are regarded as substitutes (relative to *B* and *M*).

In table 7.2 we summarize the effects of the asset shocks considered hitherto on the exchange rate and interest rate and also the effect of a change in the foreign asset on the exchange rate. The sign of the latter should be obvious from the proportional relationship between *S* and *F*. As is demonstrated in the next section the effect of changes in *F* on the exchange rate is the key dynamic relationship in the model.

The Short-run Adjustment to the Steady State

The previous section gave consideration to various asset disturbances and their effect on the exchange rate and domestic interest rate in the short run, impact period. However, as our model makes clear, such asset changes will affect real magnitudes such as the current account and savings. In this section attention is focused on the movement from the impact period equilibrium to the new long-run steady

Table 7.2 Summary of the Effects of Asset Shocks on Asset Prices in the Impact Period

Effect on	Changes in stocks			Open market operations	
	ΔF	ΔM	ΔB	$\Delta B = -\Delta M$	$S\Delta F = -\Delta M$
s	−	+	?	+	+
i	0	−	+	−	−

Source: Branson (1977).

state equilibrium following the open market purchase of domestic bonds for money. The impact equilibrium after such a shock is repeated here in the right hand of figure 7.7 as point Y.

In the left hand quadrant of figure 7.7 the pp schedule moves from pp to $p'p'$ (see discussion on page 118 above).

Although the valuation effect of the exchange rate will, on impact, give a rise in nominal wealth, it seems likely that moving to the short-run period this will be offset by the effect the exchange rate over-shoot has on the price index and thus real wealth: actual real wealth in the short-run period will fall short of desired real wealth (which, remember, is assumed constant throughout). This mismatch of desired and actual real wealth implies, via equation 7.10, that domestic residents must be saving and thus running a current account surplus (see equation 7.14) during the adjustment period. Thus the desire to restore the initial value of desired wealth can only be realized by the country running a current account surplus and accumulating the foreign asset. This is possible since in the impact period relative prices have moved in favour of the traded goods sector inducing a switch in production from non-traded to traded goods and a switch in consumption from traded to non-traded goods.

The current account surplus over time forces the exchange rate downwards (i.e. F rising, so S must be falling) leading to a diminuition of the savings rate until equilibrium is restored on the new ww curve at point z; i.e. $w'w'$ where $w = \bar{w}$ with the higher money stock.

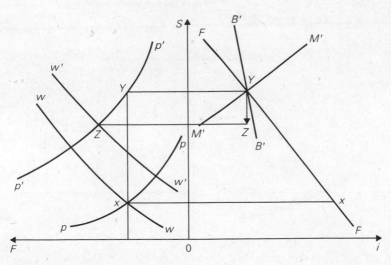

Figure 7.7   Impact and long-run equilibrium

In the right hand quadrant of figure 7.7 the *MM*, *BB* and *FF* curves all shift down from *Y* in proportion to the accumulation of *F*.

If in the initial equilibrium the price of traded goods equalled the price of non-traded goods, in the new equilibrium the relative price of traded goods will have fallen: the increase in the money supply does not lead to a proportionate increase in the overall price level. This follows since in the adjustment period the home country has been accumulating foreign assets and in the new equilibrium interest receipts on the foreign asset must be greater than the initial equilibrium. Since the current account is the sum of the trade balance plus interest earnings, and since a zero current balance is a condition of steady state equilibrium, the positive interest earnings must be offset by a fall in the real exchange rate (i.e. P^N rises relative to P^T).[6]

In figure 7.8 the adjustment profiles of the exchange rate, the trade balance and the capital account of the balance of payments accounts following the monetaty shock are plotted. Hence, after the money supply increase at time 0, the exchange rate appreciates to the new long-run equilibrium value which is, for the reasons given earlier, higher than at S_0. The deficit on the trade account for the majority of the adjustment period is possible because of the capital account deficit and the interest income on foreign bonds. The latter

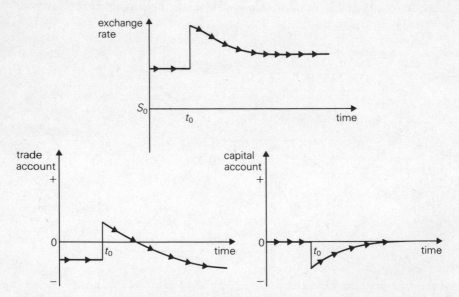

Figure 7.8   The adjustment profiles of the exchange rate, the trade account and the capital account

element allows the country to sustain a larger trade balance deficit than in the initial equilibrium.

Of the asset shocks summarized in table 7.2 we only consider the adjustment from the impact period to the long-run equilibrium for the case of the open market purchase of bonds with money. However, this shock is deemed sufficiently representative of the other shocks to allow the interested reader to trace through their implied dynamic paths. In the remainder of this section an asset shock not hitherto stressed is considered: a portfolio diversification shock to domestic from foreign bonds.

Asset Preference Shift

Say for some reason, such as a perceived reduction in riskiness or the expectation of an appreciation, that domestic bonds become more attractive than foreign bonds. What will be the implications of this for the impact period and the adjustment to equilibrium? This type of shock is illustrated in figure 7.9. At the initial equilibrium the increased demand for domestic bonds can only be satisfied by a reduction in the rate of interest giving the leftward shift in BB to $B'B'$. Equally the attempt to move out of foreign bonds can, in the impact period, only be satisfied by a leftward shift of the FF schedule. Thus the impact effect of a change in asset preference from foreign to domestic bonds results in a reduction in the interest rate and the exchange rate: from i_0 to i_1, and from S_0 to S_1.

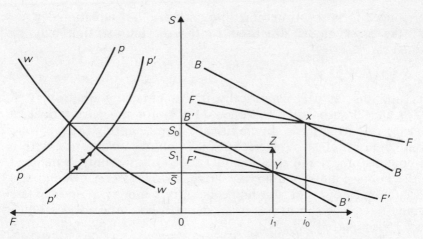

Figure 7.9   The impact and long-run effects of a change in preferences

Moving from the impact period to the short-run adjustment period we find that private sector wealth has increased due to the fall in the price of traded goods and this, for the reasons given earlier, must outweigh the wealth reducing effect of the devaluation, in home currency terms, of the stock of foreign assets. Thus w must be greater than $\bar{w}$ and agents will be dis-saving; and, via equation 7.10, consumption must rise. Further, the mirror image of the dis-saving will be a current account deficit which will be induced by the initial change in relative prices. As the stock of F is reduced over time, via the current account, the rate of dis-saving is reduced, whilst the initial exchange rate appreciation is gradually reversed until the new equilibrium is reached at $\bar{S}$. In contrast to the open market purchase of bonds, the new long-run equilibrium consequent upon the change in asset preferences must be one in which the relative price of traded to non-traded goods has fallen.

To summarize the results of this chapter thus far: first, it has been demonstrated that asset shocks emanating from money or bond markets result in exchange rate overshooting. This overshoot is, however, reversed over time as the country accumulates or decumulates F via the current account. Second, asset shocks can affect the terms of trade, or real exchange rate, in our model because of the existence of at least one outside asset: a ten per cent increase in M does not result in a ten per cent increase in the price level. Third, a current account surplus in the model is associated with an appreciating exchange rate.

Econometric Evidence on the Portfolio Balance Approach

The reduced form short-run portfolio exchange rate equation derived from the asset model discussed in the previous section may be denoted as:

$$S = f(B, M, F) \tag{7.16}$$

This equation has been empirically implemented by Branson et al. (1977) and Branson and Haltunen (1979) for the recent floating exchange rate experience. In empirically implementing the portfolio model, Branson et al. replace the small country assumption with a two country model and thus includes the foreign country's demand for the home country's domestic bond, its own 'foreign' bond and foreign money but not the home country's money as monies are assumed not to be substitutes in asset portfolios. Accordingly equation 7.16 is replaced by:

$$S = f(M, M^*, B, B^*, F, F^*) \tag{7.17}$$

In a two country setting asset accumulation emanating from the current account will have the same effect on the exchange rate as in the small country case as long as domestic residents' preference for the domestic bond is greater than their preference for the foreign bond.[7]

Branson et al. (1977), by arbitrarily dropping the B and B^* terms from equation 7.17, econometrically estimated equation 7.18

$$S = f(M, M^*, F, F^*) \tag{7.18A}$$

$$S = q_0 + q_1 \overset{+}{M} + q_2 \bar{M}^* + q_3 \bar{F} + q_4 \overset{+}{F}^* + \epsilon \tag{7.18B}$$

for the German mark–US dollar exchange rate over the period August 1971–December 1976 (the sign of the effects of asset changes on the exchange rate are represented by a positive or minus sign above the assets). The money supply terms are defined as $M1$ and the foreign assets are proxied by cumulated current account balances. Although all of the estimated coefficients have the hypothesized signs, after correction for autocorrelation only one coefficient is statistically significant. To allow for potential simultaneity bias induced by foreign exchange market intervention by the German authorities (i.e. $M = F + D$ and thus if F is changed to modify S, M will be correlated with the error term introducing simultaneous equation bias), Branson et al. (1977) estimated equation 7.18 using two stage least squares, but this did not lead to a substantial improvement of the results. In Branson and Haltunen (1979), equation 7.18 is estimated for the mark–dollar rate for the larger sample period August 1971–December 1978, but the results are very similar to those in the earlier paper. In a further paper, Branson and Haltunen (1979) estimate equation 7.18 for the Japanese yen, French franc, Italian lira, Swiss franc and the pound sterling (all relative to the US dollar) for the period July 1971 to June 1976. Their ordinary least squares results show most equations with statistically significant coefficients and signs which are consistent with the priors noted in equation 7.18. However, little reliance can be placed on their results since they suffer from acute autocorrelation. The latter could reflect a dynamic misspecification of the model or the exclusion of variables relevant to the portfolio approach. Indeed, Bisignano and Hoover (1983), in their study of the Canadian dollar, include domestic non-monetary asset stocks and report moderately successful econometric results. A further problem with the Branson implementation of the portfolio model is that the use of bilateral exchange rates and cumulated current accounts implies that third country assets and liabilities are perfect substitutes. Bisignano and Hoover (1983) use strictly bilateral asset stocks in their study and this could be a further reason for their successful results (the use of cumulated current accounts by researchers is usually out of necessity and not choice: few countries publish the details of the ownership of assets).

Alternative tests of the portfolio balance approach have exploited the insight of Dooley and Isard (1979) that the portfolio model can be solved for a risk premium. It is argued that the risk premium term, λ, in equation 7.1 is:

$$i - i^* - \dot{s}^e = \lambda \tag{7.1A}$$

a function of the factors that determine the supply of outside assets: i.e. government bonds. Thus, λ, may be written as a function of the relative supplies of bonds:

$$\lambda = \frac{1}{\beta} B/FS \tag{7.19}$$

on substituting this expression into equation 7.1A equation 7.20 is obtained:

$$B/FS = \beta(i - i^* - \dot{s}^e) \tag{7.20}$$

or in logs:

$$b - s - f = \alpha_0 + \beta(i - i^* - \dot{s}^e) \tag{7.21}$$

Thus, in order to diversify the resultant risk of exchange rate variability, investors balance their portfolios between domestic and foreign bonds in proportions that depend on the expected relative rate of return (or risk premium). Following Frankel (1983) equation 7.21 can be used to derive a generalized asset market representation of the exchange rate which is econometrically testable.

By rearranging equation 6.23 as:

$$\phi(s - \bar{s}) = \dot{p}^e - \dot{p}^{e*} - \dot{s}^e \tag{7.22}$$

and by simultaneously adding the interest differential to $-\dot{s}^e$, subtracting it from $\dot{p}^e - \dot{p}^{e*}$ and solving for s equation 7.23 is obtained:

$$s = \bar{s} - \frac{1}{\phi}[(i - \dot{p}^e) - (i^* - \dot{p}^{e*})] + \frac{1}{\phi}[i - i^* - \dot{s}^e] \tag{7.23}$$

which states that the exchange rate deviates from its long-run value by an amount proportional to the real interest differential and the risk premium. Furthermore, substituting from equation 6.24 for the long run equilibrium exchange rate, equation 7.24 can be derived.

$$s = m - m^* - \alpha_1(y - y^*) + \alpha_2(\dot{p}^e - \dot{p}^{e*})$$

$$-\frac{1}{\phi}[(i - \dot{p}^e) - (i^* - \dot{p}^{e*})] + \frac{1}{\phi}[i - i^* - \dot{s}^e] \qquad (7.24)$$

Relative bond supplies enter equation 7.24 via the last term. Thus, by substituting into 7.21 and solving for s we obtain:

$$s = \frac{\alpha_0}{\phi\beta + 1} \frac{\phi\beta}{\phi\beta + 1} m - m^* - \frac{\phi\beta\alpha_1}{\phi\beta + 1}(y - y^*)$$

$$+ \frac{\beta(\phi\alpha_2 + 1)}{\phi\beta + 1}(\dot{p}^e - \dot{p}^e) - \frac{\beta}{\phi\beta + 1}(i - i^*)$$

$$+ \frac{1}{\phi\beta + 1}(b - f) \qquad (7.25)$$

Frankel (1983) tests equation 7.25 for the dollar–mark exchange rate, January 1974–October 1978 and a representative equation is reported here.

$$s = -1.03 + 0.50m - m^* - 0.056(y - y^*) - 0.358(i - i^*)$$
$$\quad (0.18)\ (0.31) \qquad\qquad (0.21) \qquad\qquad (0.47)$$

$$+ 1.851(\dot{p}^e - \dot{p}^{e*})^V + 0.313(b^* - f)^W \qquad (7.26)$$
$$\quad (0.69) \qquad\qquad\qquad (0.05)$$

$R^2 = 0.95 \quad p = 0.92$

Standard errors in parentheses.

V = significant at the 95 per cent level and the correct sign.

W = significant at the 95 per cent level and the wrong sign.

Equation 7.26 is a test of the 'small country portfolio model' and thus b^* and f are German holdings of the domestic and home (US) bond. Referring back to equation 7.25 notice that the signs on money, income, interest rates and the inflation rate are all correct, although only the latter is statistically significant. The risk premium term, $b^* - f$, although statistically significant is wrongly signed: an increase in the foreign asset relative to the home bond leads to an exchange rate depreciation, in contrast to the prior expectation. Thus, Frankel's estimates, at best, give somewhat mixed support to the portfolio balance approach.

A version of equation 7.25 has also been estimated by Hooper and Morton (1983) for the dollar effective exchange rate, over the period

1973 (II) to 1978 (IV) and they found that the risk premium term was neither significant nor correctly signed.

In summary the above selection of empirical studies on the portfolio balance approach are not particularly supportive but perhaps this should not be a surprise: the paucity of good data on non-monetary aggregates (in particular their distribution between different countries) and the specifications of the reduced forms tested, perhaps do not give the portfolio balance approach a fair 'crack of the whip' (the issue of a risk premium is returned to in the next chapter).

Summary and Conclusions

In this chapter an asset portfolio model of the determination of the exchange rate was presented and utilized to consider various policy changes, such as monetary and fiscal policy. The model may be regarded, in terms of exchange rate theory, as 'state of the art'. It has a number of noteworthy features.

First, and in contrast to the monetary models considered in the preceding chapter, non-money assets are imperfect substitutes which allow consideration of fiscal policy, as well as monetary policy, and the effect of asset preference switches on the exchange rate. Second, a feature of the model is that the exchange rate overshoots its equilibrium value in response, say, to an expansionary monetary policy. Third, although a monetary expansion leads to an exchange rate depreciation and has a stimulative effect on the economy in the impact period, this, in contrast to the Mundell–Fleming model, is offset over time as the country runs a current account surplus which changes wealth, pushing the economy to a new long-run equilibrium. Fourth, the exchange rate in long-run equilibrium need not be consistent with ppp. This is so because if, say, the country has been accumulating foreign assets during the adjustment period interest earnings will have increased, necessitating, for current account balance, a trade deficit. The latter being induced by a change in the real exchange rate.

Notes

1 Notice, however, that the flex-price monetary model is one in which short- and long-run equilibrium coincide and thus we are always in steady state equilibrium. A common feature of steady state equilibrium in balance of payments and exchange rate models is that the current account should equal zero (more is said about 'steady' states in the rest of this chapter).

2 The monetary model outlined in the previous chapter would seem to have worked well for the dollar appreciation in 1976 and 1977. Thus although the US had a current account deficit in the period it experienced rapid income growth and, via increased money demand, it would be expected that, on the basis of equation 7.9, the exchange rate would appreciate.

3 The problem with such tests is that they are testing a joint hypothesis of perfect asset substitutability and rational expectations and thus in rejecting the joint hypothesis it is impossible to discern if this is due to imperfect asset substitutability or the irrationality of expectations or both! (More is said about this issue in the following chapter.)

4 Thus the asset demand equation should be real demands and equation 7.3 should be real wealth, but the assumed homogeneity of assets demands to wealth implies that the price deflator drops out. Wealth in equation 7.3 is also written as the sum of past savings and the history of capital gains and losses on the foreign asset. The latter element, as is shown, is one of the principal dynamic relations in the model.

5 See Tobin (1969) for a discussion of gross substitutability between bonds.

6 This result is due to Patkinkin (1965) who shows that it depends on whether bonds are regarded as net wealth by the private sector. For a discussion of this topic see Barro (1974) and Buiter and Tobin (1974).

7 In his taxonomy of portfolio balance models Frankel (1983) classifies this as the 'preferred bond habitat model'.

8 The Efficient Markets Hypothesis, Spot and Forward Exchange Rates and the Role of New Information in Foreign Exchange Markets

Introduction

In chapter 6 a number of implications of regarding the exchange rate as an asset price were considered. Since asset markets are usually regarded as efficient markets, in the sense of agents exploiting all profitable trading opportunities in the determination of asset prices (a more precise definition is given in section 1 below), it is of some interest to determine whether the foreign exchange market behaves in a manner consistent with the efficient markets hypothesis (EMH). This is the subject matter of this chapter. In section 1 some empirical regularities in the light of regrading the exchange rate as an asset price are considered. In section 2 we define an efficient market and show what implications this has for the forward market for foreign exchange. Some evidence on the efficiency of spot and forward markets is considered in section 3; such efficiency tests are pushed further in section 4 where the impact of new information in the foreign exchange market is considered.

SECTION 1 SOME EMPIRICAL REGULARITIES OF SPOT AND FORWARD EXCHANGE RATES

In a variety of preceding chapters the concept of the forward exchange rate being synonymous with the markets' expected future spot rate has been considered in various contexts. For example, in chapter 6 it was argued that spot and expected future spot and forward rates would be closely tied together. Thus, if agents revise their expected future spot rate then the current spot rate must change by a similar amount otherwise there would be large unexploited expected returns. The close correlation between actual spot and expected spot exchange rates was further illustrated using a simple monetary approach reduced form where it was demonstrated that if α_2, the coefficient on the expected change in the exchange rate, was large, the actual and expected exchange rates would have a correlation coefficient of close to unity. In figure 8.1 the relationship between the contemporaneous spot and forward exchange rates is illustrated for the UK pound–US dollar exchange rate. Notice that, as expected, the spot rate and the forward rate are closely tied together, the correlation coefficient being 0.99.

But how good a predictor of the future spot rate is the forward rate in its capacity as the expected future spot rate? In figure 8.2, by simply lagging the forward exchange rate one period, it is demonstrated that the predictive powers of the pound–dollar forward rate are not very impressive: the forward rate is a poor predictor of the future spot exchange rate. This does not, however, necessarily imply

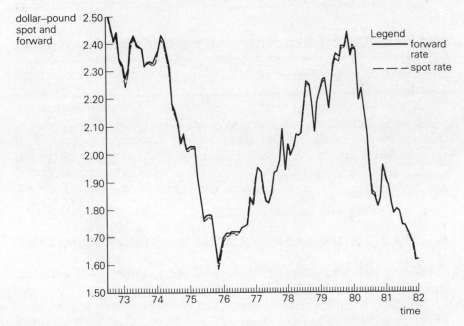

Figure 8.1   The contemporaneous spot and forward rates, dollar-pound

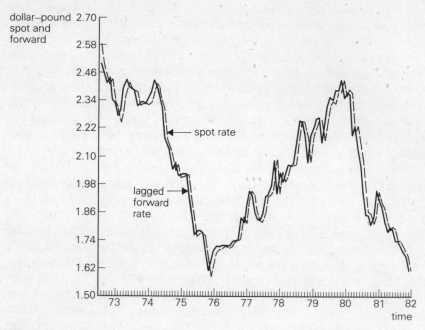

Figure 8.2   The forward rate as a predictor of the spot rate, dollar–pound

that agents have been inefficient processors of information during this period. Rather, it more probably implies that there has been a great deal of new information which has led to a divergence of the actual spot rate from the expected value set last period. This unanticipated nature of exchange rates may be illustrated further by considering the *change* in the exchange rate against the predicted changes in the exchange rate given by the forward *premium*. This relationship is plotted in figure 8.3, and it is clear that most of the change in exchange rates are wholly unanticipated. This unanticipated nature of exchange rates is discussed further in the following sections.

SECTION 2   THE EMH AND SPOT AND FORWARD EXCHANGE MARKETS

Following Fama (1970), and as stated in chapter 6, an efficient market is one which 'fully reflects' all relevant information instantly. Thus it should not be possible for a market operator to earn abnormal profits. As Levich (1979) has emphasized, in order to implement the hypothesis empirically and to make sense of the term 'fully reflect',

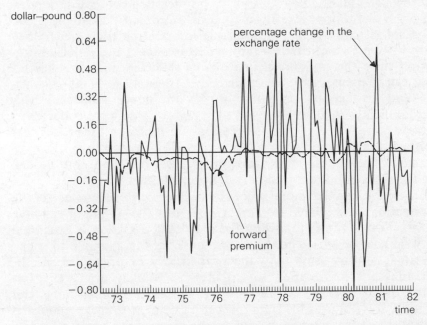

Figure 8.3 The forward premium and the percentage change in the exchange rate, dollar–pound

some view of equilibrium expected returns, or equilibrium prices, is required. Using equilibrium expected returns, for example, the excess market return on asset i is given by:

$$Z_{i,t+1} = x_{i,t+1} - E(\bar{x}_{i,t+1} \mid I_t) \tag{8.1}$$

where $x_{i,t+1}$ is the one-period percentage return, I_t is the information set, a bar denotes an equilibrium value and Z represents the excess market return. If the market for asset i is efficient then the sequence $Z_{i,t}$ should be serially uncorrelated and orthogonal to the information set (i.e. $E(Z_{j,t+1} \mid I_t) = 0$). This example makes clear that the EMH is a *joint hypothesis* because it assumes that agents in forming their expectations in period t are rational, in the sense that they do not make systematic forecasting errors, and they know market equilibrium, or expected, returns. This clearly raises an important issue for any researcher in trying to implement the EMH. Thus, a researcher, in rejecting the EMH for some asset, cannot discern if the rejection is due to the irrationality of market participants or to his mis-specification of the equilibrium expected returns.

Grossman and Stiglitz (1980) have pointed to a conundrum under-lying our definition of efficiency. For example, if asset prices *do* fully and instantly reflect all available information then presumably there will be no incentive for individuals to collect and process infor-mation since this will already have been reflected in market prices! How can market prices simultaneously reflect all relevant informa-tion *and* give agents potential profits to induce arbitrage? This paradox is in fact more apparent than real since data are collected at discrete periods and all that is necessary for market efficiency is that arbitrage has occurred within the period. This assumption allows us to analyse the effects of information on asset prices without model-ling the actual arbitrage process (see Begg, 1982).

Efficiency can be more precisely defined with reference to the information set available to market operators (i.e. I_t in our example above). For example, following Fama (1970), a market is described as 'weakly efficient' when it is not possible for a trader to make abnormal returns using only the past history of prices/returns. If, increasing the information set to include publicly available infor-mation (i.e. information on money supplies, interest rates and income), it is not possible for a market participant to make abnormal profits, then the market is said to be semi-strong form efficient. Strong form efficiency holds when it is impossible for a trader to make abnormal profits using a trading rule based on either public or private information. For the purposes of our discussion in this chapter only the weak and semi-strong form efficiency definitions will prove relevant.

As Minford and Peel (1983) point out, semi-strong form efficiency conforms most closely with the concept of rational expectations since agents are assumed to know the model generating equilibrium prices and use publicly available information in determining the expectations of the asset price. However, weak form efficiency may also be equivalent to rational expectations if agents' information set is restricted to the past history of prices due, say, to the costs of obtaining and processing the information set underlying the true economic model (see Feige and Pierce (1976)).

The above discussion about efficient markets has general applica-bility to a whole range of asset prices. We now present an application of the hypothesis to the forward market for foreign exchange. First, it is assumed that agents set the forward exchange rate, for maturity in period $t + 1$, equal to the rationally expected future spot rate for period $t + 1$:

$$E(s_{t+1} \mid I_t) = f_t^{t+1} \tag{8.2}$$

where E is the mathematical expectations operator and I_t is the information set available to agents at time t. Hereafter $E(s_{t+1}|I_t)$ will be denoted s^e_{t+1}.

In a world where speculators are risk neutral, and there are no impediments to arbitrage, such as transaction costs, speculation will ensure that 8.2 holds continuously (thus 8.2, captures our market equilibrium relationship).[1] The second leg of the joint hypothesis of efficiency is that speculators are rational and thus:

$$s_{t+1} = s^e_{t+1} + u_{t+1} \tag{8.3}$$

where u_{t+1} is a white noise error term. By using 8.2 and 8.3 we obtain the market efficiency condition under the stated assumptions:

$$s_{t+1} = f^{t+1}_t + u_{t+1} \tag{8.4}$$

which simply states that the spot rate in period $t+1$ should be equal to the corresponding forward rate plus a random error.

The sensitivity of market efficiency with respect to the assumed joint hypothesis may be demonstrated in the following way. Suppose that agents are rational, so that equation 8.3 continues to hold, but that they are risk averse and therefore to be persuaded to hold forward foreign exchange have to receive a risk premium to compensate for the uncertainty regarding the expected future spot rate. This may be written as:

$$f^{t+1}_t = s^e_{t+1} + \lambda_t \tag{8.5}$$

where following Frenkel (1981), it shall be assumed that the risk premium may be modelled as

$$\lambda_t = \alpha + \epsilon_t \tag{8.6}$$

where α is the mean of the risk premium and the term ϵ_t is a white noise error that allows for the possibility that the risk premium may vary randomly over time. Using 8.5 instead of 8.2 we obtain

$$s_{t+1} = -\alpha + f^{t+1}_t + u_{t+1} - \epsilon_t \tag{8.7}$$

where, as Frenkel (1981) notes, the forward exchange rate is a 'noisy' predictor of the future exchange rate. Thus in econometrically estimating an equation of the form

$$s_{t+1} = a + bf^{t+1}_t + \phi_{t+1} \tag{8.8}$$

if speculators are risk neutral, market efficiency implies that $a = 0$, $b = 1$ (the 'joint hypothesis' of unbiasedness), and ϕ_{t+1}, should be serially uncorrelated and orthogonal to the information set (i.e. $E(\phi_{t+1}|I_t) = 0$). If such conditions hold then the forward exchange rate is regarded as an efficient predictor of the future spot rate. If, however, speculators are risk averse we would expect a to be significantly negative and the error term to be stochastically correlated with b resulting in biased and inconsistent estimates of b and the error term to be non-white. Thus if we estimate equation 8.8 by OLS, believing equation 8.2 to hold, and find a to be statistically significant and b statistically different from unity, it would be wrong to conclude that market participants are irrational, since our results may simply reflect the existence of a risk premium as defined by 8.5. In order to allow market efficiency to encompass a risk premium, Bilson (1981) classifies equation 8.4 as the speculative efficiency hypothesis. However, in common with most other researchers we shall define equation 8.4 as market efficiency.

If the foreign exchange market is efficient, then as has been suggested, f_t^{t+1}, should contain all relevant information for forecasting the future spot rate s_{t+1}. Thus in adding information to 8.8, available to agents when forming their expectations, we should obtain statistically insignificant coefficient estimates on such information. More specifically, since the forward rate at time t summarizes all relevant information available to the market it should contain all relevant information contained in the forward rates f_{t-1}^t, f_{t-2}^{t-1} and so on, and thus adding further lagged values should not improve the equation's explanatory power. For example, in estimating equation:

$$s_{t+1} = a + b_1 f_t^{t+1} + b_2 f_{t-1}^t + \phi_{t+1} \tag{8.9}$$

market efficiency, in the absence of a risk premium implies that $a = 0$, $b_1 = 1$, $b_2 = 0$ and the error term is white and orthogonal to I_t.

Although equation 8.8 has proved the most popular way of testing the efficiency of the forward exchange market, a number of researchers have argued (see, e.g., Hansen and Hodrick, 1980 and Meese and Rogoff, 1984) that the stochastic process generating s_{t+1} and f_t^{t+1} in 8.8 may be non-stationary and therefore forward market efficiency should be tested using rates of change. Thus on subtracting s_t from s_{t+1} and f_t^{t+1} in 8.8, 8.10 is obtained:

$$s_{t+1} - s_t = a + b(f^{t+1} - s)_t + u_{t+1} \tag{8.10}$$

where, again, it is expected that $a = 0$, $b = 1$ and u_{t+1} is a white noise process and orthogonal to the information set. The relationship 8.10 is essentially that presented in figure 8.3.

As has been demonstrated in the above, one important aspect of the EMH is the error orthogonality property: the forecast error, in an equation such as 8.8 should be uncorrelated with the information set available when agents formed their expectations. The error orthogonality property may therefore be tested by regressing the forecast error, $s_{t+1} - f_t^{t+1}$, on a suitable information set, which may include past forecast errors or other publicly available information accessible to agents in period t; i.e.

$$s_{t+1} - f_t^{t+1} = a + bI_t + \epsilon_{t+1} \tag{8.11}$$

where it is expected that a and b should both differ insignificantly from zero.

Notice that in the above discussion we have been using the logarithm of the spot and forward rates, rather than their levels. The usefulness of using logarithmic transformations in efficiency tests has been demonstrated by Siegel (1972). Thus if we were to conduct our efficiency tests of, say, equation 8.8, using the levels of the spot and forward exchange rates, two different answers would be obtained depending on whether we used the home currency value of a unit of foreign exchange or the foreign currency value of a unit of home currency definitions for our exchange rates. This follows because the expectation of a variable and its inverse are *not* equivalent in levels (i.e. the mathematical expectation of s_t is not the same as $1|s_t$). Siegel's paradox is simply an application of a well known statistical theorem known as Jensen's inequality.[2]

Before considering some of the empirical evidence on the relationships considered in this section we must deal with another methodological problem, namely, the overlapping contracts issue. For example, if in testing equation 8.8 we use a forward exchange rate with a one month contract and weekly data we would expect *a priori* that the error term, ϕ_{t+1}, would be serially correlated. This follows because when the number of observations are more frequent than the maturity length the error term will not be independent of past forecast errors, but will instead follow a moving average process (of order three in terms of a one month contract and weekly data). Intuitively this may be seen by the following example. Thus, if f_t^{t+1} represents a one month period rate and we have weekly data then information that becomes available between weeks one and four will be correlated with information that becomes available between weeks two and five and so on. Thus, in any test of the EMH, care must be taken in the choice of contract length and frequency of the data.

SECTION 3 SOME WEAK TESTS: THE FORWARD RATE AS AN UNBIASED PREDICTOR OF FUTURE SPOT RATES

The majority of tests of the unbiasedness of the forward exchange rate have concentrated on econometrically estimating equation 8.8 and its equivalent representation in rates of change 8.10.[3] Equations

Table 8.1 The Forward Exchange Rate as an Unbiased Predictor of the Future Spot Exchange Rate: The Recent Floating Experience

Author	Exchange rate	Time period	a	b	DW	R^2	F	m	Estimation technique
Levich (1978)	1	March 1973–May 1978	0.017 (0.103)	0.980 (0.105)	1.51	0.81	87.6	–	OLS
	2		0.004 (0.004)	0.864 (0.171)	1.79	0.59	25.5	–	OLS
	3		0.001 (0.001)	0.997 (0.009)	1.40	0.99	204.69	–	OLS
Frankel (1979)	1	January 1974–December 1977	0.015 (0.015)	0.980 (0.020)	–	–	–	–	IV
	2		−0.237* (0.090)	0.843* (0.059)	–	–	–	–	IV
	3		−0.109* (0.052)	0.876* (0.057)	–	–	–	–	IV
Frenkel (1981)	1	June 1973–July 1979	0.030 (0.018)	0.961 (0.025)	1.74	0.95	1.86[1]	2.01	IV
	2		−0.236 (0.080)	0.844 (0.053)	2.24	0.78	4.83[1]	2.26	IV
	3		−0.021 (0.027)	0.973 (0.032)	2.10	0.93	0.51[1]	0.91	IV

Study		Period			DW	R^2	F	m	Method
Baillie et al. (1983)	1	June 1973–April 1980	0.033 (0.016)	0.956 (0.22)	1.33	0.99	2.12	—	OLS
	2		−0.174* (0.060)	0.884* (0.039)	1.85	0.99	4.57	—	OLS
	3		−0.024 (0.019)	0.968 (0.024)	1.98	0.99	0.97	—	OLS
Edwards (1983)	1	June 1973–September 1979	−0.033 (0.018)	0.957 (0.025)	1.70[1]	0.95[1]	3.52[1]	—	ZSURE
	2		−0.568* (0.179)	0.816* (0.058)	2.14[1]	0.74[1]	7.67[1]	—	ZSURE
	3		0.026 (0.027)	0.967 (0.032)	2.11[1]	0.93[1]	0.78[1]	—	ZSURE
MacDonald (1983)	1	1972 I–1979 IV (Q)	0.048 (0.03)	0.943 (0.04)	1.58[1]	0.88[1]	1.25[1]	—	ZSURE
	2		0.284* (0.11)	0.808* (0.07)	1.77[1]	0.54[1]	3.75[1]	—	ZSURE
	3		0.101* (0.103)	0.871* (0.03)	2.04[1]	0.88[1]	6.95[1]	—	ZSURE

Notes: exchange rates 1, 2 and 3 represent the UK pound–US dollar, French franc–US dollar and the German mark–US dollar respectively; DW is the Durbin–Watson statistic; R^2 is the adjusted coefficient of determination; F is an F-statistic which tests the joint hypothesis of unbiasedness; m is the Hausman specification test; standard errors are in parenthesis; superscript [1] denotes that the test statistics have been derived from OLS estimates; and * denotes rejection of unbiasedness.

8.8 and 8.10 have been tested by a large number of researchers for a variety of different currencies and time periods. As has been already indicated, if the forward market for foreign exchange is efficient we expect a to be statistically insignificant, b to differ insignificantly from unity and the error term to be serially uncorrelated. In table 8.1 a selection of evidence from the recent experience with floating exchange rates is presented.

The OLS results of Levich (1978) are supportive of the EMH: the joint hypothesis of unbiasedness cannot be rejected (the reported F statistics test this) and the residuals do not appear to suffer from first order autocorrelation (although the DW statistic for Germany falls within the indeterminate region). The problem, however, with using OLS to estimate equation 8.8, as was demonstrated above, is that if agents are risk averse then it is likely that the error term will be stochastically correlated with f_t^{t+1}, resulting in biased and insignificant estimates of b. To account for this possibility both Frankel (1979) and Frenkel (1980) use an instrumental variables (IV) estimator in their estimates of equation 8.8. Using IV, Frenkel finds that the joint hypothesis cannot be rejected and that there is no indication of first order autocorrelation. Furthermore, Frenkel uses a specification test developed by Hausman (1978) to ascertain whether using the forward rate for the expected future spot rate introduces an error in variables bias into the estimates. The appropriate test statistic is:

$$m = (\hat{b}^{iv} - \hat{b}^0)^i \, (\text{var } \hat{b}^{iv} - \text{var } \hat{b}^0)^{-1} (\hat{b}^{iv} - \hat{b}^0) \qquad (8.12)$$

where $\hat{b}^{iv}$ represents an estimate of b obtained by using instrumental variables, $\hat{b}^0$ represents the OLS estimates of b and var represents the variance–covariance matrix. The m statistic is distributed as χ^2 with two degrees of freedom under the null hypothesis. The m statistics reported in table 8.1 are insignificant and thus indicate that using the forward rate as a proxy for expectations does not introduce a significant error in variables bias into the estimates: OLS is an appropriate estimator. Frankel (1979), however, using a different sample to Frenkel, rejects the joint hypothesis for the French franc and German mark (and for two other currencies, not reported here: the Italian lira and Dutch guilder). Baillie et al.'s (1983) results, derived using OLS, indicate rejection of the joint hypothesis for the French franc (and, not reported, the Canadian dollar and Italian lira) and report the presence of first order serial correlation for the UK pound–US dollar.

Although, as Frenkel (1981) reports, the forward exchange rate in equation 8.8 may not be correlated with the error term, the error terms *across* the three equations reported in table 8.1 may be correlated, which means that OLS estimates of equation 8.8 may not be the most efficient estimates. The potential correlation of error terms across equations follows from the fact that all three currencies are directly related because they are all bilateral dollar rates. Thus, a shock emanating in the US will affect all three currencies reported in table 8.1 simultaneously. An econometric estimator which accounts for this potential correlation across equations is Zellner's Seemingly Unrelated Regression Estimator, ZSURE (see Edwards, 1983 and MacDonald, 1983 for a further discussion). Edwards (1983) reports ZSURE estimates of equation 8.8 which are unfavourable to the unbiasedness proposition for the franc–dollar (the reported DW, R^2 and F statistics are derived from the OLS estimates and the latter statistic indicates rejection of the joint hypothesis of unbiasedness).[4] MacDonald's (1983) ZSURE estimates indicate a rejection of the individual hypothesis of $a = 0$ and $b = 1$ for Germany and France.

Bilson (1981) reports estimates of equation 8.10 for a selection of nine currencies and rejects the unbiasedness proposition for two of the currencies. Furthermore, for three currencies there is evidence of first order autocorrelation which is inconsistent with the EMH.

Weak Form Error Orthogonality Tests

One crucial aspect of the EMH, hitherto not addressed is the error orthogonality property, i.e. $E(\phi_{t+1}|I_t)$. In weak form tests of this property only lagged forward rates, or lagged forecasting errors, are included in the information set:

$$s_{t+1} - f_t^{t+1} = a + b_i \sum_{i=1}^{n} (s_{t+1} - f_t^{t+1})_{t-i} + u_{t+1} \qquad (8.13)$$

where the *EMH* implies that the constant and all other coefficients should equal zero and u_{t+1} should be a white noise process.

Equation 8.9 has been tested by Frenkel (1981) for the time period and currencies reported in table 8.1, and the hypothesis of market efficiency cannot be rejected. Hansen and Hodrick (1980) estimate equation 8.13 with i arbitrarily equal to 0 and 1 using weekly data on three month forward rates for three currencies, the Swiss franc, Italian lira and German mark (all against the dollar) and find statistically significant coefficients. Frenkel (1979b) who includes a single lagged value of the forecasting error in his study of six currencies for the period January 1973–8, also finds statistically significant lagged forecast errors for the German mark–US dollar, UK pound–US dollar and Italian lira–US dollar. Gweke and Feige (1978), who also set $i = 1$ in equation 8.13, reject weak form efficiency only for one currency (the Canadian dollar–US dollar) out of seven currencies tested for the period 1972 quarter 3 to 1977 quarter 1.

Some Semi-strong Form Tests

The definition of semi-strong efficiency which was given earlier, refers to tests of the error orthogonality property utilizing more information than simply the past history of forecast errors. Hansen and Hodrick (1980) define a semi-strong form test as one in which the forecast error is regressed on the own lagged forecast error *and* lagged forecast errors from other exchange markets. Thus in a regression of the forecast error for market i:

$$s^i_{t+1} - f^i_t = a + \sum_{j=1}^{n} b_{ij}(s^j_{t+1} - f^j_t)_{t-1} + \epsilon_{t+1} \qquad (8.14)$$

on its own lagged forecast error and the lagged forecasting error from j other markets semi-strong form efficiency implies that the constant and b_{ij} terms should be statistically insignificant. For the recent floating experience, Hansen and Hodrick find that lagged forecasting errors do have significant explanatory power in the cases of the Canadian dollar–US dollar, the German mark–US dollar and the Swiss franc–US dollar exchange markets and therefore the EMH must be rejected for these markets. Gweke and Feige (1979) find that the hypothesis that a and b_{ij} are equal to zero can only be rejected for the Canadian dollar from a selection of seven currencies; however, estimating equation 8.14 for the seven currencies jointly, using ZSURE, results in the hypothesis that all the coefficients are insignificant being rejected at the one per cent level (Gweke and Feige classify this as a test of 'multimarket efficiency').

Bivariate Autoregression Approach

To many researchers, one particularly appealing feature of the rational expectations hypothesis is that it normally implies certain restrictions on a model's parameters. In the context of the spot–forward relationship Hakkio (1981) and Baillie et al. (1983) have shown that if the spot–forward relationship is modelled as a bivariate vector autoregression:

$$s_{t+1} = \sum_{i=0}^{n} a_i^1 f_{t-i} + \sum_{i=0}^{n} a_i^2 s_{t-i} + u_{1,t+1}$$

$$f_{t+1} = \sum_{i=0}^{n} a_i^3 f_{t-i} + \sum_{i=0}^{n} a_i^4 s_{t-i} + u_{2,t+1} \tag{8.15}$$

the EMH generates a set of complex non-linear restrictions between a_i^1, a_i^2, a_i^3 and a_i^4. In order to test these restrictions the model 8.15 is first estimated unconstrained then re-estimated with the constraints implied by the EMH imposed and a likelihood ratio constructed (the likelihood ratio test is essentially the non-linear equivalent of the F test in a linear model). This is the approach adopted by Hakkio (1981) who calculated the likelihood ratio for the Canadian dollar–US dollar, Dutch guilder–US dollar, German mark–US dollar, Swiss franc–US dollar and UK pound–US dollar and generally rejected the EMH for all currencies. One problem, however, with the method adopted by Hakkio is that he had to include less lagged values of s and f in his model than desirable on grounds of removing all auto-correlation. The lag length in 8.15 had to be severely limited because the non-linear restriction implied by the EMH in 8.15 became extremely complex as the lag length increased. Baillie et al. (1983) avoid this problem by estimating the system 8.15 by OLS and computing the Wald test. The latter statistic, which is asymptotically identical to the likelihood ratio test, does not require the estimation of the restricted version of 8.15. Using one month forward rates and weekly data, the Wald test was computed for four currencies, the UK pound–US dollar, the German mark–US dollar, the Italian lira–US dollar and the French franc–US dollar for the period June 1973 to April 1980 and for a further two currencies, the Canadian dollar–US dollar and Swiss franc–US dollar, over the period December 1977 to May 1980. In all cases the EMH was rejected. Attention is now focused on a discussion of the reasons for the widespread rejection of the EMH by a number of researchers.

Issues Raised by the Empirical Evidence

The broad thrust of the research reported above would seem to suggest an overwhelming rejection of the EMH applied to the forward market for foreign exchange. But as was made clear at the outset, researchers are testing a joint hypothesis and therefore rejection may be due to factors other than, say, the irrationality of market participants. It is to these factors that we now turn.

The first factor explaining the empirical invalidity of the EMH is the possible existence of a risk premium which drives a wedge between the forward rate and the expected future spot rate (see the discussion surrounding equations 8.5–8.7 above). A *constant* risk premium could be reflected in a significant constant term in unbiasedness tests. Indeed, some of the studies reviewed above do report a significant constant term (see, *inter alia*, MacDonald, 1983). But the absence of a significant constant term does not imply the absence of risk. Thus, if the risk premium varies over time this may be expected to introduce autocorrelated disturbances into estimates of the EMH. In fact a variety of researchers do report serially correlated errors (see, *inter alia*, Hansen and Hodrick, 1980 and Levich, 1978) and attribute this to the existence of a time varying risk premium.

A second possible explanation for the rejection of the EMH in the forward exchange market relates to government policy, and particularly the instability of such policy. For example, if the government's foreign exchange market intervention rule changes from period to period, market participants may not have sufficient time to learn the new policy regime and, even using all available information rationally, could induce serially correlated error terms.[5]

A third rationale for the failure of the forward market efficiency hypothesis, which is related to the previous point, is to be found in the distinction between full and partial information. For example, Minford and Peel (1983) demonstrate that if agents have incomplete information at the time the forward rate is set, the error term in an equation such as 8.8 will have a moving average error the order of which is determined by the information lag (thus incomplete information can lead to a similar error structure as in the overlapping contracts case). Thus residual autocorrelation in estimated versions of 8.8 may reflect incomplete information rather than a variable risk premium. As a consequence of incomplete information, least squares estimates of equation 8.8 will result in inefficient estimates of a and b and biased variance estimates.

The existence of transaction costs gives a fourth reason why unexploited profit opportunities may exist in the foreign exchange market. Transaction costs are an alternative way of reationalizing the significant constant terms reported by some researchers in their estimates of equation 8.8 (transaction costs may in fact result in the existence of a neutral band for forward market speculation within which it is impossible for profitable trading opportunities to be made). However, although Gweke and Feige (1979) argue that all their reported deviations from efficiency were due to transaction costs for the period of fixed exchange rates, they argue that un-exploited profits corrected for transaction costs were available for the flexible exchange rate period (they explain the latter deviations in terms of risk averse agents).

A final reason for the apparent failure of the EMH relates to the validity of the test statistics used in the econometric tests. In fact the test statistics utilized by researchers in testing the EMH are only asymptotically valid and therefore since their small sample properties are not well known care must be taken in their interpretation.

The above points tend to indicate that in setting up an efficient markets proposition we should be careful in our choice of the com-ponents of the joint hypothesis. One interesting feature, however, of the failure of the EMH, as it has been defined above, to hold is that it should be possible for at least some foreign exchange forecasters *consistently* to outperform the forward exchange rate. Thus a natural question that arises as a consequence of the above tests is: how well do the professional foreign exchange market forecasters perform? Can they beat the forward exchange rate as a forecasting mechanism? Levich (1982) compares the performances of 13 US forecasting services to the forward rate (sample period generally 1977–80) in terms of 'accuracy' and 'correctness'. The accuracy of the services is determined by computing the mean average forecast error of the service divided by the mean absolute forecast error of the forward rate. Values of less than unity indicate that the advisory service is more accurate than the forward forecast; in all cases the forecast services had a value of greater than one suggesting a lesser accuracy than the forward exchange rate. However, Levich's results suggest that many services have a high percentage of 'correct' forecasts (i.e. those that correctly predict the direction of change relative to the forward rate) not explained by change. A similar set of tests has been conducted by Brasse (1983) for a selection of eight UK fore-casting services. The tests suggest that such forecasters are less *accurate* than the forward rate but that three predict the direction of change by an amount not explained by chance.

SECTION 4 THE IMPACT OF 'NEWS' IN FOREIGN EXCHANGE MARKETS

In chapter 6 and in section 1 of this chapter the role of 'news' in explaining the unanticipated change in the exchange rate has been emphasized. Hence, even if it had been unambiguously demon-strated in the previous section that the forward rate is an unbiased forecast of the future spot rate, it is unlikely to be a particularly good forecast of the future spot rate in periods in which new information is important: although the EMH implies that anticipated changes in the exchange rate will be orthogonal to the forecast error, unanticipated changes in the determinants of exchange rates will be correlated with ϕ_{t+1} (i.e. the 'news' represents the update of agents' expectations).

The 'news' view of the determination of foreign exchange rates would seem to have wide appeal. For example, the financial columns of the daily press abound with headlines such as 'unexpectedly good money supply figures result in an appreciation of the exchange rate' and 'an unexpected deterioration in the current account led to an exchange rate depreciation'. If new information is important in foreign exchange markets then it is perhaps more appropriate empirically to implement exchange rate models, such as the monetary and portfolio approaches, in a 'news' context rather than regressing the exchange rate on the levels of, for example, relative money supplies. As was demonstrated in chapter 6, this latter approach has not been particularly successful, due mainly to the relatively low volatility of data on money supplies etc., compared to the exchange rate.

The 'news' approach may be illustrated in the following way. Assuming that agents form their expectations rationally it has been demonstrated that this implies:

$$s_{t+1} = s_{t+1}^e + u_{t+1} \tag{8.16}$$

and further, if agents are risk neutral:

$$s_{t+1} = f_t^{t+1} + u_{t+1} \tag{8.17}$$

where u_{t+1} is the forecast error. The latter term captures events unanticipated at the time agents formed their expectations and can be thought of as the effect of new information on the spot forward relationship. But how can such 'news' be modelled? First, some view of the determinants of the exchange rate is required. Say, for illustrative purposes, that the monetary model is the relevant exchange rate model and the vector z captures the influence of money supplies etc., on the exchange rate.

$$s_{t+1} = \gamma z_{t+1} + \epsilon_{t+1} \tag{8.18}$$

In forming their expectations agents use 8.18 and therefore:

$$s_{t+1}^e = \gamma z_{t+1}^e \tag{8.19}$$

Thus, on subtracting 8.18 from 8.19 the forecast error may be seen to be composed of a 'news' term (i.e. unexpected money supplies etc.) and a purely random term:

$$s_{t+1} - s_{t+1}^e = \gamma(z_t - z_{t+1}^e) + \epsilon_{t+1} \tag{8.20}$$

or if agents are risk neutral:

$$s_{t+1} - f_t^{t+1} = \gamma(z_t - z_{t+1}^e) + \epsilon_{t+1} = \phi_{t+1} \tag{8.21}$$

where the terms in parenthesis represents the 'news'. Clearly in any attempt to implement the 'news' empirically a researcher must decide on an appropriate model of the determination of the exchange rate and on some method of generating the expected values of the determining variables. As is demonstrated below, most researchers generate the expected values using regression analysis.

One of the earliest empirical implementations of the 'news' approach was conducted by Frenkel (1981). Frenkel does not specify a model of exchange rate determination but rather uses a variable which he believes reflects new information rapidly; namely, the unexpected change in the interest rate. Frenkel estimates:

$$s_{t+1} = a_0 + b_1 f_t^{t+1} + b_2 [z - z^e]_{t+1} + w_{t+1} \tag{8.22}$$

where $z = i - i^*$ and it has been assumed that agents are risk neutral (since equation 8.8 held for the period studied by Frenkel, this is not a restrictive assumption). Equation 8.22 is tested by Frenkel for the US dollar–UK pound, US dollar–French franc and US dollar–German mark exchange rates, over the period June 1973–June 1979, using essentially an autoregression to measure the expected interest differential series.[6] In all of Frenkel's estimated equations, b_2 is positive, but only in the case of one equation, reported here as equation 8.23, is b_2 statistically significant.

$$s_{t+1} = 0.031 + 0.959 f_t^{t+1} + 0.432 [(i - i^*) - (i - i^*)_{t+1}^e] \tag{8.23}$$
$$\quad (0.017) \ (0.024) \qquad (0.181)$$

Currency: US dollar–UK pound; $\bar{R}^2 = 0.96$; $DW = 1.78$;
Estimation technique: instrumental variables.

The positive association between the exchange rate and the unexpected interest differential is due, argues Frenkel, to the fact that the estimation period was one in which interest rates reflect inflationary expectations as in the flex-price monetary approach. Interestingly, when Frenkel re-estimates equation 8.22 using the actual interest differential, instead of the unexpected differential, the coefficient on the actual differential is insignificant in all cases.

Edwards (1982) estimated the FMAER[7] reduced form in a news format for the currencies considered above plus the Italian lira, over the period June 1973 to September 1979, using the ZSURE estimation. His results are generally supportive of the FMAER news equation.

A version of equation 8.21 has also been estimated by MacDonald (1983) for a selection of six currencies against the dollar (the Canadian dollar, the Austrian schilling, the UK pound, the French franc, the German mark and the Swiss franc) over the period 1972 quarter 1 to 1979 quarter 4 using the ZSURE estimator. The variables entering the z vector are home and foreign money supplies and news about these variables is generated by regressing them on such variables as the inflation rate, income, interest rates, the current account surplus and the budget deficit. The reduced form exchange rate equation tested is:

$$s_{t+1} - f_t^{t+1} = a + b_1 \sum_{i=-1}^{3} (m - m^e)_{t-i} + b_2 \sum_{i=-1}^{3} (m^* - m^{*e})_{t-i}$$

(8.24)

Following the FMAER, it is expected that domestic monetary news is positive and statistically significant and the foreign 'news' term is significantly negative; it is further expected that the lagged news term should not have a significant role to play in determining the current forecast error. A sample of MacDonald's results for the dollar–mark rate are presented here as equation 8.25:

$$s_{t+1} - f_t^{t+1} = 3.173 \ \text{DMR}_{t+1} - 0.881 \ \text{DMR}_t - 1.543 \ \text{DMR}_{t-1}$$
$$(1.18) \qquad\qquad (1.21) \qquad\qquad (1.22)$$

$$-0.013 \ \text{DMR}_{t-2} + 3.412 \ \text{DMR}_{t-3} - 2.017 \ \text{DMR}^*_{t-1}$$
$$(1.30) \qquad\qquad (1.16) \qquad\qquad (0.61)$$

$$+1.865 \ \text{DMR}^* - 0.364 \ \text{DMR}^*_{t-1} + 0.100 \ \text{DMR}^*_{t-2}$$
$$(0.64) \qquad\qquad (0.58) \qquad\qquad (0.58)$$

$$-0.344 \ \text{DMR}^*_{t-3}$$
$$(0.54)$$

(8.25)

Standard errors are in parentheses and $\text{DMR} = (m - m^e)$.

Note that period $t + 1$'s news (both home and foreign) is statistically significant, although both are wrongly signed. A further interesting feature of the results reported as equation 8.25 is the finding that lagged 'news' is statistically significant. Although publication lags could explain some lagged news terms (i.e. perhaps at lag 1) the significant lagged news terms from period $t - 4$ are harder to rationalize.

Constraints on space mean that other news studies are only briefly considered here. Dornbusch (1980) estimates a 'news' equation, for the dollar effective, yen–dollar and mark–dollar exchange rates, in which the 'news' terms are generated as the difference between bi-annual *OECD* forecasts and actual values. Results supportive of the news model are reported by Dornbusch. Bomhoff and Korteweg (1983) estimate a news equation using a multi-state Kalman filter to generate 'news' about relative money supplies, income and the price of oil for a selection of six currencies. Results supportive of the 'news' model were reported. One particularly interesting feature of the Bomhoff and Korteweg study is the finding that 'news' affects the exchange rate with long lags; in some instances there are lags of over one year before the 'news' impulses have their effect on spot rates. Branson (1983) has implemented the portfolio balance model in a news format and the results are shown to be broadly supportive of the model.

The above results suggest that the news approach to the determination of the exchange rate is reasonably well supported by the data, and future research on this topic could usefully extend the range of 'news' terms considered and the methods of generating the 'news'. One particularly interesting feature of some of the above 'news' studies is the finding that lagged 'news' has a significant role to play in determining the unexpected exchange rate component. On the face of it we may be tempted to say that such persistence effects reflects irrational information processing. However, we would be wrong so to conclude because of the arguments given above to explain the rejection of the EMH in the forward market for foreign exchange. For example, information lags, foreign exchange market intervention, the jointness of the hypothesis being tested etc., rationalize the significance of lagged 'news' in exchange rate equations. Rather than arguing that lagged news undermines the EMH, it is perhaps more pertinent to question the news framework as an explanation of exchange rate movements.

For example, in chapter 6 it was demonstrated that 'news' about expected future changes can have a powerful magnification effect on the current exchange rate resulting in it moving by a considerable amount relative to current 'fundamentals'. This clearly is fine if such exchange rate movements are justified *ex post*; however, if they are not, movements and variability of exchanges rates will be observed not justified by fundamentals, and, furthermore, such movements could have considerable resources costs. As Dornbusch (1982) points out there are essentially three reasons why expectations of the future may induce exchange rate movements *not* justified by fundamentals.

First, the exchange rate may deviate from fundamentals due to the notion of 'bubbles'.

> Here holders of an asset realize that the asset is overpriced, but are willing to hold it in the expectation that there will only be some probability of a collapse to fundamentals within a given holding period and that there is an expectation that the asset can be passed on with capital gains sufficiently large to reward the risk of a collapse.

The phenomenon of bubbles is frequently discussed in the press. To many the recent ascent of the dollar, 1980–5, is a classic example of a speculative bubble. An empirical framework to test for bubbles has recently been provided by Flood and Garber (1982). A useful area for future research would be the application of this framework to tests of the existence of bubbles in foreign exchange markets.

A second reason for the deviation of the exchange rate from fundamentals could simply be that market participants have the 'wrong' model of fundamentals and their expectations based on the wrong model will affect the actual exchange rate or, even if they possess the correct model, market participants may be swayed by fashions as to which variables are 'newsworthy'. For example, in one period current account 'news' may be fashionable, in the next it may be fiscal or monetary discipline.

Expectations about the possibility of governments changing their intervention rules (i.e. foreign exchange market intervention or more generally their monetary policy rule) give a third reason for dis-equilibrium exchange rate movements. This is the so-called 'Peso' problem (see, for example, Blanchard, 1982). In this perspective exchange rates are influenced by current fundamentals but also by agents' expectations that these fundamentals may change, with given probabilities in certain directions. Thus market participants may make a particular policy, such as the support of an exchange rate, impossible to follow simply because they *believe* it cannot be followed.

The corollary of the effects of the above 'misguided' expectations is that they may force unjustified changes in economic policy and this instability of policy results from the instability of expectations and not vice versa.

SECTION 5 SUMMARY AND CONCLUSIONS

In this chapter the empirical validity of a number of propositions pertaining to the EMH have been examined.

As has been demonstrated, the available evidence would seem to question the efficiency of the forward market for foreign exchange. However, it was stressed that researchers are testing a joint hypothesis and that rejection of the EMH does not necessarily imply irrational information processing. Indeed, a number of explanations, consistent with rational behaviour, were outlined such as the existence of risk, government intervention and the distinction between full and partial information.

Modelling unanticipated exchange rate changes using new information does appear to have been a relatively fruitful area and gives scope for further work of a refining nature. Attention was, however, drawn to the fact that it may not be 'news' alone that drives the unanticipated exchange rate. Rather, such features as bubbles, Pesos and irrelevant information may also have influence on unanticipated exchange rates. Empirical testing of such concepts would seem to be an important area for future research.

Notes

1 Frenkel and Razin (1980) demonstrates that if prices are stochastic this may drive a wedge between s_{t+1} and f_t^{t+1}, but that in practice this effect is likely to be insignificant.

2 For a discussion of Siegel's paradox see, *inter alia*, McCulloch (1975), Roper (1975), Boyer (1977) and Stockman (1978).

3 In MacDonald (1986) the evidence on a somewhat weaker test of the predictive powers of the forward rate is given: namely, whether the mean forecast error differs significantly from zero. The extant empirical evidence from this test is supportive of the EMH.

4 Interestingly, Edwards finds that the lira–dollar rate failed the market efficiency test when OLS was used but passed the test when ZSURE was used.

5 The effect of regime changes on agents' optimal use of information and the implications this has for the error orthogonality property is discussed in Friedman (1979).

6 In fact $i - i^*$ was regressed on a constant two lagged values and the forward rate, f_t^{t+1}.

7 FMAER stands for the Flexible Price Monetary Approach to the Exchange Rate.

9 Recent International Monetary Arrangements

Introduction

Many economists were of the opinion that the gold standard imposed too harsh a financial discipline on domestic economies and that output and employment were sacrificed for the maintenance of external equilibrium. This view, along with the experience of the 1930s, provided the motivation to devise a new *managed* international monetary system, but one which was still linked to gold to secure price stability and which retained pegged parities for currencies. The managed elements of the system came in the provisions for adjusting the parities of currencies and for supplementing international reserves through borrowings from a new international organization, the International Monetary Fund (IMF). This new system, the Bretton Woods System (BWS) called after the place where the arrangements were finalized, represented a partial move away from gold.

This system, however, evolved in a manner unforeseen by its designers. Too little use was made of the provisions which permitted discretionary management. The parities for currencies were changed too infrequently and the demand for additional international reserves was met not by extra borrowing facilities at the IMF or even by gold but by vastly increased dollar holdings. The flood of dollars which engulfed the world economy in the early 1970s and which could not be exchanged for gold from the US reserves because of the latter's inadequacy, led to mistrust in the dollar and to a series of crises which wrecked the system. From the turmoil there emerged a flexible exchange rate system and, somewhat surprisingly, not a lesser role for the dollar but rather the demonetization of gold.

Thus when the Bretton Woods System proper came to an end in the early 1970s, the world had moved even further away from gold, the parities for currencies were no longer fixed and borrowing facilities at the IMF were not, despite the introduction of Special Drawing Rights, the main source of international liquidity.

Section 1 of this chapter outlines the origins, objectives and evolution of the Bretton Woods System – the system which never really operated in the way that had been planned but gave the institutional setting in which the USA was to exercise dominant financial power. Section 2 examines the dollar standard as it developed in the 1960s, while section 3 reviews the role of the IMF in more recent years. The final section of the chapter sets out a model of the optimal amount of international reserves.

SECTION 1 THE BRETTON WOODS SYSTEM TO 1971

As early as 1941 plans were being prepared in the UK and the USA for the post-war economy. These plans were heavily influenced by the experience of the 1930s which had witnessed the Great Depression and the collapse of the gold standard. During that decade, in an attempt to maintain employment levels, countries had engaged in trade protection and in competitive devaluations. These expedients, though, served only to destroy world trade and to prolong and deepen the Depression.

The principal monetary institution created at Bretton Woods in 1944 was the IMF. The first of the Articles of Agreement of the IMF set out the objectives of the new international monetary system. They can be summarized as follows:

(1) to promote international monetary co-operation by consultation and collaboration on international monetary problems;
(2) to facilitate the balanced growth of international trade and high levels of employment and real income;
(3) to promote exchange rate stability;
(4) to establish a multilateral system of payments for current account transactions;
(5) to give confidence to member countries by making available the IMF's resources with adequate safeguards; and
(6) to shorten the duration and lessen the degree of disequilibrium in the balance of payments.

Action was most clearly visible on objectives (3) and (5). Member countries were required to state par values for their currencies in terms of gold and then to intervene in the foreign exchange market to keep the market exchange rate within one per cent of the par value by adding to, or reducing, foreign exchange reserves. In practice members expressed the par value of their currency in terms of the US dollar as the US was ready to convert dollars into gold at the price of $35 per ounce. This is the so-called 'asset convertibility' of the dollar. The system had the characteristic of a gold-exchange standard, with the dollar, in the early years at least, preferable to gold, as reserve dollars could be deposited in America earning interest.

The IMF's resources came from the members' subscriptions or quotas which were related in size to a country's economic importance. The quotas were paid one-quarter in gold and three-quarters in the member's currency. The size of a quota determined both a country's voting rights at IMF Executive Board meetings and the scale of borrowing. The quotas are reviewed at intervals of five years and a four-fifths majority is required in favour of any change. This was the one provision in the agreement available to the IMF for increasing international liquidity.

The Early Role of the IMF

In 1952 the IMF introduced a general policy for the use of its resources as well as commencing surveillance of members' macroeconomic policies. The latter now involves annual consultation between the IMF and each of the members on balance of payments and domestic macroeconomic policies and it has become a principal means of attaining the first objective of Article 1. With regard to resource use the IMF announced 'tranche' arrangements under which countries could borrow. The right to the first, or gold tranche (now called the reserve tranche), was automatic. A country could also request access to four further tranches, each 25 per cent of quota, so that total borrowing could amount to 125 per cent of a country's quota. Borrowings on these four credit tranches were conditional upon the country pursuing certain economic policies stipulated by the IMF and on repayment within three to five years. As a result of several new lending facilities introduced in the 1970s and 1980s it is now possible for a country to borrow conditionally up to four and a half times its quota. These now form 'the heart of the Fund's financial assistance' (de Vries, 1985). Also introduced at this time was the so-called stand-by arrangement, which is a line ot credit, only drawn upon if required. The very fact of its existence helps to restore confidence in a country's currency, while only a small commitment charge is involved if foreign currency is not in fact drawn. Between 1953 and 1984 there have been 546 stand-by agreements for SDR49 billion out of total cumulative borrowing from the IMF over this period of SDR87 billion (IMF 1984).

The Heyday of the Bretton Woods System

Though the Bretton Woods system existed from 1945 to 1971 the main conditions necessary for its operation lasted for at most about a decade from the late 1950s; as mentioned before, current account convertibility was only widely achieved at the end of the 1950s, the convertibility of the dollar into gold ceased in 1971 and, by 1973, most major countries had renounced par values for their currencies. Moreover, as discussed in section 2 below, the US dollar came to play such a predominant role as a reserve asset – a role that was not envisaged in 1944 – that some authorities have described the international monetary system at this time as being a 'dollar standard'.

The 1960s had witnessed a period of rapid growth of world production and international trade. The decade, however, was not without its problems. There was concern about the disruptive effects of short-term capital movements, especially on the key currencies – the dollar and sterling – which were held as international reserve assets. Doubt about the foreign payments position of a reserve currency country led to outflows of short-term capital, depleting its reserves and putting the currency under even greater speculative pressure. In an effort to cope with this, in 1961 the IMF extended the use of its resources to help members in difficulty because of short-term capital outflows.

Secondly, there was concern in some quarters about the adequacy of international liquidity, as the ratio of international reserves to the value of imports for all countries declined from 73 per cent in 1954 to 51 per cent in 1961 and 35 per cent in 1968 (IMF, 1970a). To deal with this problem the IMF concluded the General Arrangements to Borrow (GAB) with the ten major industrial countries, the 'Group of Ten' or G10, made up of the USA, the UK, West Germany, France, Italy, Japan, Canada, the Netherlands, Belgium and Sweden. (In 1964 Switzerland, not an IMF member, joined the arrangements). The GAB allowed the IMF to borrow from members experiencing payments surpluses to assist members suffering capital outflows. Thus GAB had the undesigned effect of negating the Scarce Currency Clause: the IMF could now obtain a potentially scarce currency for use by another country without the need for currency revaluation. The sum involved was $6 billion and the scheme was entirely for the benefit of G10, which formed an exclusive club.

The GAB were significant in two further respects. They represented the first occasion on which the IMF borrowed to supplement its resources and as such they have been the forerunner of other borrowing arrangements such as the oil facilities (1974–1976) and the supplementary financing facility (1979). Secondly, they had an important political dimension, by promoting consultation among G10 members who soon came to influence Fund policy on many matters. For example, the main negotiations leading to the creation of SDRs in 1969 took place within the G10. The activities of G10 led to the formation of the Group of 24, among developing countries, in 1971. One commentator has gone so far as to say that the GAB 'can also be viewed as an additional defence of an essentially conservative, strong country oriented economic order which weakened possible pressures for reform which might otherwise have been taken more seriously' (Brett 1983). In the 1970s the GAB declined in relative size and importance, and were significantly reformed in the early 1980s as described below.

The Introduction of Special Drawing Rights

Against a background of inadequate growth in gold production, studies commenced within G10 in 1963 on the balance of payments adjustment process and on the probable future needs for international liquidity. Discussions on the latter topic were widened in 1966 to include the Executive Directors of the IMF and at the annual meeting of the IMF at Rio de Janeiro in 1967 a draft outline for a scheme of Special Drawing Rights was produced. After some amendments by Ministers of the G10 in 1968 the Fund submitted to members a proposal to amend the Articles of Agreement to permit the IMF to operate a Special Drawing Fund in addition to its General Fund. This was accepted in 1969 and the first allocation of SDRs took place in 1970.

Four main issues arose in the course of the protracted discussions over the creation of SDRs (Tew 1982). The first concerned the question of membership. Initial proposals were for a membership restricted to the rich industrial countries but in the end it was accepted that all members of the IMF should be eligible to participate in the scheme. Secondly there was the issue of the 'link'. This was the suggestion that reserve creation should be linked to the provision of aid to developing countries: the new reserve asset could be distributed to developing countries and thereafter be 'earned' by developed countries through balance of payments surpluses. As it transpired the SDR scheme was designed not to cause a permanent transfer of resources from one country to another.

The third issue was whether there was in fact any need to create a new international reserve asset since significant symptoms of strain in the form of trade and payments restrictions, rising unemployment or falling prices were hard to detect despite the slow rate of growth of international reserves in the mid- and late 1960s.

Finally, there was considerable dispute as to the nature of the reserve asset required. The essence of the matter was whether it should represent unconditional or conditional liquidity. Most countries favoured the former, but some opted for the latter, so that the actual scheme became something of a compromise: SDRs may be used without prior consultation but members are required to maintain a certain minimum percentage of their cumulative allocation of SDRs. There was also debate on the question of backing for the asset. Most European countries favoured backing the asset with a mixture of reserve currencies other than sterling and the dollar, i.e. it should be a composite reserve unit. In the event the SDR has turned out to be an accounting creation without any backing.

SECTION 2 THE DOLLAR STANDARD

The word 'standard' refers to the dollar as the *ultimate* standard of value. That is, the dollar as a 'world money', performing all the functions of money: as a standard of value (or numeraire), a store of value and as a medium of exchange. This had not been the intention at Bretton Woods when the world powers devised an international monetary system for the post-war world. At Bretton Woods gold had been chosen as the ultimate 'money'.

However, as indicated above, international monetary arrangements did not work out as the Fathers had planned. The dollar was so sought after by America's trading partners that it quickly rose to a position of pre-eminence. One view has it that 'for twelve years after World War II, the world was unambiguously on a dollar standard; the gold convertibility of the dollar was incidental and *irrelevant*' (Ruff, 1967, p. 3, italics added). If this was true then it is hard to see that the Bretton Woods system ever did operate as envisaged. However, as Triffin and others were to argue, towards the end of the 1950s the question of the convertibility of the dollar into gold was becoming a major problem for the gold-exchange standard; such a major problem, indeed, that the system was bound sooner or later to collapse. In fact, from 1967 onwards several major central banks agreed with the US *not* to exchange their unwanted dollar holdings for American gold in order to relieve the downward pressure on US gold reserves which was threatening the asset convertibility of the dollar. What is important here is that the agreements *not* to exchange dollars for US gold caused a partial *de facto* demonetization of gold – i.e. gold was withdrawn as a means of settling international debts. Accordingly, it is justifiable to date the rise of the dollar standard from the mid-1960s. But Tew (1977) prefers to apply a more exacting criterion: 'The Bretton Woods system came to an end in August 1971 [when President Nixon closed the gold window] and was succeeded by a rather different pegged-rate regime, which we shall refer to as the dollar standard' (p. 53). Here the dollar standard's origin is dated from the *de jure* demonetization of gold.

Early Views on the Dollar Standard

Despres, Kindleberger and Salant (1966) – later referred to as DKS – and Kindleberger (1965) performed the service of being amongst the first to point out the international reserve-creation process that had developed outside of the plans laid down at Bretton Woods. These views were quickly challenged, as is discussed below, but a new mode of thinking about the international monetary system was brought into play. For DKS, Triffin's apocalyptic view of the collapse of the international monetary system was really a misunderstanding of how the reserve-creation process worked in practice. For them the creation of dollar reserve assets was contained within a 'steady-state', self-regulating system. The basis of this system was the USA's role as an *international financial intermediary*.

US balance of payments deficits were *not* the cause of a problem but, rather, the result of the operation of the USA's role as a financial intermediary. The USA's official settlements balance of payments deficit was due to a deficit on financial transactions (short- and long-term capital together) that exceeded the *surplus* on current account transactions. The USA was then a net accumulator of claims on the rest of the world (through the current account surplus) a feature which should have bred confidence in the value of the dollar according to DKS. However, large net *long-term* capital outflows exceeded the surplus on goods and services and appeared to be financed by net *short-term* capital inflows.

The big question was: 'were these short-term capital inflows placed voluntarily or involuntarily by European investors and central banks?' DKS said that they were voluntary. According to them, the parallel long- and short-term capital flows between America and Europe were caused by differences in liquidity preference between the two continents. DKS argued that Europe had high liquidity preference – a feature which led to a spectrum of low short-term and high long-term interest rates in European capital markets. America had low liquidity preference which resulted in the interest rate structure being twisted in the direction of relatively (to Europe) high short-term and low long-term interest rates. Accordingly, if international capital markets were open, beneficial flows of short- and long-term capital between Europe and America were bound to arise. 'Beneficial' because the flow of American long-term capital to Europe helped to reduce long-term interest rates in Europe and so stimulated investment and economic growth. In the meantime the Europeans satisfied their high liquidity preference by placing deposits in American financial markets. This counter-flow of short-term capital certainly helped to finance US long-term capital outflow, but it was in no sense an involuntary act on the part of the Europeans. Rather, the capital flows were an equilibrating response to fundamental economic realities, namely, the different interest rate structures. Thus, DKS were driven to the conclusion that 'the US is no more in deficit when it lends long and borrows short than is a bank when it makes a loan and enters a deposit on its books' (1966, p. 526). America was the world's banker, and like any banker it provided liquidity to depositors (i.e. the short-term capital inflows) and loans to borrowers (the long-term capital outflow). The US was a financial intermediary performing intertemporal asset conversion for the Europeans.

Criticisms of the 'Financial Intermediary' View

Unfortunately for the stability of the international monetary arrangements, the dollar standard was less automatic than DKS had supposed. Halm (1968), Aubrey (1969) and others made several relevant critical points:

(1) the USA could not be unconcerned about its balance of payments deficits, for it was vulnerable to 'a run on the bank'. The international monetary system and the USA as the world's banker had no 'lender of last resort'. The international monetary system might, after all, become unstable if Europe was in fact accumulating dollars involuntarily and wished to turn them in for US gold.

(2) Given volatility in short-term interest rates, together with different governmental objectives for local interest rates – related to domestic employment and inflation considerations – it would be impossible to rely upon a world structure of short-term interest rates which would ensure that the USA's balance of payments deficits would be automatically financed. What this amounts to is saying that Europe might not always want its monetary policies governed by the imperatives of the US balance of payments and monetary policy. The search for monetary independence could threaten the stability of the automatic dollar standard.

(3) European countries were well aware that some of their dollar reserve accumulations were involuntary. De Gaulle, for example, objected to American political hegemony and financial predominance and accused the Americans of buying-up Europe on the cheap – a view which was articulated at length by Servan-Schreiber in his book *The American Challenge* (1968). It was argued that America was over-spending abroad – on the war in Vietnam, on direct foreign investment in Europe and on foreign aid (which was an integral part of US foreign policy). This over-spending, rather than Europe's high liquidity preference, accounted for the build-up of dollars in Europe's foreign exchange reserves. And much of this build-up was involuntary.

(4) As there was evidence that European financial markets were efficient financial intermediaries and that the use of US financial markets involved foreign exchange risk, it is hard to see why Europe should want to use the USA as a banker. Financial intermediation could be done well and at less risk at home.

The weight of these points is to bring gold back into focus at the centre of the post-war international monetary system. The dollar, although a key currency, could not yet be recognized as the system's pivot – alone performing the functions of an international money. The so-called asset convertibility of the dollar (into gold) remained as an important issue in the 1960s and was to remain so until 1971. The dollar had not yet become the ultimate reserve asset.

Another View of the Dollar Standard

A US role of financial intermediary relying upon differences in American and European liquidity preferences is not necessarily required as an explanation of the growing importance of the dollar as an international reserve asset. Rather, the international demand for dollars can be explained with reference to the concept of the demand for money. Money has been defined thus: 'money is what money does': and what money does is to perform the well known functions mentioned earlier.

The Demand for Dollars

It is of crucial importance that, by definition, a medium of exchange must be acceptable in payment of debts. In an international context, the international money must be a *convertible* currency, that is, it must be possible to exchange it legally for other currencies. Until 1959 the US dollar was the only major convertible currency and so was the only contender for the role of an international money. Other currencies could not be used because governmental restrictions upon their use prevented them being generally acceptable in payment of international debt.

As a convertible currency it was (and still is) convenient to use the dollar to finance international trade. So dollar working balances were built up for this purpose. And this happened on a large scale in the financing of trade between 'third countries' – the dollar was a *vehicle currency*.

The dollar retained its role as the major vehicle currency even after major currencies became convertible in 1959, for the interbank system was already geared to using dollars as a means of settling international debts. In effect, the transaction costs of exchanging, say, Dutch guilders for Austrian schillings were lower when using the dollar as a vehicle then directly exchanging guilders for schillings (Magee and Rao, 1980). The banks' portfolio management costs are lower when the portfolio is made up largely of dollars than if it is made up of several dozen currencies. Also, with the dollar as the vehicle currency, banks in any country needed to establish correspondent relationships with banks only in the US instead of in every country which had a convertible currency.

The dollar as an international numeraire has advantages in use by both the private sector and between central banks. In the private sector many major primary products are quoted in dollar prices mainly because the USA is a major producer and/or consumer of primary products. Similarly with oil – by value the single most important commodity in world trade. Thus, using the dollar as a unit of account yields simple and effective international communication of price quotations.

Outside of private international trade, and even when gold was nominally the commodity-base numeraire, the dollar quickly took over this role. The reason is straightforward: the dollar was convertible into gold at $35 per ounce and other countries found it convenient to peg their exchange rates in terms of gold through the dollar. That is, other countries quoted par value exchange rates against the dollar and, since the dollar price of gold was fixed, therefore, against gold. The dollar came to take on the so-called 'n^{th}' currency role.

Since the dollar was (and still is) used for foreign exchange market intervention, i.e. as a medium of exchange, it was concomitantly used as a store of value. The medium of exchange and store of value functions of any money are intertwined because the process of exchange takes place over time. The dollar, until the 1960s was a good store of value, given: (a) the relative stability of the US price level, which made the dollar stable, measured in terms of the quantity of US goods and services which it could purchase; and (b) the fact that interest was paid on central bank dollar deposits in the USA.

The store of value function of the dollar is enhanced by the USA's dominant position in world trade. The geographic structure of a country's imports can be an important factor affecting its choice of foreign exchange reserve assets. A country will naturally want to hold the currency of its largest trading partner because even if this partner devalues, the value of reserves in terms of future imports would be unchanged. Thus, with the USA easily the dominant country in world trade, most countries would prefer to hold dollars as foreign exchange reserves.

McKinnon (1969) comments that it was not surprising that the dollar began to predominate over gold as a central bank reserve asset. Gold was not a numeraire in international trade but, as explained above, the dollar performed that role. In fact some 60 per cent of world trade is invoiced in dollars, the rest in local currencies (Magee and Rao, 1980). Gold clauses in contracts just do not arise. Nor was gold a medium of exchange in the private sector. The dollar as a convertible currency has superior liquidity while gold, at the very most, is a 'near-money', and to be used must first be exchanged for dollars or some other currency. Also, for the period of the 1950s and 1960s it was possible to argue that the dollar was a superior store of value because interest was paid on it while gold, fixed in price, attracted no interest.

The Supply of Dollars

That the supply of dollar reserve assets is *demand* determined was implicit within the Despres, Kindleberger and Salant view of the USA's role as a financial intermediary. This is a major claim in favour of the dollar standard, provided that the US pursues a policy of monetary stability – an argument which was first put forward by McKinnon (1969).

Dollar reserve assets are supplied through the USA's basic balance of payments deficit, viz.:

$$(X - M) - LTC = STC + \Delta G \tag{9.1}$$

where X is exports; M, imports; LTC, long-term capital flow: STC short-term capital flow; and ΔG the change in reserves. Balance of payments deficits (left-hand side) could be financed by STC inflow (a positive item) or decreases in reserves (also a positive item). If the left-hand side is negative the right-hand side must be equally positive.

The most important point is that with pegged exchange rates the short-term capital inflow would take the form of foreign countries increasing holdings of dollar foreign exchange reserves when placed in the US by central banks. Central banks would make net purchases of dollars in order to peg the country's currency's exchange rate against the dollar. These dollars would then be placed in the USA to earn interest.

The supply of dollar foreign exchange reserves is demand determined because any country could, within limits, choose the extent of its own balance of payments surplus or deficit. For example, if it wished to reduce the rate of growth of reserves it could cut interest rates and adopt other means of inflating the domestic economy, which would normally reduce the size of its balance of payments surplus. Conversely, reserves could be increased by adjusting the domestic economy so as to run a balance of payments surplus. Or, domestic interest rates could be raised to encourage borrowing from the USA. In principle, all dollar accumulation could be viewed as voluntary. The USA's role in this system was to practice *benign neglect*, allowing other countries to determine the US balance of payments.

Reserve Creation and US and World Price Levels

The world price level is connected to the US price level by two routes. The strength of these connections was greater in a world of adjustable peg (but mainly fixed) exchange rates. But the connection is still there today for exchange rates are not allowed to float completely freely: central banks still intervene in foreign exchange markets, running up or down their dollar exchange reserves.

The US price level is important to the world price level because, firstly, the US is a dominant supplier or buyer in many international markets and through commodity arbitrage (i.e. the international movement of commodities from low cost areas to high cost areas) US prices are bound to influence price levels in competitor and supplier countries; and secondly, the US price level influences the supply of international liquidity. Thus, with a stable US price level and pegged exchange rates, inflation in Europe would make European countries less competitive with the USA. Europe would eventually experience balance of payments deficits and foreign exchange reserves would fall, as with the MABP (chapter 5). Sooner or later this would be taken as a signal to governments to adopt anti-inflationary economic policies. Hence, European price levels could not rise much above the (assumed) stable US price level. Conversely, if Europe had a falling price level (or one rising less quickly than that of the USA), increasing competitiveness relative to the USA would lead to balance of payments surpluses and to accumulation of dollar foreign exchange reserves. Again, sooner or later, rising foreign exchange reserves would cause an increase in European money supplies, lower interest rates, higher expenditure, economic expansion and (probably) a rising price level. Thus the European price level could not fall much below the stable US price level.

It should be clear, therefore, that stability of the world price level, under the pegged exchange rate dollar standard extant until spring 1973, required stability of the internal value of the dollar. A stable US price level would provide the link between the monetary and real spheres, much as gold was supposed to have done under the gold standard. But with the dollar standard, and given a stable US price level, it was the stable price of *all* US traded goods and services which governed the world price level.

The Dollar Standard 'On the Booze'

In 1972 Haberler in an article entitled 'Prospects for the Dollar Standard' wrote that 'the greatest, nay indispensable, American contribution to the working of the system is to curb inflation' (p. 4). But the USA was already failing in this duty. The nub of the problem was that it was becoming increasingly expensive for the USA to manage its economy in a non-inflationary manner so as to provide the 'ballast' that would have stabilized the world price level. At first the cost of failure to stabilize the US price level could be measured by the loss of gold reserves through the payments deficits. At $35 per ounce gold was becoming increasingly undervalued compared with the general price level. Moreover, the price of keeping American inflation down could also be measured in terms of rising unemployment and lost output – a price which successive administrations became increasingly reluctant to pay.

The US surplus on goods and services fell steadily from 1964 onwards and reserve losses were contained only by smaller deficits on financial transfers. In 1970 the dam broke and the large balance of payments deficit flooded dollars into foreign exchange reserves around the world. In failing to stabilize the price of US goods, the stable link between the monetary and real spheres was broken and the world inflation of the 1970s was set in motion.

The widespread move to floating exchange rates in the spring of 1973 can be viewed as occurring as a result of the price instability that the dollar standard was imparting to the world economy. Since the US was no longer able to provide price level stability, some countries chose to do so themselves. This is the underlying reason why the West Germans, for example, floated their exchange rate against the dollar. By decoupling the German price level from the American, the Germans could attempt themselves, through strict financial policies, to provide a stable link between their own localized monetary and real spheres of economic activity.

Commenting in 1983 on the huge US payments deficits, *The Times* of London wrote:

> It is a commonplace that a country with a large current account deficit should have a weak currency. There is no doubt that this simple principle applies very effectively to France, Italy and dozens of smaller deficit nations around the world. But it does not seem to work with the United States. The American deficit next year will be at least five times the size of the French, but the dollar is at the top of the foreign exchanges' popularity list while the franc is near the bottom ... Fifty years ago, when President Roosevelt and his Treasury Secretary, Morgenthau, were manipulating the gold price from day to day, Keynes described American policy as 'a gold standard on the booze'. Today we have a grossly overvalued dollar, record real interest rates, the largest budget deficit ever known and the prospect of a current account shortfall which is a multiple of the worst previously registered by any nation. The combination may fairly be described as the dollar standard on the booze.

It has been 'on the booze' for a decade or more and the world community is still vainly seeking an international reserve asset and reserve-creation system that will guarantee price stability.

SECTION 3 THE IMF TRIES TO PICK UP THE PIECES

The Failure of the 'Grand Design' (1972-4)

While the world economy was experiencing international monetary turmoil between 1971 and 1973, discussions were taking place at several levels to design a new monetary constitution for the world. One suggestion was for an SDR standard: the SDR would be used as the numeraire for exchange rate parities and as the major reserve asset, while the growth in demand for international reserves should be met by the managed creation of more SDRs. Eventually in September 1972 the Governors of the IMF set up an *ad hoc* committee, the Committee of Twenty (C20), with a wider membership than G10, since developing countries were represented, to consider reform of international monetary arrangements.

The C20 failed to create agreed rules for a new international monetary system for a variety of reasons. The three major groupings of participants were interested in different objectives. The major preoccupation of the US was to obtain symmetry of adjustment obligations between surplus and deficit countries by introducing trigger adjustment criteria. The US wished to promote more frequent exchange rate adjustments by surplus countries than had been the case up to 1971. The Europeans and Japanese wished to remove some of the advantages – seigniorage and ability to avoid adjusting payments deficits – conferred on reserve currency countries and pressed for symmetry between reserve currency countries and others. The third group, the developing countries, wanted a greater transfer of real resources to promote development via the 'link', when new SDRs were created. The outcome of these conflicting interests was that 'there was no agreement on a set of rules for assigning adjustment responsibilities, no design of a viable adjustment mechanism, no introduction of an SDR standard, no substitution account [for dollars] and no curb on the asymmetries' (Williamson, 1977).

The C20 proposed that the positions of developing countries be examined in the new conditions created by the 1973 oil crisis, world inflation and floating exchange rates. As a result a joint committee of Governors of the World Bank and of the IMF on the transfer of real resources to developing countries was founded in October 1974. The position of gold was also to be reconsidered and the IMF's Articles of Agreement had to be amended since floating rates were not currently permissible. This was done in 1976 and came into operation in early 1978, so that now countries can operate any exchange rate system which they like. Floating is legalized in the new Articles, while gold, the numeraire under the old Articles, is dethroned. Members have an obligation to promote stable exchange rates by fostering orderly underlying economic, financial and monetary conditions and the IMF has to exercise firm surveillance over exchange rate policies.

The Evolving Roles of Gold and the SDR

The status of gold has steadily diminished between 1944 and 1976, though gold still plays an equivocal role in international reserves. As we have seen, in the Bretton Woods Agreement gold was both the numeraire of the system and the basic reserve asset with its value defined by the parity for the dollar.

In addition to its official use, there was also the private use of gold, with gold available from 1954 through the London gold market. Until 1960 the London market price was the same as the official price but in late 1960 and much of 1961 the market price exceeded the official price as demand for gold increased in the belief that its price was to rise to augment international liquidity.

To preserve equality between the market price and the official price, the central banks of the USA and of the major Western European countries formed a 'gold pool' to supply the London market with gold. Private demand for gold grew throughout the sixties, and from 1966 onwards it exceeded the output of new gold, so that gold reserves had continually to be used to hold the price at $35 per ounce. After the devaluation of sterling in 1967, the private demand for gold rose dramatically in the expectation that the dollar might also have to be devalued, so that by March 1968, the cost to central bank gold reserves was so great that the gold pool arrangements had to be suspended. Until the abolition of the official price of gold in 1978, the market price of gold exceeded the official price of gold used in the settlement of debts between countries. Although until 1971 the higher market price for gold was an incentive for central banks to change their dollar holdings for gold from the US reserves, countries refrained from doing this on a large scale because of the repercussions it would have had on US gold reserves. This restraint did not prevent the termination of convertibility of the dollar into gold by the USA in 1971, while by the Smithsonian agreement the gold price was raised to $38 per ounce. The price was further raised in 1973 to $42.22 per ounce, a price at which the USA would neither buy nor sell gold, since the dollar remained inconvertible.

At the meeting of the interim committee at Jamaica in January 1976 gold was further downgraded, and this was enshrined in 1978 in the Second Amendment to the Final Articles. The official price of gold was abolished, as were all its monetary uses at the IMF. Central banks were allowed to buy gold at any price they wished, so that inter-bank transactions became possible. A decision was made to return one-sixth of the IMF's gold holding to the members and to sell off another one-sixth with the profits from the sale (excess of market price over official price) to be used for a fund to help the poorest countries, this being action on a C20 proposal.

The status of gold is now ambiguous. Though demoted at the IMF, it can be included in a country's reserves valued at market price and used in settlements between countries. However, given the great variability in the free market price, countries are likely to be unwilling to use it in official settlements, since they might sell at the wrong time. It can also be used as backing for foreign loans.

The Second Amendment to the IMF Articles, as well as demoting gold, sought to promote the SDR, so that it became the principal reserve asset in the international monetary system. The regulations surrounding the use of SDR are now less restrictive. Members may discharge many obligations to the fund in SDRs. SDRs may now be transferred between members by agreement, even if these are not required for reserve reasons. The IMF may also permit members to use SDRs in operations other than those specifically authorized by the articles (Gold 1978). In addition to the use of SDRs by countries at the IMF, 14 prescribed official institutions hold and use SDRs. The SDR is now becoming more widely used as a unit of account for private financial instruments, e.g. in bonds and syndicated loans, because it is more stable in value than individual currencies. It is, however, certainly not the major reserve asset and does not look as if it will become so in the near future.

This has been explained (Hood, 1983) firstly by the fact that it seems inappropriate to create additional SDRs at a time of inflation, since it might add to the inflation. Secondly it also seemed wrong to create more unconditional liquidity at a time when the IMF is imposing stiff conditionality on countries using fund resources to get them to adjust their economies. It is also the case that interest in the SDR wanes with the strength of the dollar. Only when the dollar is weak, as it has not been since 1981, is there an interest in having an alternative asset to hold.

To make the SDR the main reserve asset would require giving the IMF control over world liquidity and its growth. No such political will exists at the moment. All that seems feasible at present is to encourage the wider private use of SDRs and to give thought to how the private creation of SDRs, produced by combining the five currencies in their correct proportions, could be linked to official SDRs at the IMF.

The Role of the IMF After the Abandonment of the Adjustable Peg

Though the IMF has to exercise surveillance over the exchange rate policies of its members, its regulatory activities have come to receive less emphasis than its financial functions; lending has become a primary activity, with the fund both augmenting its own resources by borrowing and acting as an intermediary between lenders and borrowers.

When the first oil price shock plunged the rest of the world into current account deficit with OPEC members, the IMF recommended that these countries should finance their deficits rather than attempt current account adjustment by deflation or currency depreciation. The bulk of such financing was done through private markets but the IMF itself established two 'oil facilities' in 1974 and in 1975, largely financed by borrowing from the OPEC members. 1974 also saw the creation of the Extended Fund Facility through which the IMF offered assistance for structural adjustment where there was serious imbalance in production and trade or where slow growth and weak balance of payments prevented the pursuit of an active economic development policy. The IMF was thus moving into 'supply-side measures' and what, hitherto, had been World Bank territory.

With the Supplementary Facility of 1977, again financed by borrowing from member countries, the Fund could lend multiples of quotas to countries facing serious payment imbalances. The 1970s also saw the creation of a Subsidy Account to reduce the cost of drawings under the 1975 oil facility by low-income developing members, while the Trust Fund, financed from the Fund's gold sales, was a source of loans for developing countries.

Under the enlarged access policy of 1980 the maximum total amount available to a member from credit tranches, the Extended Fund Facility and the Supplementary Financing Facility has been set at 450 per cent of quotas repayable over three years.

In 1983 the GAB arrangements were reformed and the funds made available have increased from $6 billion to SDR17 billion. Whereas before 1983 only the G10 plus Switzerland could borrow under the

GAB arrangements, the reform extends the right to borrow to other members of the IMF. The pressure for this reform and for the quota increase of 47 per cent to SDR90 billion at the end of 1983 arose from the international debt crisis of 1982–3. The Fund played a crucial role in a series of ad joc rescue packages for debtor countries as it alone could provide finance in support of adjustment programmes in debtor countries and act as a catalyst for other private and official lenders. The Fund's resources were then seen to be inadequate. In addition the Fund has borrowed from the Bank for International Settlements, Saudi Arabia and some other countries.

Although since early 1984 the Fund has increased resources through enlarged quotas and the various borrowing arrangements mentioned above, Ainley (1985) and others have argued that the enlargement of GAB in preference to a larger quota increase (which had been opposed by the USA and Germany), could be interpreted as the acceptance of a conservative financing role for the Fund since it is the GAB member countries which retain ultimate control over the new GAB resources and not the Fund with its more widely dispersed membership.

SECTION 4 THE OPTIMAL VOLUME OF LIQUIDITY IN THE WORLD
by Robert Shaw

Just as domestic money has a social productivity by releasing resources which would otherwise have been devoted to barter and by permitting specialization and division of labour, so too does international liquidity. Its use to maintain a fixed parity helps to reduce uncertainty and instability in the international economy so that specialization and trade are encouraged on a wider international scale.

It is conceptually possible to derive a world demand for international reserves, and this is represented by the curve *MSB* (the marginal social benefit from reserves) in figure 9.1. On the vertical axis the marginal cost of creating reserves it also measured. On the horizontal axis an (abstract) reserve asset, which could be supplied either by gold (at a fixed market price) or by an international fiduciary reserve asset like SDRs, is measured in millions of units. It is assumed that the marginal cost of gold production rises, while that of the fiduciary asset is low and constant.

The intersections between the respective marginal cost curves and the *MSB* curve give the quantity of each type of asset which would be demanded. Since it seems reasonable to assume that gold produc-

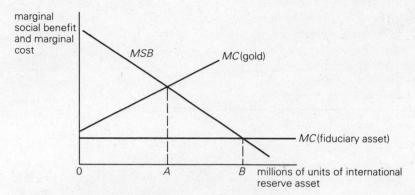

Figure 9.1   Optimal international reserves (1)

tion uses more real resources, a smaller quantity *OA* of the asset would be optimal if its source were gold, than if the fiduciary asset were used, when the quantity would be *OB*.

The fiduciary asset is superior to gold in that it gives the world a larger quantity of a good at a lower price. A larger volume of reserves should enable the world economy to operate at a higher level of activity with greater fixity of exchange rates and less uncertainty in international trade. As the volume of world trade grows, the *MSB* curve will move rightwards continually, but this would leave unaltered the superiority of the fiduciary asset as a source for international liquidity.

A fiduciary asset is always likely to be superior to a commodity reserve asset, since the production of the latter will involve higher resource costs. Two considerations apply to the choice between possible fiduciary assets, e.g. SDRs and dollars. Assuming both are under responsible control, so that the rate of growth of supply can be kept at about the rate of growth of world trade, cheapness of production and in the running of the system would be one criterion. The second would be seigniorage, i.e. the right to the difference between the spending power of the asset and its cost of production. It might be cheaper to run an entirely dollar standard, but this would probably be unacceptable to all except the US, for to gain the dollars required as reserves, the rest of the world would have to part with goods and services, which would reduce its well-being but increase that of the US. It is for reasons of seigniorage that the rest of the world is likely to prefer an international reserve asset such as the SDR, in whose seigniorage they would share.

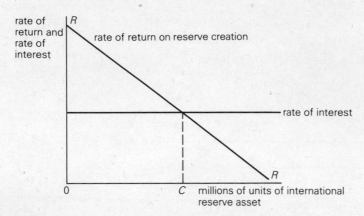

Figure 9.2   Optimal international reserves (2)

The creation of a reserve asset from whatever source represents an investment of real resources and for all of society's resources to be optimally allocated the rate of return on reserve creation must be equal to that at the margin elsewhere in the world economy. If capital markets are efficient, the going rate of interest can be taken to measure the rate of profit elsewhere, and the optimal amount of reserve creation can be alternatively represented as in figure 9.2.

The intersection of the rate of return schedule with that for the rate of interest gives the optimal volume of reserves, *OC*. If figure 9.2 relates to a fiduciary asset the volume *OC* in figure 9.2 will be identical to *OB* in figure 9.1, for the two figures are related to each other, the connection being as follows. If the rate of return were to rise elsewhere in the economy, this would be represented in figure 9.2 as an upward shift of the rate of interest line, giving a new equilibrium quantity of reserves to the left of *OC*. In terms of figure 9.1 greater profitability elsewhere in the economy will mean that resources will be attracted to these activities by higher factor payments. To retain resources in reserve creation will require the payment of higher transfer earnings to factors of production. This raises marginal cost, so that the intersection of *MC* (for fiduciary assets) with *MSB* will move to the left, and fewer international reserve assets will be produced.

One complication in the analysis is the rate of interest paid to holders of fiduciary assets. This seems to suggest that the *MSB* curve in figure 9.1 should be raised vertically to account for this payment with the resulting intersection with the *MC* curve determining the creation of more than *OB* resources. This procedure would be illegitimate for the following reasons. The *MSB* curve takes account of the increase in efficiency in the world economy because of the existence of reserves; this is a net gain to the world. The interest payments do not represent a net gain to the world; they are gains to the recipients, but losses to the payers, with the two cancelling each other out.

The Optimal Volume of Liquidity: Two Qualifications

There are two arguments which suggest that the optimal volume of liquidity might well be less than *OB* in figure 9.1. These are the dangers of world inflation and problems arising from inconsistencies in the macroeconomic policies of countries.

If international reserve assets were increased until their marginal social benefit equalled the marginal cost of production, this might cause such an increase that it would feed through to money supplies and consequently to inflation. This argument is advanced by proponents of the international quantity theory, alternatively known as international reserve monetarism. For its operation it would require a stable demand function for reserves and appropriate domestic monetary expansion in the face of an excess of reserves and a reduction when reserves decline. There are studies (Frenkel, 1980 and Bilson and Frenkel, 1979) which suggest that despite the change from fixed to flexible exchange rates there is still a stable reserve demand function. Heller (1976) has also attempted to quantify the link between reserve growth and inflation. He found that a ten per cent increase in reserves resulted in a three to four per cent increase in the world monetary base, which subsequently showed up within four years as a three to four per cent increase in global inflation, so that increases in reserves could be a significant cause of world inflation.

It has also been argued (Jones, 1983) that international reserve constraint can be beneficial, for it can implicitly co-ordinate the stabilization actions of interdependent but non-co-operative nations. The argument is developed in a two country model with fixed exchange rates where the objective is to minimize the variance in real output experienced by the two countries. If the two countries are co-operative and each takes account of the repercussions of its stabilization policies on the other, then it is easier to design a consistent set of policies to maintain income levels if actions are not constrained by a shortage of reserves. If, on the other hand, the countries do not co-operate in devising their policies, a shortage of reserves reduces the range of actions available to each country, making it easier for each country to guess the action likely to be taken by the other. Without this constraint the countries could engage in a wider range of policies, less easily anticipated and inflicting costs on the other.

If the lessons are applied to the real world, while the countries are more than two, their interests are sufficiently divergent to make it likely that the conflict model would be more appropriate than the co-operative model, in which case reserve tightness would be desirable.

The Desirable Characteristics of a Reserve Asset

Experience shows that whether the world operates a system of flexible exchange rates or fixed rates, international reserves are required. It is necessary not only to have the appropriate (or optimum) volume of international liquidity but to use a reserve asset which has inherently desirable characteristics. These include the ability of the assets to inspire confidence, to stabilize output and prices and to be produced cheaply and in an equitable manner.

Lack of confidence in a reserve medium is marked by shifting to another asset. The only way in which confidence can be guaranteed is if there is only one reserve asset, which, for example, could be gold or a single currency or a fiduciary asset created by an international institution such as exists in the form of the SDR.

In addition to maintaining confidence, the reserve asset should help promote stability of output, prices and employment. At the minimum this requires that the asset should not be produced in such a way that it causes a monetary shock. Gold could be deficient in this respect if there were a major discovery,and the supply of dollars to the rest of the world rose too sharply in the early 1970s. Indeed it could be argued that the creation of the reserve asset should be contra-cyclical, so that creation is increased in recession and restricted in boom times. Under the gold standard, gold production was contra-cyclical. A shortage of gold put downward pressure on prices, including those of inputs into gold production so that the profitability of its production rises and larger quantities are mined and refined. On the other hand, too much gold via the international quantity theory will raise prices, including those of inputs in gold mining so that profitability and production declines. In practice the effect was not significant because of the downward rigidity of prices and because the volume of resources devoted to gold mining has been too small to have an impact on the world economy. Given the lags in the economic system and the lack of success of contra-cyclical policy at the national level, the safest procedure would be to lay down a rule that reserve creation proceed at a steady and moderate rate, such as the long-run rate of growth of international trade. While this could be achieved with an asset like the SDR, it is more difficult in the case of a currency. While the growth of the money supply within the country of issue could be slow and steady, its availability to the rest of the world depends on the size of the reserve currency country's payments deficit.

Thirdly, it is desirable that the reserve asset be produced as cheaply as possible. This rules out the choice of commodities as reserve assets since they are costly to produce in terms of resources used as compared to fiduciary assets. If, however, the reserve asset is produced at much below its exchange value, seigniorage will accrue to its issuer. This argues against the use of a national currency which would confer gains upon the issuing nation and in favour of a reserve asset created by an international organization, so that the seigniorage can be distributed more equitably, e.g. in proportion to a nation's foreign trade or as part of a policy of aiding less developed countries by favouring them in the distribution of the asset.

10 The Eurocurrency System

Introduction

In this chapter the nature of the most important private sector international financial innovation in the last 25 years or so is investigated – the Eurocurrency banks and the network in which they operate, the Eurocurrency system. Eurocurrencies, the most important of which is the Eurodollar, are defined and the effect of the Eurocurrency system on world money supply, world inflation, the operation of domestic monetary policy and the Bretton Woods parity grid system are explained. The size of the Eurocurrency market is shown to be vast and to touch upon most countries in the world.

The controversy over how best to model, or show how the Eurocurrency system works, is investigated at some length. The main conclusions drawn are that the Eurocurrency system is a highly effective system for managing international debt, that it has not been responsible for the creation of new money and so cannot be blamed for causing the world inflation which became a problem of increasing magnitude not so long after the Eurocurrency markets came into existence. This view contrasts sharply with some earlier views which saw the Eurocurrency banks as engines of money creation which needed to be controlled, primarily by new banking laws, if world inflation was to be reduced.

Eurobanking Defined

A Eurocurrency bank is an intermediary in non-domestic financial markets which are commonly described as 'external' or 'offshore' markets. The Eurocurrency market is made by banks that accept time and other interest earning deposits and make loans in a currency other than the country in which they are located. Hence, Eurodollars are dollar deposits in commercial banks situated outside the USA and Euromarks are Deutschmark deposits in banks located outside West

Germany. There are several Eurocurrencies besides the US dollar and West German mark; however, the dollar predominates, accounting usually for between 72 per cent and 80 per cent of Eurocurrency bank liabilities. Marks (with about 10 per cent of the total), Swiss francs, Japanese yen, sterling, French francs and Dutch guilders make up the remainder of the Eurocurrencies. Since the US dollar is so predominant, the discussion here focuses on the Eurodollar market but its mode of operation is little, if at all, different from those of the other Eurocurrencies. As is explained below, Eurodollar deposits remain the liability of *domestic* American commercial banks. The circulation of Eurodollar deposits from one owner to another takes the form of liability transfers on the books of American commercial banks. Dollar bills do not actually move from one Eurobank's vault to another's to any significant extent in the Eurodollar market.

The prefix 'Euro' is not strictly accurate as Eurodollars and other Eurocurrencies are also the assets or liabilities of banks located outside Europe. Indeed, European Eurocurrency banking centres, notably London, Luxembourg, Paris and Frankfurt, accounted for just 62 per cent of the Eurocurrency market in 1982. Offshore banking centres (Bahamas, Singapore, Bahrain, Hong Kong, Cayman Islands, Panama and Netherland Antilles) accounted for a further 22 per cent and North America and Japan the remaining 16 per cent. The prefix 'Euro' was first appended because the external currency markets originated in Europe in the 1950s, and, despite extensive geographical diversification, the term has not, in common usage, been replaced.

The Origin of the Eurodollar Market

The origin of the Eurodollar market can fairly accurately be dated to the years 1957 and 1958. In these years two important events occurred that sparked the Eurodollar market into life. In 1957 the Bank of England introduced tight controls on non-resident sterling borrowing and lending by UK banks. In order to retain their position in the financing of world trade, the UK banks turned to the US dollar. Then, in the following year, major European currencies were made convertible, so allowing banks in these countries to hold freely dollar accounts rather than being required to exchange dollars with their central bank for local currencies. The first of these two factors increased the demand for dollar balances by non-US commercial banks while the second increased both the demand and supply of what had become Eurodollars. In 1958 the Eurodollar market amounted to less than $1 billion. It was to grow at an annual average compound rate of over 20 per cent during the next 25 years or so. By 1983 the *net* size (i.e. gross liabilities minus interbank loans) of the Eurodollar market approached $760 billion dollars to which could be added about $200 billion of other Eurocurrencies.[1]

The second of these two events, Europe's move to currency convertibility, is viewed by Hewson and Sakakibara (1975a, p. 4) in somewhat dramatic terms: the advent of Eurocurrency finance was the form taken by

> the internationalization and liberalization of short- to medium-term international capital . . . in this respect the decade of the 1960s and early 1970s should be viewed as the transition period from US dominated and tightly 'controlled' international economic system to a 'freer' system where the US influence is less dominant.

The achievement of convertibility by Europe was itself an expression of Europe's economic progress from the dark days of the early post-World War II years, and this improvement was also shown in the growth of Europe's GDP relative to that of the USA.

The rapid growth of the Eurodollar market rests upon its efficiency in performing financial intermediation between ultimate lenders and borrowers – multinational corporations and other private sector entities, governments and governmental bodies such as UK local authorities and nationalized industries in many countries, and some central banks. Commercial banks operate a large *interbank* market in Eurodollars which is deserving of a short digression.

Interbank liabilities amount to over one-half of the Eurobanks' gross liabilities. In the interbank market funds flow from one bank to another. There are important reasons for this: first, banks will sometimes borrow in the Eurocurrency market to satisfy local national bank regulations on cash or liquidity ratios – this is known as 'window dressing'. Secondly, funds flow from Eurobanks with surplus deposits to those which have identified non-bank investment outlets. Thirdly, Eurobanks arbitrage short-term capital to high interest rate convertible currency countries (depending upon the configuration of forward exchange rates). Most arbitrage capital moves through the Eurocurrency markets and most of the deposit funds are short-term.

Returning to the main theme of this section, the competitive efficiency of the Eurobanking system is indicated by the narrowness of the spread between the interest paid by the Eurobanks to depositors and that charged by them to prime borrowers compared with banks in national money markets. Usually interest rates charged on Eurodollar loans are expressed as a percentage above the London

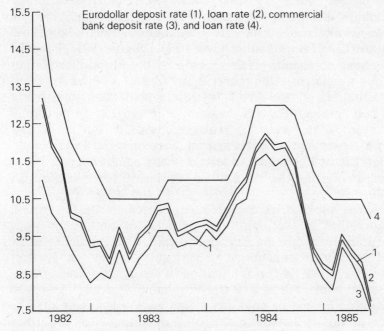

Figure 10.1   Dollar and Eurodollar interest rates

interbank *offer* rate (LIBOR).[2] For example, in early 1983 US commercial banks charged a spread of about two per cent to prime
domestic borrowers above deposit rates but, during the same period,
Eurobank syndicated[3] international loans were made separately to a
Norwegian company and the City of Barcelona at $\frac{5}{8}$ per cent above
LIBOR. Figure 10.1 shows that Eurobanks consistently pay higher
rates of interest to depositors and charge lower rates to depositors
than do US commercial banks.

There are two categories of factors which largely account for the
relative efficiency of Eurobanks as international financial intermediaries: first there are those factors related to certain bank regulations which apply to national commercial banks but not to Eurobanks; and secondly, there are factors related to economies of scale
in Eurobanking. Eurodollar loans are generally very large – over $1
million – and sometimes they are for sums one thousand times larger.
Hence, for a given level of loans, Eurobanks' administrative costs will
be lower than those of domestic banks.

A banking regulation of some historical importance to the growth
of Eurobanking is the US government's Regulation Q which limited

the rate of interest which US banks could pay on dollar deposit and saving accounts. US domestic banks were effectively hindered in competition for dollar deposits with Eurobanks as Regulation Q did not apply to the offshore banks. Two other US government regulations also served to encourage the growth of the Eurodollar market and to reduce significantly the role of New York as a centre for international capital. First, the 1963 Interest Equalization Tax, introduced to help protect the US balance of payments from capital outflow, meant that foreign borrowers could no longer borrow cheaply in the New York capital market. Secondly, the 1965 Voluntary Foreign Credit Restraint Guidelines (made compulsory in 1968) were aimed at limiting the amount of lending to foreigners by US banks.

However, the role of these three regulatory elements in the growth of the Eurodollar market, although initially of importance, was essentially transitory, for the Eurodollar market continued to grow even after they were abandoned. The regulatory law of greatest importance, therefore, is the application of reserve requirements to US commercial banks but not to the Eurobanks. Indeed, Eurobanks are not required by law to hold any liquid reserve assets at all. The importance of this is that the Eurobanks' operating costs are lower than those of domestic banks because the latter have to hold low or zero-interest earning assets as part of the reserve requirement while the Eurobanks do not. Hence, one of the principal effects of these banking regulations, especially Regulation Q and the application of reserve asset requirements, was to induce many US domestic commercial banks to establish branches or subsidiaries outside of the jurisdiction of US and other countries' banking laws which in certain respects applied to resident and not 'offshore' banks.

An additional explanation of the growth of international banking is from the side of industrial economics. The modern theory of the multinational enterprise (MNE) explains the growth and spread of these firms in terms of market failure. Returns on firm specific knowledge, or intangible assets, such as patents and trade marks, managerial skills, marketing skills and, very important in the case of banking, specific knowledge of a client's business, can be obtained in international markets in various ways. The three options are exporting and licensing (both of which rely upon market relationships) and direct foreign investment (which involves a hierarchical relationship between head office and the branch or subsidiary). When the markets of the former are imperfect and costly to use, firm specific knowledge may be exploited through the direct foreign investment alternative. The firm or bank goes multinational in order to avoid the costs

of using the market (Rugman, 1981 for example). Thus, bank regulations have, to some extent, increased the degree of imperfection in
US and other national money markets. Becoming a Eurobank was a
means of capturing business (and profits) which was denied by bank
regulations, e.g. the collection of dollar deposits by US Eurobanks
at competitive interest rates above Regulation Q ceilings. A related
explanation links the rapid spread of US Eurobanks to the spread of
US multinational enterprise non-banks. A bank develops detailed
knowledge of a client's business, objectives and mode of operation
('first mover' advantage) and 'it enjoys a transactional advantage for
supplying the same service to the MNE's foreign subsidiaries' (Caves,
1982, p. 11). In effect, the familiarity of the bank with the MNE
reduces the cost of doing business (e.g. inferring the riskiness of a
loan) and so a competitive advantage is conferred on this bank.

One problem that lies with the reasons which have been given so
far for the growth of the Eurocurrency market is that separately and,
perhaps, together, they do not give a full explanation of the rapid
growth of Eurocurrency assets and liabilities which has been sustained
for a period of more than a quarter of a century. Attention is now
turned to rival theories which try to explain the Eurocurrency
growth phenomena. In the process a deeper appreciation will be
gained of the operation and economic implications of the Eurocurrency markets.

The Eurodollar Credit Multiplier

Understanding how the Eurodollar system plays the role of financial
intermediary, creates credit and finances and manages international
debt is important because without this understanding policy analysis
of the Eurodollar and Eurocurrency markets and policy-prescription
virtually meaningless. Indeed, hot disputes arise on policy-related
matters between different analysts who model the Eurodollar market
in different ways.

This section is primarily concerned with the issue of whether the
Eurodollar market can create credit in a manner analogous to national
(or closed) commercial banking systems, and whether any part of
this credit creation is in the form of money creation. A distinction is
drawn between 'money', a medium of exchange, and 'credit', the
postponement of debt repayment, or transfer of purchasing power.
Three models are discussed: those of the Eurodollar market as a
fractional reserve banking system: secondly, as a partial banking

system; and, thirdly, as a debt management system. It is shown how credit is created in each and the dispute over credit creation versus money creation is pointed out. Also, as a preliminary matter, the definition of the 'Eurodollar' is made more explicit.

The Eurodollar Market as a Fractional Reserve Banking System

A clear statement of this analogy was given by Klopstock (1968, p. 6):

> The Eurodollar expansion is in theory similar to the one that is familiar in the creation of credit in the US on the basis of a given amount of excess reserves ... In theory, this process, would give rise to a series of dollar loans and deposits abroad based on one dollar deposit in the US.

This expansion process is easily understood with reference to the schema laid out in table 10.1. In table 10.1 it is supposed that an American non-bank institution, Exxon Corporation, transfers, by writing a cheque, $1 million from its account with Chase Manhattan Bank (CMB) in New York to a time deposit account with Lloyd's Bank International (LBI is a British Eurocurrency bank) in London. Table 10.1, parts A and B show the transfer taking place on the books of CMB, and section C shows the change in LBI's assets and liabilities as a result of the transfer by Exxon Corporation. It is assumed that LBI cannot find an immediate 'ultimate' customer for its new asset (the $1 million demand deposit with CMB) and quickly re-lends it on the *interbank* market to Manufacturers Hanover (MH, another Eurocurrency bank) – section D – which requires funds for on-lending to an Italian import agency. The latter is the 'ultimate' borrower, in need of funds to meet invoice obligations.

At this point four important points about the nature of the Euro-dollar system can be made: first, a Eurodollar is a deposit on the books of a US bank. Secondly, Eurodollar *circulation* takes place on the books of American banks. In table 10.1, CMB's $1 million liability is seen moving from the account of Exxon Corporation to LBI and on to MH. For this reason it would be quite wrong to think of dollars 'fleeing to Europe in brown leather satchels' (McKinnon (1979), p. 209). Thirdly, an *interbank* market in Eurodollars exists in order to transfer funds between those Eurobanks which have accepted deposits and those that have identified profitable outlets but might be short of funds. Fourthly, notice that for each ultimate borrower (the Italian importer) there is an ultimate saver (Exxon Corporation). The Eurodollar banks play an intermediary function.

Table 10.1 Eurocredit Expansion in a 'Fractional Reserve Banking' Model

Chase Manhattan Bank

(A)   *Assets*   *Liabilities*
      $1 million $1 million
      (loans and reserves)   (Exxon Corporation)

(B)   *Assets*   *Liabilities*
      $1 million $1 million
      (loans and reserves)   (Lloyds Bank International)

Lloyds Bank International

(C)   *Assets*   *Liabilities*
      $1 million $1 million
      (demand deposit with CMB)   (time deposit of Exxon Corporation)

Manufacturers Hanover

(D)   *Assets*   *Liabilities*
      $1 million $1 million
      (demand deposit with CMB)   (time deposit of LBI)

(E)   *Assets*   *Liabilities*
      $1 million $1 million
      (loan to Italian importer)   (time deposit of LBI)

Note: If the Italian importer's creditor redeposits with a Eurobank, Exxon Corporation's initial $1 million deposit (or a part of it) with LBI will pass through a similar chain of banks and borrowers: only, most probably, the 'names' will be changed.

This has led some observers to question the inflationary impact of the Eurodollar system for, so far in our example, there is no increase in (world) liquidity. But as yet the story of multiple credit creation is incomplete: a natural, indeed, vital, question is to ask what happens to the dollars when the Italian importer settles the invoices due?

Least interesting is if the Italian's purchases are from a US exporter who deposits the $1 million in the US domestic banking system, for then the dollars are lost to the Eurobanks. More interesting is what happens if the exporter (an American or otherwise) *re-deposits* all or a part of the $1 million with a Eurobank? Then the credit-chain of table 10.1 can be repeated (with different names perhaps) again and again.

Thus, re-depositing with Eurobanks will cause multiple credit expansion on the basis of Exxon Corporation's original $1 million deposits. What determines the extent of the credit multiplier in the Eurodollar system? Proponents of this view of the credit multiplier in the Eurodollar system (for example, Klopstock, 1968; Swoboda, 1968; Carli, 1971; and Makin, 1972) have all drawn the analogy with credit creation in 'closed' fractional reserve national banking systems. Here, the formula for the credit multiplier is well understood and can be written as:

$$\frac{\Delta D}{\Delta R} = K = \frac{1}{r + c - rc}$$

where ΔD is the change in deposits caused by an initial change in reserves, ΔR, K is the credit multiplier, r the banks' reserve ratio, and c is the public's cash ratio (i.e. cash/deposit ratio).[4] One change needs to be made to the meaning of the symbols in this equation to make it appropriate to the Eurodollar market: c becomes the loan-retention ratio (e.g. the proportion of the $1 million not redeposited with Eurobanks after stage E in table 10.1).

Estimates of the Eurodollar credit multiplier using the fractional reserve banking methodology have varied widely, as table 10.2 shows. The reasons for this need not be discussed here except to point out that conceptual definition and statistical measurement of D and R are in practice by no means straightforward. It might also be because the fractional reserve banking analogy is not entirely appropriate.[5] However, the discovery of large values for the Eurodollar multiplier gave rise to the fear that the Eurodollar system had an inflationary potential. It only needs to be noted here that the act of re-depositing with Eurobanks is an act of saving so there is no presumption that credit creation in the Eurodollar market must increase (world) aggregate demand and necessarily have an inflationary potential.

Table 10.2 Estimates of the Eurodollar Credit Multiplier

Klopstock	(1968)	0.50–0.90
Machlup	(1971)	2.00
Carli	(1971)	3.00–7.00
Makin	(1972)	18.45
Hewson and Sakakibara	(1975b)	1.0
Lee	(1973)	1.51
Friedman	(1969)	Large

The Eurodollar Market as a Partial Banking System

Friedman (1969) and Mayer (1970) retained the conception of the Eurodollar market working upon a fractional reserve base, but viewed the credit creation process somewhat differently. The starting point of their conception was to recognize that the Eurobanks accepting dollar deposits were really an extension of the US banking system. That is, the Eurodollar system was a 'partial banking system'. The credit creating potential of Eurobanks rests as before upon their reserve and currency retention ratios. However, the *net* credit creating potential of the Eurodollar banking system depends upon its credit multiplier relative to that of the US domestic banking system. The presumption was that the Eurobanks' credit multiplier was larger than that of the US domestic banks. The reason for this contention was that Eurobanks held lower reserve ratios than did US domestic banks. This was because the latters' reserve ratio was governed by law while the formers' were not; secondly, Eurobanks' deposit liabilities were less liquid than those of US domestic banks and so were less likely to be called at short notice for repayment; and thirdly, a Eurobank could itself readily call up reserves at short notice by borrowing in the inter-bank market. Thus, Mayer explained

> allowing for the fact that the Eurodollar banks in London are free from reserve requirements ... This means that a shift by non-banks of their deposits from other banks to the Eurobanks in London will now be a way of circumventing reserve requirements and will amount on an international basis to an increase in the overall credit-granting potential (1970, p. 14).

Or, put another way, if a deposit of high powered money was shifted from a US domestic bank to a Eurobank, the credit creating potential of the latter would be greater than the credit reducing effect on the former; in net terms, credit would be created.

The Analogy Challenged Despite the appeal of these two related models of the Eurodollar market, based upon the analogy with the operation of domestic commercial banking systems, it is doubtful that they are entirely appropriate. Lutz (1974) challenged the applicability of the analogy, arguing that re-depositing in a national banking system is a function of the means of payment (cheques) but re-depositing in the Eurodollar market is a matter of choice dependent upont the advantages of doing so – the interest paid and convenience yield. Lutz viewed the multiplier process in the Eurodollar market as analogous *not* to multiple creation of demand deposits (new money) but to multiple creation of time deposits (savings). Enzig (1970) was of the same opinion because 'for all practical purposes Eurodollar transactions are *loan* transactions in terms of dollars' (p. 154, italics added).

It has also been argued that as the degree of maturity transformation performed by the Eurobanks is quite small these banks can have little scope for liquidity creation (Hewson and Sakakibara, 1975b and Hewson, 1976, for example). That is, the Eurobanks tend to match the assets and liabilities of each maturity: e.g. maturities of less than eight days, eight days to one month, one month to three months etc. . . .[6] The importance of this is that *net* liquidity creation by the Eurobanking system must be very limited. Again, it is argued, in effect, Eurobanks are passing on to borrowers assets of given maturities which have already been set aside by depositors.[7]

A Eurodollar Money Multiplier? Indeed, whether the Eurodollar *credit* multiplier is also a *money* multiplier has been left by many writers as something of an open question. Most often the multiplier is referred to as a 'credit multiplier' and the question of whether this multiplier is also a 'money multiplier' is left unaddressed. However, even drawing the analogy with domestic fractional reserve commercial banking, with their powers of multiplying demand deposits (M_1), comes pretty close to admitting that the Eurodollar system creates money. If so, the inflationary potential is obvious.

It has also been pointed out that although Eurobanks are called 'banks' they are, in fact, *non-bank* financial intermediaries (Dufey and Giddy, 1978). As such the Eurobanks *substitute* for, rather than add to, domestic credit intermediation. For example, banks dealing in the Eurodollar market have initially to attract dollar deposits from rival financial institutions before simply on-lending these funds to borrowers. Essentially, Eurodollar credit substitutes for domestic dollar credit one-for-one. The Eurodollar credit multiplier is unity (or less) and the concept of a Eurodollar money multiplier is just not relevant. This last point is so, as was pointed out earlier, because the Eurobank's liabilities are not money: as time deposits they cannot be spent before being turned into cash or demand deposits with a US clearing bank.

The inflationary potential of Eurobanking, therefore, must be limited to the effect which the existence of these institutions might have on the velocity of circulation of money. It is true that there might be some effect here. A holder of an idle demand deposit with a US clearing bank might be induced by the interest rate offered to transfer this deposit to a time deposit account with a Eurodollar bank. The clearing bank's liability is simply transferred from the account of the private depositor to the account held with it by the Eurodollar bank. US money supply – M_1 – is clearly unchanged. However, the Eurobank, having accepted a deposit, will seek an ultimate customer (leaving the inter-bank market aside) who, presumably, will spend the borrowed funds. In this way an idle time deposit at a US clearing bank will be put into circulation and the velocity of circulation of money will increase. However, this effect is thought by commentators to be of limited significance.

Eurobanks as a Debt Management System

While the 'fractional reserve banking' analogy had a powerful appeal that remains popular even today, almost from the very beginning it had its detractors (Einzig, 1970 and Lutz, 1974 for example). The main point of their criticisms was that Eurobanks accepted *savings* and made *time deposit* loans and that this process was quite different to credit creation in the US commercial banking system where the banks liabilities are a means of payment. Hogan and Pearce (1982) have provided a systematic explanation of the Eurodollar banking system as an international system for managing debt. They are quite scathing about the money multiplier concept of the Eurobanking system: 'the truth is that money is money and debt is debt while neither is both' (p. 76). The essence of Hogan and Pearce's argument is that the spectacular growth of Eurodollar debt is due not to multiple money creation through a fractional reserve banking money multiplier, but rather, to the persistence of the *same* group of countries being in balance of payments deficit while another group is in persistent balance of payments surplus. The schema laid out in table 10.3 makes this point clear. (Other aspects of international debt are discussed in chapters 11 and 12.)

The world is divided into just three countries which for convenience we shall call the 'USA', 'Latin America' and 'Europe'. The 'USA' is always in balance of payments equilibrium, 'Latin America' is in persistent payments deficit while 'Europe' has a persistent payments surplus. Eurobanks are in existence and they are assumed to hold assets and liabilities after a transfer to them of $100 million by a US non-bank. In year 1, 'Latin America' has a balance of payments deficit of $100 million which, given the assumptions, must be matched by a $100 million European payments surplus. If 'Latin America' financed its payments deficit from foreign exchange reserves and the next year corrected the deficit, the Eurobanks

Table 10.3 Balance of Payments Disequilibria and the Growth of Eurocurrency Debt

EUROBANKS HAVE $100M TO LEND*

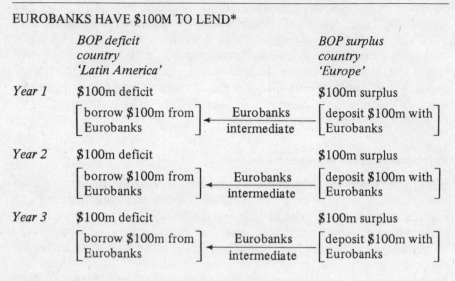

	BOP deficit country 'Latin America'		*BOP surplus country 'Europe'*
Year 1	$100m deficit		$100m surplus
	[borrow $100m from Eurobanks]	← Eurobanks intermediate	[deposit $100m with Eurobanks]
Year 2	$100m deficit		$100m surplus
	[borrow $100m from Eurobanks]	← Eurobanks intermediate	[deposit $100m with Eurobanks]
Year 3	$100m deficit		$100m surplus
	[borrow $100m from Eurobanks]	← Eurobanks intermediate	[deposit $100m with Eurobanks]

EUROBANKS AFTER THREE YEARS

Assets	*Liabilities*
$300m ('Latin American' loans)	$300m (European deposits)
$100m (deposits with US banks)	$100m (US non-bank's deposits)
$400m	$400m

Note: *A US non-bank is assumed to transfer funds from a chequing account with a US commercial bank to a Eurobank. The Eurobank's assets at this stage read: assets $100m (deposit with a US commercial bank); liabilities $100m (deposit of the US non-bank).

Source: Following W. P. Hogan and I. F. Pearce, *The Incredible Eurodollar* (Allen and Unwin, London, 1982).

would not be called upon. They would have no function to fulfil. However, it is assumed that 'Latin America' borrows $100 million from the Eurobanks, so financing its payments deficit, and does nothing to correct that payment's deficit. 'Europe' too allows its payments surplus to persist from one year to the next, and deposits the $100 million payments surplus with the Eurobanks because they offer the most advantageous terms. The circuit is thus primed to run on year after year: table 10.3 shows just three years of payments disequilibrium.

Eight important points concerning the operation of the Eurodollar market can be made with reference to table 10.3:

(1) Eurobanks assets take the form of loans to 'Latin America' ($300 million) and deposits with a US bank ($100 million), and after three years total $400 million.

(2) The *size* of the Eurodollar market is growing by $100 million per annum and after three years totals $400 million whether measured in terms of the Eurobank's assets (as in the first point) or liabilities, $300 million to 'European' depositors and $100 million to the original US non-bank depositor.

(3) It is made clear that annual growth in the size of the Eurodollar banking system is governed by the size of world balance of payments deficits.

(4) Eurodollar debts will continue to grow so long as balance of payments deficits persist.

(5) The growth of Eurodollar debt is non-inflationary, or at least it is in terms of table 10.3. For each amount borrowed there is an equal amount saved: 'Latin America's' excess of spending over income is matched by 'Europe's' excess of income over spending. The recycling of payments surpluses does not lead to an increase in world aggregate demand. Hogan and Pearce have qualified this point, pointing out that 'the growth of international debt can continue without new money creation anywhere. On the other hand, if governments do create new money it is as likely as not that some of this will find its way into the hands of the Eurobanks where it may serve to generate even greater trade deficits and, *ipso facto*, an even faster growing total of international debt' (1982, pp. 83–4). But the Eurobanks play an intermediary role; money creation is initiated elsewhere.

(6) Eurodollar debt is the debt of 'Latin America' and nobody else.

(7) Notice that growth of the Eurodollar market does not need either the creation of new dollars by the USA's Federal Reserve System or even a US balance of payments deficit. Indeed, in our example, it did not even need a US balance of payments deficit for the Eurodollar market to spring into life.

(8) As Hogan and Pearce observed, 'there can be no increase in debt without a flow of money' (1982, p. 80). The flow of money in question is the $100 million asset that the Eurobanks hold on the books of a US commercial bank. This money is constantly flowing through the Eurobanks to 'Latin America' and is redeposited with them by 'Europe'. 'Latin America's' creditors

though, are the Eurobanks only in the sense that the Eurobanks play an intermediary function. The ultimate creditor,
which has reduced spending below income, is 'Europe' and this
would be true whether the Eurobanks played an intermediary
role or 'Europe' lent directly to 'Latin America'.

Money and Credit Creation Again

When account is taken of the view that the Eurobanks are a debt
management system and of the fact that Eurodollar liabilities do not
serve as a means of payment it becomes clear that Eurobanks are
akin to non-bank financial intermediaries. These can create assets and
liabilities by making loans and accepting deposits, as was shown
earlier, but this is not the same thing as creating means of payment,
i.e. money. To explain: demand deposit liabilities (chequing accounts)
of commercial banks to their customers are means of payment, so *if*
in the schema laid out in table 10.3 the Europeans' assets of $300
million were demand deposits, the Eurobanks liabilities would be in
the form of money. If this were the case (which it is not) then observation of the ratio of the Eurobanks liabilities ($300 million) to their
money asset base ($100 million) might give an idea of the size of the
Eurodollar multiplier. However, the vast bulk of Eurobank liabilities
are *time deposits* (i.e. without chequing account facilities). If the
European depositors wanted to spend their savings with the Eurobanks they would need first of all to turn them into a spendable
form – cash or demand deposits upon which they could draw
cheques. The story could end here; the Eurobanks do not create
money because their liabilities are not money. Multiplication of their
liabilities is not the same thing as multiplication of the money stock.
To spend their savings the depositors with the Eurobanks must some-
how turn their deposits into deposits with American banks with
chequing account facilities. Let us see how this might be done.

If the European depositors wished to withdraw their $300 million
of assets, the Eurobanks could pay over, at most, $100 million of
money to the European depositors as, in our example, this is the
total amount of their demand deposits held with US commercial
banks (and even that is conditional upon the Eurobanks not having
already paid these deposits as new loans to Latin America). The
Eurobanks might borrow the shortfall (of $200 million) from the
US domestic banks. What would be the effect of this on the outstanding stock of dollars? If the US commercial banks were fully
'loaned up' (i.e. their liabilities were already at the limit governed

by the legal or prudential cash or liquidity ratio), then the $200 million of loans to the Eurobanks would need to be diverted from loans to other customers. Clearly, there is no money creation here. Alternatively, the US banks might not be fully loaned up, in which case lending to the Eurobanks would provide an opportunity for US commercial banks to create new money. But, to be clear, it is the US banks with their chequing account facilities which create the new money, not the Eurobanks. Besides, in the circumstances, had the Eurobanks not existed and the Europeans held time deposits directly with US commercial banks, their switch to demand deposits would have created new dollars just the same.

Summing Up on Eurodollars and Inflation

It was pointed out earlier that at first credit creation in the international Eurodollar system was modelled as if it were a fractional reserve banking system. Certainly, some monetary officials, bankers and academic economists were concerned that liquidity creation in the Eurobanking system might be excessive and, ultimately, inflationary. Nor, it was thought, could central banks influence this money creation process without, for example, imposing reserve requirement ratios on the Eurobanks. Worry over the effects of Eurobanking was enhanced by the observation that the growth of Eurodollar liabilities and worldwide inflation was the common experience of the last quarter century.

However, several reasons have been given which suggest that Eurobanking has *not* been a cause of money creation or worldwide inflation. First, even in the fractional reserve banking system analogy (table 10.1), it was shown that for each borrower of Eurodollars (with spending greater than income) there must be a re-depositor holding savings with Eurobanks. Thus, Eurobanking intermediation does not necessarily increase the level of world aggregate demand. This point was, perhaps, even more forcefully made in the discussion of the Eurobanks as a debt management system.

Secondly, as all but an insignificant proportion of the Eurodollar banks' liabilities are time or call deposits and not demand deposits, multiplication of the former does not necessarily increase the quantity of circulating medium (money on the M_1 definition). That is, a distinction was drawn between multiple *credit* creation and multiple *money* creation. Thirdly, attention needs to be drawn to the fact that each central bank has at its disposal means of sterilizing the effects of foreign capital inflow on the domestic money supply.

However, as argued in the next section, the development of the Euro-markets has had important implications for the role and effectiveness of monetary policy at the national level.

Euromarkets and the Move to Floating Exchange Rates

While the regime of fixed exchange rates was still in effect, one of the main problems that arose from the growth of the Eurodollar market was the reduced effectiveness of domestic monetary policy (Klopstock, 1968; Swoboda, 1968; Mayer, 1970; Hewson and Sakakibara, 1975b). Mundell had shown (see chapter 3) that with fixed exchange rates monetary policy would have no long-term effectiveness but that it might have some influence over interest rates and domestic economic activity in the short term. However, this short-term effectiveness depended upon international capital being less than perfectly mobile in response to national interest rate differentials. By analogy, like the level of water in two connected barrels, if the gauge of the connecting pipe is narrow, it would take some time for the levels to even out should somebody add to or take away from one of the barrels a bucket full of water. The relevance of the analogy is that in the short term a central bank could have some effective control over national monetary aggregates and interest rates. However, if international capital mobility was increased (the gauge of the connecting pipe widened) as transactions costs were reduced by efficient financial intermediation by Eurobanks, then, as an instrument for influencing real economic activity, monetary policy would become less efficient.

The Eurobanks' principal function is to intermediate capital around the world. In other words, one of the main effects of the Eurobanking system was to raise international capital mobility by reducing transactions costs. In the 1960s this was clearly recognized by central banks and, in an attempt to drive a wedge between domestic and foreign interest rates, several 'mild' foreign exchange control devices were introduced. But the central bankers were never really convinced that they could mount really effective controls. As Klopstock (1968) observed: 'not the least of the reasons for this reluctance [to use controls] has been the suspicion that another control device would do no more than lead those most affected to discover some other means of escape' (p. 23) and others have made essentially the same point. Hence, faced with increased international capital mobility in the 1960s, central bankers had to recognize that national money markets were becoming more integrated. And, because of this, the possibilities of conflicts between the imperatives of 'internal' and 'external' balance were increased. Thus, for example, a country might wish to reduce domestic interest rates in order to stimulate economic activity, while the foreign account might require higher interest rates in order to stimulate capital inflow.

In the context of increased international capital mobility, therefore, greater co-ordination of macroeconomic policy was required so as to maintain the Bretton Woods fixed exchange rate regime itself. This was because large interest rate differentials between national money markets would lead to interest arbitrage, and the money flows through the foreign exchange markets would strain the ability of central banks to maintain their pegged exchange rates.

Hence, towards the end of the 1960s three factors came together which ultimately contributed to the end of fixed exchange rates. These were, first, increased international capital mobility; secondly, recognition that foreign exchange controls could not be effective; and thirdly, advice from the monetarist school that effectiveness of monetary policy could be at least partially regained if the exchange rate was allowed to float.

Conclusions

This chapter has discussed the development of thinking on how best to model the Eurocurrency system. This was the main task because only through understanding how the system works can its effect on the world economy be properly understood. Merely, noting that the Eurocurrency system is large and has grown annually at very high rates can tell little, if anything, about its effect on world inflation or the world economy in general. The main conclusions to be drawn are that Eurobanks are really non-bank financial intermediaries and that the Eurocurrency system is best viewed as a debt management system that has grown up because of the persistence of balance of payments disequilibria. The persistence of these disequilibria had simultaneously set up a demand for and supply of Eurocurrencies. The demand comes from those countries in balance of payments deficit and the supply from those in surplus. It is also concluded that the Eurocurrency system does not create money and that it has not of itself had an inflationary impact upon the world economy. Indeed, it is noted that as the Eurobanks only organize the passing on of savings by one group of countries to 'deficit spending' countries, their intermediation does not imply that world aggregate demand must be increased with an accompanying inflationary potential.

However, this is not to say that the Eurocurrency system is unimportant, for the increased mobility of international capital, which the Eurobanks have engendered by lowering transactions costs, has been a factor in the decision taken, in the early 1970s, to adopt floating exchange rates in place of the Bretton Woods parity grid system.

Notes

1 Calculation of the size of the Eurocurrency market is not straightforward, depending upon definitions and coverage. Morgan Guaranty and the Bank for International Settlements estimates are not identical but are of the same order of magnitude.
2 LIBOR is calculated as the average offer rate of certain major Eurobanks located in London.
3 A syndicated loan is where a group of banks make a loan to a single borrower. Syndicated loans are typical of Eurodollar loans.
4 The derivation of this formula is given in most intermediate macroeconomic textbooks, for example Glahe (1977), chapter 8.
5 Despite this, the fractional reserve banking analogy is retained in textbooks on international money such as Crockett (1977) and Williamson (1983).
6 This fragment of maturity structure is taken from that used by the Bank of England (see *Quarterly Bulletin*).
7 Hewson and Sakakibara defined the liquidity multiplier as:

$$\frac{1}{1-s(1-r)} \cdot (L_D - L_1)$$

where r is the Eurobanks reserve ratio; s the non-bank public's re-deposit ratio; L_D is the weighted average liquidity of deposits; and L_1 the weighted average liquidity of loans. Thus, if the liquidity of deposits and loans is the same, the Eurobank's liquidity multiplier is zero.

11 The IMF and the Third World

Less developed country (ldc) members of the IMF are easily the most frequent users of IMF conditional loans. However, the terms and conditions attached to these loans are often regarded by them as being too harsh and imposing unacceptable economic and political costs. Sometimes potential borrowers will not accept the IMF's conditions and will turn a loan down. Some borrowers fail to abide by the loan conditions and have the credit-lines cut off. However, many other ldcs accept and abide by the IMF's conditionality clauses and adjust their balance of payments to sustainable levels.

This chapter discusses the economic reasoning behind and criticism of the IMF's approach to balance of payments adjustments, and considers the effects of the IMF's 'medicine' on the members' balance of payments and general economic performance. The chapter opens with a brief discussion of ldc exchange rate arrangements. This subject is interesting because payments deficits could not arise if exchange rates were allowed to float freely. Why do all ldcs operate pegged or managed exchange regimes? The second section considers the IMF's role in balance of payments adjustment, states the IMF's objectives and the policy means chosen to attain those objectives. As the IMF's view of balance of payments adjustment is rooted in economic theory, the main outlines of that theory – the monetary model developed by J. J. Polak (1957) – are also set out. Following this there is a brief account of the 'structuralist school's' criticism of IMF policies, and the debate between the two sides is considered in a schematic economic model. The final sections of the chapter explain why the IMF is so often concerned with including clauses in its conditional loans which aim at reducing price distortions. The discussions here is set at both the theoretical and empirical levels. The main conclusion to this latter discussion is that price-distortions hinder economic growth, with the implication that the IMF is generally correct to pursue policies which reduce their severity.

Ldc Exchange Rate Arrangements

Most ldcs peg their exchange rates to another currency or to a basket of currencies. This preference can be explained in terms of the strong likelihood that ldc exchange rates, if allowed to float, would be unstable because of the existence of short-run inelastic domestic supply and demand functions and associated 'J' curve effects on the balance of payments. Dependence of many ldcs on one or a few exported commodities and, sometimes a narrow geographic base of export markets, also makes them vulnerable to fluctuations in export earnings. Moreover, as it is true that the domestic money and capital markets of most ldcs are not well integrated with international financial markets (Black, 1976), swings in the balance of payments cannot be financed by responsive international capital flows.

As no ldc allows its currency to float freely, the pegging (or managed-floating) of their currencies has the inherent danger that real effective exchange rates will diverge, perhaps markedly, from purchasing power parity. Indeed, several ldcs have, from time to time, allowed their currencies to become heavily over-valued and this has had detrimental consequences for their balance of payments and economic performance. When this happens, the ldc concerned may approach the IMF for loans, and when these loans are to be made from 'upper credit tranches', the IMF will make them *conditional* upon the implementation of certain adjustment policies.

The IMF: Its Role

The role of the IMF in the international financial and economic system was discussed at some length in chapter 9 and only the barest essentials need to be mentioned here. The IMF's main objectives when confronted with a member country seeking funds to finance a balance of payments deficit is to restore payments equilibrium as quickly as possible: one Fund staff member has written *'the unique function of the Fund is to promote the adjustment process'* (Dale, 1983, italics added); and another embroiders the point: 'The ultimate aim of Fund financial assistance is to restore viability to the balance of payments in the context of price stability and sustained economic growth, without resort to measures that impair the freedom of trade and payment' (Guitián, 1981).

The IMF has an array of instruments (or policies) from which it can select in order to obtain its main objectives. The main ones are:

(1) Monetary control, usually by setting ceilings on domestic credit expansion.
(2) Devaluation.
(3) Reduced price distortions, e.g.
   (a) higher energy prices, and reduced food subsidies;
   (b) interest rate reform;
   (c) trade liberalization.
(4) Wage freezes.
(5) Ceilings on growth of net foreign indebtedness.

Very important are demand management policies. The IMF's view is that domestic demand (or 'absorption') must be constrained to a level consistent with the level of domestic production plus any sustainable net capital inflows, otherwise a balance of payments deficit is unsustainable. Important among 'demand management policies' is the control, or restriction, of domestic bank credit expansion. Selection of this policy instrument, and the setting of targers for domestic credit expansion (DCE) follows from the IMF's analysis of the causes of payments deficits, an analysis which is rooted in the monetary approach to the balance of payments (see chapter 5). In the following section of this chapter the fundamental monetary model that has been used by the IMF – the Polak model – is set out, and the importance of controlling the domestic money supply shown. Use of monetary policy instruments is often accompanied by targets for public sector borrowing, i.e. fiscal targets which are often set in terms of target levels of aggregate government spending and income and sometimes with reference to spending levels on various public sector programmes and tax-revenue schemes.

However, for balance of payments adjustment to be anything other than temporary,the IMF often seeks the attainment of certain other objectives:

(1) Improved resource allocation: the view is that this will lessen the constraint on the level of domestic demand imposed by a *given* availability of resources. The policies used here usually involve exchange rate adjustment, interest rate adjustment and other price-adjustment policies, especially public sector pricing and subsidies.
(2) From the late 1970s the IMF has given attention to 'supply side' measures – so as to reduce the payments constraint on demand from the side of increased domestic production from *enhanced* domestic resources. This is especially important where the root causes of ldc payments deficits lie in external events

(such as higher energy prices), which are structural, rather than reversible, in character. Such structural deficits can be reduced by increasing domestic supply (e.g. of energy resources) rather than by simply cutting domestic demand.

This distinction between 'supply-side' and 'demand-side' measures is somewhat false, however, as measures taken by governments in conjunction with IMF conditional loans will often simultaneously affect both sides. For example, reduced fiscal deficits, an apparent 'demand-side' measure, can reduce domestic interest rates paid by private sector borrowers and act as a spur to private sector production. Or, as is discussed below, devaluation, especially when accompanied by monetary and fiscal restraint, which may be regarded as a 'demand-side' measure, also has the 'supply-side' consequence of inducing the reallocation of resources towards the traded goods sector – which is necessary if balance of payments deficits are not to be removed entirely by a reduced domestic demand.

These IMF policy tools are by no means universally accepted as ideal; dissenters include the recipients of IMF conditional loans, who are required to implement what they see as harsh economic policies, and a group of economic theorists who are known as the *'structuralist school'*. A later section of this chapter is concerned with assessing at theoretical and empirical levels the economic merits of the IMF's policies and the relevance of the arguments put by the structuralist school against them. The weight of this evidence is shown to support the IMF's position rather than that of its critics. First, though, attention is paid to the monetary model which for almost three decades has strongly influenced the IMF's approach to balance of payments adjustment.

The IMF's Monetary Approach to the Balance of Payments

In the early days the IMF sought a robust theory of the balance of payments upon which a consistent set of adjustment policies could be based. In 1957 Fund staff-member J. J. Polak published what became widely known as the 'Polak model' (Polak, 1957). The basic underlying assumption of this model, largely taken over and applied by the IMF with some modifications, is that balance of payments deficits have common causes and that payments adjustment can be most efficiently achieved by applying the limited set of adjustment policies mentioned in the previous section.

The IMF's approach to balance of payments adjustment is not strictly 'monetarist' in character, although it is based upon an assumption (supported by empirical evidence) that the demand for money is a stable function of a few economic variables and, accordingly, that the velocity of circulation of money is also stable. Hence, changes in money supply have predictable effects on nominal national income. However, in applying his version of the quantity theory of money to open economies Polak employed a Keynesian economic concept – the marginal propensity to import. As is spelled out below, an increase in money supply, or, rather, the component of it which is under the control of the 'local' monetary authorities (domestic credit expansion), will affect the levels of nominal national income, imports, the balance of payments and foreign exchange reserves according to the value of the marginal propensity to import.

The Polak Model

Polak's model is based upon the quantity theory of money $M_0 V = PY$. The starting point of the analysis of the relationship between money and income, imports and the balance of payments is that (a) V is assumed to be stable; and (b) in an open economy, M_0 (the money supply) is *endogenous* – i.e. not entirely under the control of the monetary authorities. It is true that the monetary authorities can control to some degree the rate of DCE (domestic credit expansion). However, the other component of domestic money supply, the net foreign assets of the (consolidated) banking system – i.e. foreign exchange reserves – is not directly under their control as it depends upon the balance of payments. Thus, an increase in DCE, setting off a rise in spending and imports, will worsen the balance of payments and foreign exchange reserves and money supply will fall. Clearly, only if exports equalled imports at all times would DCE directly determine domestic money supply. Accordingly, an important variable in the Polak model is the marginal propensity to import, for it determines the extent to which any increase in domestic credit and spending leaks abroad.

The model is described by the following set of equations:

$$Y_t = Y_{(t-1)} + DCE_t + X_t - M_t \tag{11.1}$$

$$\Delta M_{0t} = (Y_t - Y_{(t-1)})K \tag{11.2}$$

$$M_t = m Y_{(t-1)} \tag{11.3}$$

$$X_t = \bar{X}_t \tag{11.4}$$

$$DCE_t = \overline{DCE_t} \tag{11.5}$$

$$\Delta M_{0t} = DCE_t + \Delta F_t \tag{11.6}$$

$$\Delta F_t = X_t - M_t \tag{11.7}$$

Equation 11.1 shows that the level of income in period t is equal to the previous period's level of income if DCE_t and $(X_t - M_t)$ equal zero. Equations 11.4 and 11.5 indicate that exports (X) and DCE are exogenous; equation 11.3 shows that imports are a function of the last period's income $(Y_{(t-1)})$, m is the marginal propensity to import. Equation 11.2 shows that the absolute change in money stock is proportional to the change in income. The proportionality factor, K, is the fraction of money national income held in money balances (i.e. $K = 1/V$). Equation 11.6 shows that the growth in money supply (ΔM_{0t}) is equal to DCE plus the change in net foreign exchange reserves (ΔF_t); and equation 11.7 shows that the change in reserves is a function of $X_t - M_t$.

Since there is only one leakage from the circular flow of income in the domestic economy – imports – the multiplier effect on income of an autonomous change in exports or DCE is equal to $1/m$. It is important to notice that imports are a lagged function of income, so that the effects of a change in exports or DCE take time to work themselves out – adjustment trajectories of income, imports, money supply and foreign exchange reserves can be calculated. The calculation of these is straightforward given the value of m. In figure 11.1 increased spending on imports lags increases in income by one-quarter of a year.

Supposing a permanent $1 million increase in exports beginning in the first quarter and that $m = 1/10$, income will rise by $1 million in the first quarter. In the second quarter, $9/10 million of this increased income will be spent at home and $1/10 million on imports – income will increase by $1 + 9/10 million. In the third quarter, the domestic recipients of the $9/10 million induced expenditure of the second period will in turn spend 9/10ths with residents and 1/10th on imports; income will have increased to $1 + 9/10 + (9/10)^2$. This process will continue into the future, with the increase in income in any quarter, n being calculated as:

$$\$1 + 9/10 + (9/10)^2 + \ldots + (9/10)^{n-1}$$

Income will asymptotically approach its new equilibrium, which is $1 \times 1/m = \$10$ millions higher than its initial level.

Part (B) of figure 11.1 shows what happens to the current account of the balance of payments quarter by quarter. The rise in imports is calculated simply as m times the change income. Finally, part (C) shows the *aggregate* change in the level of foreign exchange reserves on a quarterly basis. Reserves increase according to the difference between exports and imports. Since the velocity of circulation of money (or, K) is fixed, money stock must have increased in propor-

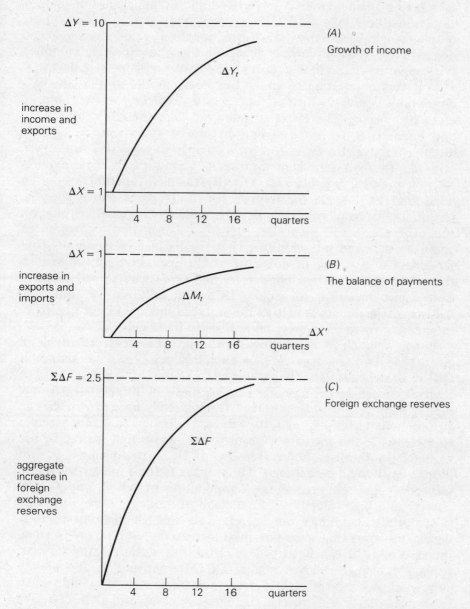

Figure 11.1 The Polak model: autonomous increase in exports and positive DCE

tion to income. As expenditure lags income by one-quarter year, $K = \frac{1}{4}(V = 4)$ and given $\Delta Y = \$10$ million, the change in money stock must be $10/4 = \$2.5$ million. And how has this increase in the money stock been achieved? From equation 11.6, given that no domestic credit expansion has occurred, the whole increase in money is through the rise in foreign exchange reserves – figure 11.1 part (C).

It is very interesting to apply the Polak model to the case of a developing country which is *financing a fiscal deficit by domestic credit expansion.* The effect on income, and, therefore, on money and imports, is the same as in the case of an increase in exports discussed above. However, foreign exchange reserves will run down, at a rate that will ultimately approach the rate of DCE. As exports are not affected, in figure 11.1 part (B), the $\Delta X'$ function lies on the horizontal axis, while the import function climbs above it – the resulting balance of payments deficit reduces reserves. Reflection on this observation will show that there is a danger that a government could be deceived into thinking that the balance of payments consequences of a policy of domestic credit expansion are not serious for, in the early quarters, imports exceed exports by a small amount. Conversely, measures to reduce DCE will only slowly contain a balance of payments deficit as the induced income effect of slower monetary growth on imports takes time to build up.

But how much DCE can a country afford? Can it afford any at all given that DCE reduces foreign exchange reserves? The answer is that it all depends upon the rate of export growth, the target level of reserves chosen by the monetary authorities and the ratio of national money supply to annual imports.[1] It has already been shown that an autonomous increase in exports will cause foreign exchange reserves to increase. If this increase were to a level above that desired by the monetary authorities, some measure of DCE (to finance a budget deficit, say) could be engaged. Thus, if the ratio of money supply to imports is low (because of the combination of a high import propensity and high velocity of circulation of money), a given increase in exports will produce only a relatively small increase in reserves. Given this somewhat small potential increase in reserves, only a small increase in DCE can be afforded. Otherwise, despite rising exports, foreign exchange reserves might fall. Alternatively, if the money supply–import ratio is high, a given increase in exports would yield a large potential rise in foreign exchange reserves, and DCE could be correspondingly higher.

Several important points can be drawn from the Polak model which highlight the role of monetary variables in determining the balance of payments:

(1) Domestic credit expansion plays a crucial role in determining the balance of payments. A too rapid rate of expansion will cause large payments deficits.

(2) The effects of changes in autonomous variables (such as the level of exports or DCE) take time to build up and in the early stages these effects may be misleadingly small. For example, a monetary authority may be led to over-expand credit on the basis of an early observation that recent increases in credit had had little effect on the balance of payments.

(3) An autonomous expansion of exports does not have a lasting effect on the balance of payments surplus. Thus, expansionary DCE policies based upon an early, large balance of payments surplus, would eventually lead to serious payments difficulties.

(4) Import barriers can have no *lasting* effect on the balance of payments, as imports will rise with induced income effects. A country beginning with a payments deficit will end up with a payments deficit even though import barriers have been imposed. Income will be higher, but, as discussion later in this chapter shows, the accompanying price distortions may reduce the rate of economic growth.

(5) With floating exchange rates 'excessive' DCE will lead to currency depreciation. If the nominal exchange rate is not allowed to depreciate sufficiently (either because it is pegged to another currency or because the government operates a system of managed floating), 'overvaluation', measured by the real exchange rate, will accompany the payments deficit. An appropriate remedy would be a combination of restricted DCE and depreciation of the nominal exchange rate.

Structuralist Arguments Against IMF Adjustment Policies

The structuralists' case against the routine application of 'standard' IMF adjustment packages in ldcs is that their economic structures are quite different from those of developed countries, and that, as a group, they are themselves structurally diverse. Adjustment packages that might work well when applied to dcs, or even to *some* ldcs, are likely to be ineffective, or worse, to have severely detrimental effects when applied in *most* ldcs.

Taylor (1983), noting that ldcs are structurally diverse, points out that 'no single set of institutions or equations can capture all of this variety' (p. 191). He develops several macroeconomic models which incorporate many different structural characteristics. Manipulation of these models yields a wide variety of results with, very importantly, virtually no outcomes being determinate on the basis of *a priori* economic reasoning. Different assumptions about key parameter values can yield policy outcomes quite counter to those asserted by the IMF. By way of example:

(1) a *reduction* in money supply could be inflationary if 'interest rate cost push' is strong. This might arise if firms have to hold large stocks of circulating capital financed by borrowed money.
(2) devaluation can worsen the current account deficit (an example of 'elasticity pessimism') and cause a reduction in the rate of economic growth. This latter effect could stem from the effect of reduced real wages on the level of aggregate demand. Reduced spending by workers may not be made up by higher spending by other 'classes', so that aggregate demand and economic growth rates fall.
(3) If food subsidies are reduced as a part of a programme of reduced government expenditure, the demand for non-food goods would be reduced if the demand for food is inelastic. Growth-incentives would also be reduced and the rate of economic growth would suffer.

Some country studies and, indeed, comparative economic assessments by the IMF itself, lend support to the structuralist's case that the IMF should tailor its adjustment policies to suit the specific circumstances of individual ldc applicants for IMF conditional credits. Green (1983) argued that an IMF credit-adjustment package for an Extended Fund Facility loan in 1981 was refused by the Tanzanian authorities because the IMF did not take account of microeconomic and structural issues particular to the Tanzanian economy. The argument was that the devaluation demanded by the IMF was inappropriate as a means of improving the current account deficit. Export bottlenecks existed and required imports to alleviate them, while any temporary gains from devaluation would be quickly wiped out by the inflation brought on by the devaluation. In the case of Jamaica it has been argued that the conditions for IMF loans negotiated during the 1970s showed pro-market bias and operated under the assumption that markets worked efficiently (Sharpley, 1983). The government pointed out that devaluation would not work because of the low price-elasticity of demand and supply for exports.

Structuralists Versus the IMF: The Case of Devaluation

The IMF's case for and the structuralists' case against devaluation as a means of adjusting balance of payments deficits can be contrasted in a simple model. The model is based upon the following three assumptions:

(1) the economy is divided into two sectors:
   (a) *non-traded goods (NT)*, such as housing and other items of social infrastructure, many services and, very often, commodities which are produced and consumed only in the domestic (possibly village) economy;
   (b) *traded goods*, a major export industry based upon a raw material produced in a mineral or agricultural sector, together with a sector of limited scale producing import-competing goods.
(2) Perfect mobility and constant productivity of factor inputs when they move between industries *within a sector*. This is the basis of the division of the economy into the two sectors.
(3) Diminishing marginal productivity of factor inputs when they move between sectors, so that the production possibly curve between traded and non-traded goods is convex to the origin.

Given the underlying production and utility functions, the levels of production and consumption will depend on the relative prices of traded and non-traded goods (measured in local currency).

The Case for Devaluation

Figure 11.2 shows a production possibility curve for a country which happens to be running a balance of payments deficit: at the relative price ratio tt between NT and T goods production is at point P, consumption at point C and the payments deficit measured in terms of local currency is AC – that is, consumption of traded goods is greater than domestic production.

Currency depreciation would, if it successfully raised the relative price of traded goods in local currency terms, correct the payments deficit for:

(1) The higher relative price of traded goods reduces the demand for them and raises the demand for non-traded goods; point C moves northwestwards.
(2) Production of traded goods would rise as the higher relative price increases profitability in that sector. The reverse happens to profitability in the non-traded goods sector; point P moves southeastwards.

The equilibrium relative price $t_1 t_1$, is where production is at P_1 and consumption at C_1; with $P_1 = C_1$, the balance of payments

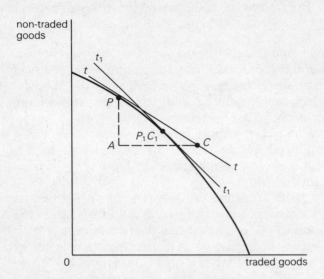

Figure 11.2   Balance of payments adjustment with resource mobility

deficit is removed and, as the country is producing on its production possibility curve there is no unemployment.[2]

Structuralist and Other Criticisms

A general point that is often raised with regard to currency depreciation is that it can be quickly offset by inflation: successive devaluations cause excessive inflation. Empirical evidence, however, shows that nominal exchange rate depreciation does generally cause the real exchange rate to depreciate, even after three years, so that devaluation can alter the relative prices of traded and non-traded goods (Donovan, 1981, and references therein).

Structuralist arguments against currency depreciation usually revolve around factors such as *import dependence* and *resource immobility*, particularly between the traded and non-traded goods sectors. These can be treated as arguing that the production possibility curve is degenerate: in the extreme case of zero resource mobility, it becomes a rectangular box with one corner at the point where domestic production just happens currently to lie. Resources cannot be reallocated from the non-traded goods to the traded goods sector (an important adjustment mechanism in the case made above for the effectiveness of currency depreciation).

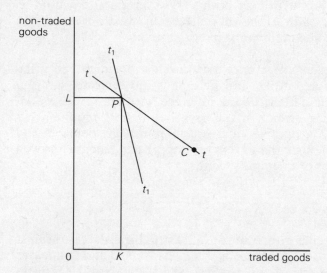

Figure 11.3   Balance of payments adjustment with resource immobility

In figure 11.3, where the rectangular production possibility curve reflects the assumption of perfect resource immobility, production and consumption are initially at *P* and *C* respectively with a payments deficit. An appropriately chosen devaluation could reduce consumption of traded goods and, at *P*, the payments deficit would be removed. However, the whole burden of this adjustment is on the consumption of traded goods. This is unwelcome, structuralists argue, in circumstances such as:

(1) *Food import dependence:* reduced availability and higher price of food has *inegalitarian* income-distributional consequences as the poor spend a larger proportion of their income on food than do the rich.
(2) *Input–import dependence* (where imported capital goods etc. are vital to the domestic economy): reduced availability of traded goods would:
    (a) if vital to production of non-traded goods, move production to a point somewhere on the line *PK* – there would be unemployment in the non-traded goods sector;
    (b) if vital to production of traded goods, move production to a point somewhere on the line *LP* with unemployment in traded goods sector;

(c) if vital to production in both sectors, production would lie somewhere within the degenerate production possibility curve with unemployment in both sectors.

Structuralists conclude, therefore, that devaluation might be inflationary, and, therefore, futile, and even if it did serve to reduce a balance of payments deficit, could interfere with the processes of development planning (which often lays out import requirements and, along with unfavourable domestic and foreign demand and supply elasticities, defines the extent of import dependence) as well as inducing high rates of unemployment.

Some Empirical Evidence

Empirical evidence tends *not* to support the structuralists' case against devaluation. Even so, the evidence is somewhat mixed and still leaves room for arguments against the application of 'standard' IMF packages to all ldc borrowers from the fund. For example, table 11.1 shows real export growth improved both in the short run (one year comparison) and long run (three year comparison) following devaluation. However, as in the case of other economic magnitudes, the improvements were not achieved in all of the 12 countries which had accepted IMF upper credit tranche loans during the 1970–6 period. For the group as a whole, real import growth actually increased following devaluation, a feature which reflects both the removal of certain import barriers and the improved (in the short run only) rate of real GDP growth. The improvement in the real trade balance is particularly sharp: in the three years prior to devaluation it worsened at a rate of 2.1 per cent per annum, to be turned around to improve at a rate of 2.5 per cent per annum in the subsequent three years. The turnaround was even sharper in the short run. However, where the success of IMF adjustment packages can be most seriously questioned is in relation to the reduction of inflation and impact on real GDP growth. Only marginal gains were made in reducing inflation, from a group inflation rate of 96 per cent of the average for non-oil ldcs one year before adjustment to only 89 per cent in the post-adjustment year; and in the long run the improvement was only marginally better than this – from 100 per cent to 87 per cent of the average. The performance of real GDP is even more questionable: while growth improved in the short run (from 80 per cent to 110 per cent of the average for non-oil ldcs), it worsened in the long run (from 87 per cent to 76 per cent of the average).

Table 11.1 Economic Performance Before and After Implementation of an IMF Adjustment Package During 1970-6[a] (per cent per annum)

	Before adjustment	% of world average	After adjustment	% of world average
Real exports (X)				
One-year comparison	−1.3	–	9.2	–
Three-year comparison	0.3	–	6.5	–
Real imports (M)				
One-year comparison	1.1	–	3.5	–
Three-year comparison	3.2	–	4.0	–
Real trade balance (M − X)				
One-year comparison	2.4	–	−5.1	–
Three-year comparison	2.1	–	−2.5	–
Inflation				
One-year comparison	14.3	96	15.7	89
Three-year comparison	12.8	100	17.3	87
Real GDP				
One-year comparison	3.5	80	5.6	110
Three-year comparison	4.5	87	3.9	76

Source: Donovan (1981).

Note: [a]Twelve countries agreeing to implement IMF adjustment packages, including devaluation.

Adjustment and Income Distribution

Devaluation

The effect of devaluation on income distribution is not at all clear despite structuralist claims that devaluation will have inegalitarian effects on income distribution. In a simple one sector, two class (wage-earners and capitalists) model where all goods are traded goods, devaluation raises the profitability of exporting by raising the domestic currency price of exportables relative to nominal wages. This would be likely to redistribute income in an inegalitarian direction. However, matters are not as simple as this, as consideration of a two sector (traded and non-traded goods), three class (wage-earners, traded good sector capitalists and non-traded good capitalists) model shows.[3]

Devaluation will reduce the balance of payments deficit if resources can be squeezed out of the non-traded goods sector and put to work in the traded goods sector producing exports and/or import substitutes. This movement of resources will come about if profitability in the traded goods sector rises relative to that of the non-traded goods sector. Devaluation raises the domestic currency price of tradeables, and profits in the traded goods sector will rise if output-prices rise relative to input-prices (assumed to be made up entirely of nominal wage costs). Reduced profitability in the non-traded goods sector occurs as wages rise relative to the prices of non-traded goods.

Hence, the effect of devaluation on the real wage is ambiguous.[4] If non-traded goods take up a large share of wage earners' consumption, the effect of devaluation on the real wage may not be to reduce it and it might even increase! But, it might be asked, since an effective devaluation requires a rise in exports relative to national income, where is the consumption squeeze felt? The answer must be: if not on real wages, then on capitalists' profits in the non-traded goods sector.

Further complications in the analysis of the effect of devaluation on income distribution can be seen by referring to the literature of development economics. As before, devaluation works by altering the *internal* terms of trade in favour of the traded goods sector. This ratio is also known as the 'up-country terms of trade' and is regarded as being important to economic growth performance in less developed countries (Myint, 1964). The non-traded goods sector, or the 'traditional sector', is known to be made up of several classes – landless labourers, self-employed farmers and petty tradesmen and labour-employing capitalistic farmers, to mention just three. Nor is the traded-goods sector, or the 'modern sector', any less complex, with labour itself passing through a spectrum of classes from the newly arrived urban non-wage-earning migrant subsistence labourer to the fully wage dependent longer-established urban worker (Sinclair, 1978).

To promote economic growth the internal terms of trade would have to be turned against the traditional sector so that economic surpluses could be extracted for investment in the modern sector. A similar process is at work when devaluation is used to correct a balance of payments deficit. The deficit represents net foreign investment in the country – use of foreigners' savings – and an effective devaluation will have the effect of replacing this net foreign investment with surpluses extracted from the domestic economy. *A priori* it is quite impossible to tell which classes – rich or poor – will benefit or suffer from the devaluation. The outcome depends upon too many factors. For example, if agricultural crops are sold only or mainly on local markets, as in Indonesia and Bolivia, the relatively higher price of traded goods will tend to squeeze real incomes in the farming sector; but if a large proportion of crops are exported, as in Ghana, farming sector real incomes will tend to rise following a devaluation (Johnson and Salop, 1980).

Such is the complexity of the income distributional effects of devaluation in ldcs, together with the array of fiscal measures which governments can, and do, employ along with a devaluation, that the outcome for income distribution is likely to be more a matter of political choice than the workings of crude economic forces. Devaluations in Latin America might have produced inegalitarian outcomes because the military dictatorships in power there favour the rich, while the more egalitarian results of devaluations observed in Malaysia may be explained by the observation that the poorer income groups there are better represented in government (Cline, 1983).

Credit and Fiscal Policies

As a part of an adjustment package the IMF usually couples restrictive credit and fiscal policies with devaluation. The array of fiscal policies that can be deployed to reduce government expenditure and/ or raise public sector income is broad, and the choice will sometimes have clear income-distributional consequences. Reduced price subsidies, particularly on food, will tend to reduce the real income of the poor more than that of the rich. But other considerations are also important, as Johnson and Salop (1980) have pointed out. If egalitarian objectives are important, deep cuts may be made in the income of high-ranking, relatively highly paid, civil servants. The incidence of higher taxes is another critical consideration: the egalitarian element resulting from an IMF devaluation-budget balancing package will be increased when the government chooses to levy increased taxes on the higher income earning groups in society. Similarly, with credit policies the government's choice of policy-composition is important. Policies taken to reduce the extent of 'financial dualism' (Myint, 1971 – see also the references to McKinnon later in this chapter) where cheap credit is channelled to large firms and higher income groups in the urban sector at the expense of higher interest rates charged to rural, poorer, borrowers, if they can borrow at all, will have the effect of moving income distribution in an egalitarian direction by removing a regressive interest rate subsidy to the rich.

Distortions and Economic Performance

IMF thinking on the selection of adjustment policies is guided not only by macroeconomic models of balance of payments adjustment, but also by microeconomic considerations. The key microeconomic consideration is that price distortions, especially negative real interest rates and over-valued real exchange rates, are detrimental to efficient resources allocation and, ultimately, economic growth performance. However, IMF attempts, through loan conditionality clauses, to make prices reflect scarcity value, often run into a barrage of criticisms. The main problem is that vested interests in ldcs, especially in import-competing sectors, which are effectively subsidized by cheap capital funding and cheap foreign exchange, are close to government and, naturally, complain when they see that the subsidies might be taken away.

In this section we shall discuss, first, theoretically, why distorted real interest rates and real exchange rates are economically detrimental; and secondly, we shall show empirically that, generally, countries which have experienced relatively few price distortions have experienced higher rates of economic growth. The empirical evidence is relevant to the discussion over choice of trade-bias regime. Export promotion (competition on world markets) is usually associated with relatively low levels of price-distortion, while import substitution (behind tariff walls) deliberately introduces price distortions to the economy.

Negative Real Interest Rates

For optimality, interest rates should be at the level where savers' time preference (the rate of interest at which future consumption is discounted) is equal to the rate of return on investment. Since consumption is unlikely to have reached satiation point in any ldc, time preference must still be positive – at the margin present consumption is preferred over future consumption and real deposit and borrowing interest rates should be positive. Only investment projects which yield positive real rates of return should be undertaken. Accordingly, when real rates of interest are observed to be negative a distortion is likely to be present. In a sample of 37 ldcs taken in June 1979 all but six countries had negative real deposit rates of interest (IMF 1983b).

Negative real interest rates are often associated with financial repression (McKinnon, 1973; Shaw, 1973). Government regulations over the private sector financial system can be so severe as to reduce the efficiency of private intermediation as a conduit between savers and investors. Reserve requirements imposed on the commercial banks – the major component of the private financial sector in ldcs – can be extremely high, perhaps in the order of 50 per cent or more. High reserve ratios (with the commercial banks required to hold low- or zero-interest earning public debt with the central bank) act as a tax on these banks and enable the central bank and the government to obtain a part of the private sector's economic surplus, which is held in liquid form with the banks owing to the narrowness of capital markets. In these circumstances, a strong positive relationship between the bank's *real* lending rate of interest and the rate of inflation, as well as a negative relationship between inflation and the *real* deposit rate of interest has been shown to exist (McKinnon, 1981). When inflation is high the government effectively imposes an inflation tax on the banks' reserve holdings as well as all holders of local currency. If the banks are to make modest profits, they must recoup this 'tax' from their clients – the depositors and the borrowers. This is done by means of a wide spread between the nominal rates of interest paid by the banks to depositors (which will be kept low) and those paid to the banks by borrowers (which will be correspondingly high). If inflation was to be higher still, the inflation tax on the banks' non-interest earning compulsory reserve assets will also be increased. So, again, the 'tax' must be recouped with an even larger spread between deposit and loan rates. Whatever financial surpluses are extracted from the banks – to finance fiscal deficits – must, in turn, be extracted from their clients. The principal inefficiency is that low real *deposit* rates of interest discourage saving while high real *loan* rates discourage borrowing and investment.

Overvalued Real Exchange Rates

A country's real exchange rate will become overvalued when its rate of price inflation relative to that of its trade partners exceeds the rate at which the nominal exchange rate is allowed to depreciate. This often happens, causing real exchange rate overvaluation, in ldcs. It has the effect of transferring income from the export sector (often agriculture) to the non-traded goods sector, so encouraging growth of the latter to the detriment of the former.

The persistence of overvalued real exchange rates requires the introduction of administrative means to allocate scarce foreign exchange resources, otherwise the excess demand for foreign currencies would cause nominal and real exchange rates to depreciate. However, the efficiency of such administrative allocations is questionable – even in a country such as India, which can boast a relatively well developed administrative infrastructure. A study of India's import licensing system showed that the authorities operate with far from complete information on optimal foreign exchange allocation; substitute administrative rules of thumb for economic criteria; are subjected to corruption; and impose long delays between application for and granting of import licenses (Bhagwati and Desai, 1970).

Price-distortions and Economic Performance: Evidence

Opposing views on the role of protectionism and government intervention in the economy and the choice of 'inward' or 'outward' looking development strategies have been referred to above. As the validity of these opposing arguments cannot be judged on theoretical grounds alone, appeal must be made to the empirical evidence. Fortunately several comprehensive cross-sectional studies have been made of the relationship between economic performance and economic policy in ldcs.

In an important study Agarwala (1984) tested the relationship between the degree of price-distortion and economic growth performance in a group of 31 ldcs. Price-distortion (in the sense of market prices not equal to marginal production costs) is difficult to measure, so proxy measures were devised. The proxies were the level of effective and nominal protection, the amount of deviation in real effective exchange rates from base period purchasing power parity, the degree of negativity of real interest rates, the level and amount of acceleration in inflation rates, qualitative assessments of distortions in labour markets, and the size of the downward squeeze on rates of return on marketable infrastructural services. In each of these categories, each country was classified as displaying high, medium or low distortion. The study found that low price-distortion countries had *higher* rates of economic growth, exports, savings propensity, return on investment and growth rates of agricultural and industrial sectors than did either the high or medium price-distortion countries. Another important finding was that, if anything, high price-distortion was associated with *more unequal* income distribution.

Balassa (1978) studied the relationship between export incentives, export growth and economic growth in eleven ldcs in the period 1960–73. The findings support the view that export orientated, minimal protectionist – low price distortion – economic policies promote growth of both exports and GDP. During 1966–73 export growth was highest in the three ldcs which most nearly approached the free trade model (Singapore, Taiwan and Korea[5]). In the earlier period, 1960–6, the five countries with the highest incremental export–output ratios also had the highest growth rates of manufacturing, while the two countries with the lowest also had the lowest manufacturing growth rate. Krueger (1978), in a study of ten ldcs, also found a positive statistical relationship between the growth rate of exports and the growth of GDP. Moreover, those countries which adopted export promotion policies were shown to experience more rapid growth rates of manufactured exports.

Balassa (1982) repeated the earlier study for a group of 19 sub-Saharan African countries with broadly similar findings. Countries which could be described as broadly 'market orientated' (nine in number) coped with the effect of the 1973 oil price shock much better than did 'interventionist countries' (ten in number). The latter group resorted to considerably enhanced levels of external borrowing, running their debt service ratio up to 24 per cent in 1978 compared with 11 per cent in 1973, a deterioration that was worsened by declining shares of their export markets. 'Market orientated' countries *improved* export market shares considerably and by this means alone financed over 40 per cent of the adverse balance of payments effects caused by the external (oil price) shock. Their debt service ratio actually *fell* from 14 per cent in 1973 to 12.5 per cent in 1978.

Improved export performance by 12 ldcs which have pursued progressively more open trade policies has been shown by Havrylyshyn and Alikhani (1983). This group is following about a decade behind the original 12 newly industrializing countries. Indeed, seven of the nine which happen to be included on Agarwala's distortion index show low degrees of price-distortion. In fact, the above citations support findings published by Kravis as long ago as 1970. He showed that in the 1960s the ldcs which experienced rapid export growth did so because they competitively increased market shares in traditionally exported goods markets as well as successfully diversified into the export of new products. Those ldcs which failed to increase competitiveness or to restructure exports also failed to achieve satisfactorily high rates of export growth.

The Order of Liberalization

While it has been argued that low-distortion economies have 'performed' better than high-distortion economies it does not necessarily follow that the *immediate* removal of all distortion creating policies is desirable. Rather, some thought must be given to the sequential order in which economic reforms are best implemented.

The critical financial features of many Third World countries, especially in the 'Southern Cone' of Latin America during the 1970s and into the 1980s, were:

(1)   A large fiscal deficit of 20 per cent or more of GDP.
(2)   High rates of monetary expansion and inflation reaching 800 per cent per annum or more.
(3)   High real and nominal loan rates and low deposit rates of interest.
(4)   An export sector suffering from an over-valued real exchange rate.
(5)   A proliferation of controls over foreign trade and inward and outward capital flows.

These financial problems stem largely from the persistence of large fiscal deficits. As was pointed out earlier in this chapter, the government obtains funds in addition to tax receipts and other incidental income by requiring private banks to hold zero or low nominal interest earning reserve requirements. With high rates of inflation the 'tax' on the banks (and holders of domestic currency) is high and, for reason of sustaining profitability, they must open a gap between their loan and deposit rates of interest. Faced with these interest rates the natural response of the non-bank public would be to turn to international capital and money markets where deposit rates of interest are higher and loan rates lower.

The problem that this private sector response induces, however, is that the size of the 'inflation tax' base – local currency and local currency deposits with the domestic banking system – is narrowed. A higher 'inflation tax' rate is needed to finance a given fiscal deficit and inflation must accelerate further.

For democratic governments the foregoing are symptoms of a terminal illness: military dictatorships took over in Chile in 1973 and Argentina in 1976, and in many other Latin American countries one military government has followed another. Usually the new governments promise to restore economic and financial stability as a means of legitimizing their ascent to power.

There are four broad areas where reform measures need to be taken:

(1)   internal finance, especially the fiscal deficit and the 'inflation tax';
(2)   exchange rate policy:
(3)   liberalization of foreign trade;
(4)   liberalization of exchange controls.

It may seem to be desirable immediately to remove controls on international capital movements, thus allowing residents to borrow abroad and so provide funds for capital accumulation and to contribute towards financing the fiscal deficit. McKinnon (1982) and Edwards (1984) among others have argued that such an approach would be disastrous. First, capital inflow would cause the exchange rate to appreciate and the wrong resource reallocation signal to be given. The non-traded goods sector would tend to expand and the traded goods sector contract. Additionally, capital inflow would tend to worsen the borrowing country's debt service problem.

Secondly, capital outflow would increase as residents sought to diversity their portfolios. As residents could now choose to hold foreign currency, the domestic currency base upon which the inflation tax is levied would narrow. As a consequence of this, with the fiscal deficit still large, the rate of 'tax', or, 'inflation', would have to increase again.

Perhaps the best explanation of the correct order of financial liberalization is provided by McKinnon (1982). Figure 11.4 and the following discussion is based upon this. Financial reform should begin where the financial problems are ultimately derived – the fiscal deficit. The deficit is the factor driving inflation and causing policies to be adopted which repress domestic finance and require the imposition of foreign exchange controls. Accordingly, in figure 11.4 phase I in the order of liberalization begins with the government significantly reducing the fiscal deficit to perhaps one per cent of GDP or less. If this is achieved the government's need to borrow from the domestic banking system declines, and the high reserve requirement can be much reduced. This in turn will allow the banks to lessen the wedge between their deposit and loan rates.

In figure 11.4 it can be seen that during phase I, even though inflation has begun to fall, it still far exceeds the world rate. Phase II – the initiation of a trade reform programme – is the next step in reducing inflation towards the world level. With the removal of tariffs and quotas commodity arbitrage can begin to exert its influence on the domestic price level: the importables sector will be opened up to the discipline of foreign competition.

Until phase III exchange rate policy has been passive with the nominal rate roughly following the rate of inflation. But now exchange rate policy should become active, the objective being to influence inflationary expectations and so to bring the rate of inflation down. The government should pre-announce a schedule of intended nominal exchange rates setting the currency on a downward crawl of diminishing size. If inflationary expectations are led

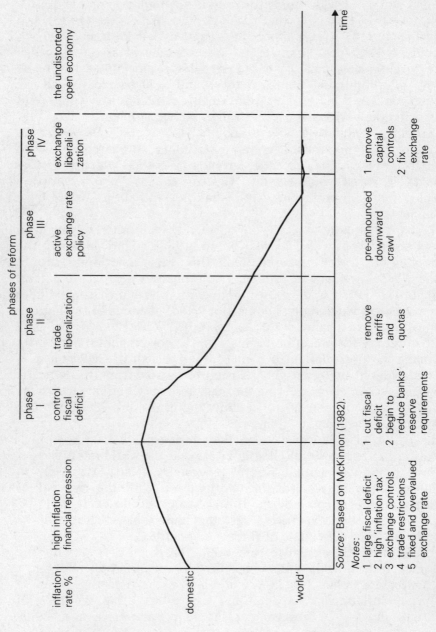

Figure 11.4 The order of financial liberalization

downwards, inflation should also fall, so the real exchange rate should not become over-valued.

Finally, in phase IV, when domestic inflation has converged with the world rate of inflation, the exchange rate should be fixed and exchange liberalization can be put into effect. With the 'inflation tax' only a memory, the banks' reserve requirements will not need to be set at abnormally high levels and the wedge between the commercial banks' loan and deposit rates will have narrowed appreciably. Capital flows, inwards as well as outwards, will no longer distort the exchange rate or interfere with a process of inflationary financing which is anyway not required. Now, with an 'open' capital account, capital flows will regulate the rate of domestic monetary expansion in a way that should keep domestic inflation close to the world rate.

Notes

1 From the equation set and the earlier discussion, it can be deduced that the growth of money supply (M_0) depends upon the increase in exports, the multiplier effect of increased exports on income, and the velocity of circulation of money (V) which determines by how much money must grow to obtain a constant V at the higher income level. Thus:

$$\Delta M_0 = \Delta X \times \frac{Y}{M} \times \frac{M_0}{Y}$$

Therefore:

$$\Delta M_0 = \Delta X \times \frac{M_0}{M}$$

Since DCE is assumed here to be zero, the increase in M_0 is entirely in the form of increased foreign exchange reserves. Hence, the growth in foreign exchange reserves is determined by export growth and the ratio of money supply to imports.

2 Two further points are relevant to the adjustment process. First, currency depreciation will have the effect of reducing the real value of the money supply, and this induced 'expenditure reducing' effect will also tend to improve the balance of payments. Flexible prices are needed to maintain full employment. Secondly, in figure 11.2, with production and consumption at their initial levels (P, C) there is an excess supply of non-traded goods equal to PA; the downward pressure on the relative price of non-traded goods would have resource allocation and consumption allocation effects similar to that of currency depreciation.

3 Labour is assumed to be mobile between sectors while capitalists are not.

4 The real wage can be calculated as the nominal wage index divided *by* the index of the weighted average price level, where the weights, correspond to the share of traded and non-traded goods in wage-earners' consumption. Cline (1983) provides the following equation from which the effect of devaluation on real wages can be calculated.

$$\dot{w}^* = \dot{w} - a_T d - a_{NT} \dot{P}_{NT}$$

where $\dot{w}^*$ is the percentage change in the real wage, $\dot{w}$ is the percentage rise in the nominal wage, a_T the share of tradeables, a_{NT} the share of non-tradeables and d is the percentage devaluation.

5 The view that Korean economic performance has been improved by the adoption of export promotion policies and low degrees of price distortion is supported by the findings of Westphal (1978) and Kincaid (1983).

12   International Debt

This chapter provides an analysis and a record of the events which culminated in the international debt crisis of the late summer of 1982 when the largest debtor country – Mexico – could no longer service its debts on the contractual terms to which it had agreed. Mexican debts had to be rescheduled by the several hundred international banks which had made loans to it and this was then quickly followed by 25 other reschedulings concerning mainly Third World countries.

The chapter is divided into 11 sections. The first provides a theoretical description of the proximate causes of the growth of national and governmental international indebtedness. As the two 'oil price shocks' of 1973 and 1979–80 are major contemporary events contributing to the growth of international indebtedness, especially among the non-oil less developed countries, their impact is assessed in two sections and Third World debt prior to 1973 described. Comecon debt is also briefly assessed. Measures of the burden of debt service – repayment of interest and principal – are also considered and the debt service ratio (debt service–export earnings) explained. Capital 'flight' has increased the difficulty of servicing foreign debts for several Latin American governments, and this subject is scrutinized.

The final three sections of the chapter consider some important issues from the side of the international banks. Why did they go on lending to the debtor countries even as the debt problem was obviously becoming unmanageable on the terms originally agreed? A following section points out that the debt crisis is 'systems-related', i.e. it is one of the international banking system and probably could not have arisen if loans had been raised by the issue of bonds rather than through the raising of bank loans. The final section considers three views of the nature of the debt 'crisis' as well as some proposals for its solution.

Some Theory

The increase in a *country's* net foreign indebtedness is equal to the sum of the current account deficit and net long-term capital inflow. The proximate causes of the first component, the current account deficit, are:

$$(M - X) = (I - S) + (G - T) + R_F \tag{12.1}$$

where R_F is net interest paid on foreign indebtedness and the other symbols have their usual meaning.[1] Hence, if the long-term capital account is balanced, net foreign indebtedness will increase if the private and governmental sectors taken together are in financial-flow deficit and this deficit is not offset by net interest *earnings*. Indeed, if a debtor's interest payments are not to be capitalized – that is, added to debt outstanding – net interest payments need to be offset by a financial-flow *surplus* on private and government account.

Anything which causes I to rise relative to S, or G relative to T – such as an increase in the propensities to consume or of government spending respectively – will tend to increase the size of the current account deficit as will a rise in the rate of interest paid on foreign loans. These elements in the worsening debt position of nine Latin American countries are discussed in some detail below.

We also desire to show the proximate causes of increased *governmental* foreign net indebtedness (i.e. public and publicly guaranteed debt), as a country's 'debt problem' can be more that of governmental debt than of national net indebtedness. The proximate causes of increased governmental indebtedness are derived in the following way:

$$\Delta F = BoP = \text{current account} + \text{capital account} \atop \text{surplus} \qquad \text{surplus} \tag{12.2}$$

where ΔF is the increase in offocial foreign exchange reserves, and *BoP* the balance of payments on official settlements account. The capital account surplus can be decomposed into three elements yielding:

$$\Delta F = BoP = \text{current} + \text{net long term} + \text{government} \atop \text{account} \quad \text{private capital} \quad \text{foreign} \atop \text{surplus} \quad \text{inflow} \quad \text{borrowing}$$
$$- \text{gross private short-term} \atop \text{capital outflow} \tag{12.3}$$

Rearranging (12.3) yields, what we are interested in is:

government = current + ΔF + gross private short-term
foreign   account   capital outflow
borrowing   deficit

               − net long-term
                 private capital
                 inflow   (12.4)

Hence, a government's foreign borrowing will, *ceteris paribus*, be greater, the larger is the current account deficit, or the increase in foreign exchange reserves or gross private capital outflow, and the smaller is the level of net long-term capital inflow. However, the increase in a country's *net* foreign indebtedness is determined only by the sum of the current account deficit and net long-term capital inflow, as both an increase in reserves and gross private capital outflow provide the country with offsetting claims on foreign resources. Looked at another way, a government's foreign borrowing may be offset to some extent by the sum of the increase in foreign exchange reserves and gross private capital outflow. However, in practice it can matter a lot which of these latter two items predominates as far as a government's debt service 'problem' is concerned. If gross private capital outflow is large a government may still face debt service difficulties even though net indebtedness had not increased by very much. This is simply because it was unable to use the interest-income earned by residents on their foreign private investments to service public and publicly guaranteed foreign debts.

Measuring the Debt Burden

Various measures have been devised to gauge the extent of the burden of debt and debt service on borrowing countries. One of the most important is the ratio of a country's debt service (interest and repayment of maturing debt) on public and publicly guaranteed debt to annual export earnings. This is *the* debt service ratio. But quoting Dornbusch (1984) on the experience of just one major debtor country: 'the Brazilian experience brings out particularly clearly the fact that we do not have a sensible model of the optimal level of external debt'. However, a high debt service ratio can mean that a country is vulnerable to adverse changes in its foreign trade sector. A sudden fall in export earnings or rise in expenditure on 'necessary' imports (caused by a crop failure or higher oil import prices, for example) may leave a country with few substitution possiblities because of the large fixed nominal obligation to service foreign loans. Default on debt service payments may be threatened and this in turn would prejudice potential creditors against future loans. Then, without access to foreign loans and savings, a country's rate of economic growth would be constrained by the level of domestic savings.

A problem with these proxy measures for the debt burden, however, is that they often do not reflect the whole complex of factors which determine a country's ability to service its outstanding debts.

The ability to increase export earnings is clearly a major factor that determines whether an external debt service obligation becomes a burden. A country may be able to earn insufficient foreign exchange because of structural factors such as inelastic foreign demand for its exports or immobile domestic resources which prevent a rapid expansion of the export sector. A high degree of unforeseen fluctuation in export earnings makes external debt management difficult, especially when foreign exchange reserves – owned or borrowable – are small. Again, structural factors such as foreign demand elasticity and lengthy domestic supply gestation periods are important here, as are fluctuations in the level of foreign demand associated with the business cycle. Moreover, attempts to stabilize market prices by the use of quotas or buffer stocks have been unsuccessful. Nor have compensatory finance arrangements such as the IMF's Compensatory Finance Facility or the EEC's Stabex done anything like enough to compensate developing countries during periods of shortfalls in export earnings.

The willingness of existing lenders to roll-over maturing debt is important to a country's ability to service debt and to manage a high debt service ratio (see 'the lenders' trap' below). For a long time oil-rich Mexico, with high potential foreign exchange earnings, had little difficulty in rolling-over debt while countries with bleak export potential suffered great difficulties in servicing relatively small debts because new loans could not be raised on a sufficiently large scale.

The term structure of debt repayments also impinges on the debt burden question. For example, when repayments are bunched in time, a temporary decline in export earnings could set off a debt crisis if banks were discouraged from making new loans by current difficulties to repay these debts. A more disbursed term structure of debt repayment would be preferred to a bunched pattern.

Debt Service Ratios

Notwithstanding these difficulties, table 12.1 shows the debt service ratio for each of 21 major ldc borrowers in 1983. At 154 per cent

Table 12.1 Debt Service Ratios and Estimated Gross External Debt and Debt Service of 21 Major LDC Borrowers

	Gross external debt at end-1982 $ billions	Debt service in 1983, % of exports[a]	
		Total	Excluding rollover of short-term debt
Latin America			
Argentine	38.0	154	88
Brazil	85.5	117	67
Chile	17.2	104	54
Colombia	10.3	95	38
Ecuador	6.6	102	58
Mexico	80.1	126	59
Peru	11.5	79	47
Venezuela	29.5	101	25
Subtotal	278.7	117	56
Asia			
Indonesia	25.4	28	14
Korea	36.0	49	17
Malaysia	10.4	15	7
Philippines	16.6	79	33
Taiwan	9.3	19	6
Thailand	11.0	50	19
Subtotal	108.7	36	14
Middle East and Africa			
Algeria	16.3	35	30
Egypt	19.2	46	16
Israel	26.7	126	26
Ivory Coast	9.2	76	34
Morocco	10.3	65	36
Nigeria	9.3	28	14
Turkey	22.8	65	20
Subtotal	113.8	58	16
Total of 21 ldcs	501.2	71	30

[a] Interest on gross debt plus all maturing debt, including amortization of medium- and long-term debt and all short-term debt as percent of exports of goods and services, including net private transfer payments.

Source: Morgan Guaranty (February 1983).

Argentina's debt service ratio meant that annual interest payments and repayment of maturing debt far outstripped the country's annual total export earnings. Even when short-term debt – which could be somewhat uncertainly assumed to be automatically 'rolled over' by the lending banks – is netted out, Argentina's debt service ratio was still 88 per cent.

At one time – in the 1950s – the major lending institutions such as The World Bank thought that a 15 per cent debt service ratio was about the *highest* that a debtor country could safely go. By that standard all but one of the countries in table 12.1 faced severe debt service difficulties in the 1980s. Two related points are: first, while debt service ratios were high in all 21 countries listed in table 12.1, they were highest in Latin America; it is true that the 'debt crisis' was mainly of Latin American borrowers and the international banks which had made loans to that continent. Secondly, international debt is highly concentrated by borrowing country: these 21 countries accounted for about five-sixths of all ldc debt outstanding. The rest of the non-oil ldcs – 70 or 80 countries – carry relatively little external debt. What debt they do owe is mainly to official lenders – governments and the World Bank and its offshoots such as the IFC – for the international banks have never found them to be an acceptable credit risk.

At the most highly aggregative level, it is easy to see why debt service ratios came to be so high. Unless real interest rates were to fall enough – and they increased in the 1980s – the debt service ratio must increase if the growth rate of total external debt is higher than that of exports. Of the 21 major ldc debtors, in all but five cases in the six years prior to summer 1982 debt growth easily outstripped export growth. (Moreover, in three of the five exceptions, export earnings were to suffer from the effect of falling nominal and real oil export prices on the growth of their export earnings (Morgan Guaranty, June 1983).

Growth of Non-oil Less Developed Countries' Debt 1973–82

The growth of non-oil ldc debt during the period 1973–82 is shown in figure 12.1. The growth profile of total debt outstanding is steep, as is the 'bank loans' component. Grants and concessional loans from OECD countries increased very little over the period. The shifting proportion of bank loans (which rose) and official development assistance (which fell) is one reason for the worsening debt positions of the non-oil ldcs during the last 15 years or so. The terms and con-

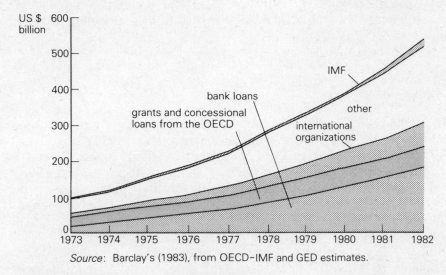

Source: Barclay's (1983), from OECD–IMF and GED estimates.

Figure 12.1 Growth of non-OPEC developing countries' debt (medium- and long-term

ditions – particularly interest rates and grace and amortization periods – are much less favourable on bank loans than on grants and loans from foreign governments.

Three of the most important external influences on the non-oil ldcs' deepening current account deficit during the 1973–82 period were: first, the sharp increase in oil prices in 1973 and again during the two years 1979 and 1980 (see discussion below); secondly, a sharp increase in real interest rates from 1980 onwards to historically high positive levels, reversing the circumstances of the mid-1970s when they had been negative; and thirdly, deterioration in their terms of trade. Improvement in the terms of trade after the first oil 'shock' had contributed to a reduction in the size of the current account deficits in the mid-1970s, but sharp deterioration recurred as oil prices again increased at the end of that decade and the world economic slump of 1980–2 deepened.

Rising debt service ratios increased the perceived riskiness of bank lending to ldcs and the rate of growth of gross bank claims on these countries fell very sharply from almost 40 per cent per annum in 1978 to about 20 per cent in 1982. Interest payments were also rising. This latter development was reflective both of the worldwide disinflationary process beginning in the early 1980s and of higher risk-related markups on loans to ldcs. The combination of these developments led to *net* financial transfers to ldcs becoming severely squeezed.

Comecon Debt

The debt problems of these countries, as a group, have never been so serious as those of Third World countries, in particular the Latin American group. The ratio of total debt to (hard currency) export earnings in Latin American peaked at almost 400 per cent in 1983, but reached only about 210 per cent for the Comecon group in 1978. Between that date and 1984 the debt service ratio of each of the seven Comecon countries fell and is, anyway, generally much lower than for the most of the 21 less developed countries listed in table 12.1. However, both Poland – on several occasions – and Rumania have had to have their debt repayments rescheduled and Hungary has had to resort to IMF and BIS 'bridging' loans. Despite these experiences, however, the Comecon countries took action earlier and have been more successful in coping with their external debt obligations and – Poland apart – have not been too worrisome a problem for the international banks.

The Transfer Problem and the First Oil Shock (1973)

The impact of higher oil prices in 1973 on the oil importers' debt position can be analysed within the context of the co-called 'transfer problem' model. J. M. Keynes and B. Ohlin discussed the transfer problem with reference to Germany's First World War reparations payments. They debated how a *financial* transfer of war reparations levied on Germany would result in a *real* transfer of resources to the recipient countries. A 'financial transfer' is nothing more than a running up of foreign debt – an issue of 'IOUs'. But with a 'real transfer', real resources (and services) are internationally transferred and debts are either not run-up or are paid off.

The balance of payments effect of the sharp rise in oil prices in 1973 can be viewed similarly. The sudden rise in oil prices acted like a tax upon the oil-importing countries payable to the members of the OPEC. In equation 12.1, the real oil price rise increased the current account payments deficit as expenditure on imports rose with the higher price of imported oil. On the right hand side of that equation, higher expenditure on oil served to increase the combined financial flow deficit of the private and public sectors. The counterpart to the larger current account payments deficit was – in equation 12.4 – increasing government net indebtedness as the current account deficit increased and foreign exchange reserves were run down.

OPEC members meanwhile were experiencing large current account surpluses and so accumulated claims on foreign resources. They made large deposits of surplus dollar earnings with the international banks which played an intermediary role between the oil-exporter creditor nations and the oil-importer debtors to whom the banks made loans. The role of the Eurocurrency banking system in the international intermediation of funds between nations is discussed in chapter 10.

However, these financial transfers to OPEC could result in real transfers in the same direction only if the oil importers began to correct their current account deficits. Until such time the oil price 'tax' would be paid by international borrowing – ultimately, mainly out of OPEC's very own payments surpluses deposited with the international banks. The size of the oil price 'tax' in real terms was large: the non-oil ldcs' terms of trade *vis-à-vis* the oil exporters had deteriorated sharply from an index value of 100 in 1973 to only 40 in 1974. The oil importers needed to export 2.5 times by volume as many goods and services per barrel of imported oil in order to pay for the more expensive oil imports without incurring further increases in their foreign debts. As far as the non-oil ldcs were concerned, they did not make real transfers of resources to the oil exporters in 1974 or 1975, but they began to do so in 1976. Such was the extent of the reduction in their current account deficits that a large real transfer had been accomplished as early as 1977 (Hallwood and Sinclair, 1981). These developments helped to alleviate somewhat the non-oil ldcs' growing debt problem.

The Second Oil Shock (1979–80) and its Aftermath

Such was the success of the non-oil ldcs in cutting their current account deficits in the mid-1970s and the efficiency of the international banking systems in recycling 'petro-currency' – as the oil exporters' deposits with them became known – that the call on IMF standby purchases was much reduced. Indeed, one monetary expert quipped that the IMF in 1978 had become an 'academic institution'! But 1979 heralded the second oil 'shock'.

In 1978 'marker crude' stood at $12.70 per barrel, increasing to $32.00 in 1980 – as it happened a smaller percentage increase than during 1973. However, while earlier in the decade the non-oil ldcs were able to avoid a debt crisis, this time they did not.

There are four main reasons why the events of 1979 and the early 1980s led to a major debt 'crisis' while those of 1973 and the mid-1970s had not. First, in the earlier period world inflation was high and accelerating and real interest rates paid by debtors fell and eventually became negative, but the reverse was true in the early 1980s as the world economy moved into a disinflationary phase. Secondly, the world economic recession of 1975 was neither so deep nor so prolonged as that of 1981–2, so debtor country export earnings did not suffer so badly as in the later period. Thirdly, debt service ratios were lower in the earlier period. Finally, the first oil shock happened to coincide with peak levels of non-oil ldc real foreign exchange reserves which both encouraged banks to lend and provided a reserve of funds with which they could purchase imports.

Table 12.2 shows that the world recession 1981–2 is estimated to have contributed about $100 billion to the increase in the non-oil ldcs' debt outstanding of $482 billion between 1973 and 1982) as relative commodity export *unit values* (the terms of trade) and *volume* declined. Higher real interest rates contributed another $41 billion. But Cline (1984) estimated that over the period end-1973 to 1982 as a whole it was higher real oil prices which were the single largest proximate cause of the non-oil ldcs' growing external debts – contributing some $260 billion.

Table 12.2 The Effect of Exogenous Shocks on the External Debt of Non-oil ldcs

Effect	Amount ($ billion)
Oil-price increases in excess of US inflation, 1974–82 cumulative	260
Real interest rate in excess of 1961–80 average: 1981 and 1982	41
Terms of trade loss 1981–2	79
Export volume loss caused by world recession, 1981–2	21
Total	401
Memorandum items	
Total debt: 1973	130
1982	612
Increase: 1973–82	482

Source: Cline (1984).

Foreign Borrowing and Capital 'Flight'

In the late 1970s in the Southern Cone of Latin America (Argentina, Chile and Uruguay) capital flows – inward as well as outward – were largely freed of restrictive regulations. An important outcome was that there was a massive surge of capital inflow into these countries – well in excess of the needs to finance the current account deficits. In Argentina's case, between 1978 and 1983, foreign indebtedness increased by $36 billion, which was much more than the aggregate, $13 billion, current account deficit for these years (Morgan Guaranty, 1985). In the case of Chile, capital inflow surged from $1.25 billion in 1979 to $4.5 billion in 1981, during which time the current account remained in surplus (Edwards, 1985). For Latin America (excluding Central America), during 1978–83 new foreign borrowing exceeded the current account deficit plus changes in official reserves by $50 billion. (Bank for International Settlements, 1984.) Why did this happen and where did the excess funds go go?

The release of pent-up domestic demand for foreign loans brought about by financial liberalization was the main reason for the surge in foreign borrowing by Southern Cone countries. Capital flight largely accounts for the excess of capital inflow over the needs of current account financing plus any foreign exchange reserve accumulation. These two apparently contradictory events – a combined surge in capital inflow and outflow – are quite easily explained.

Following Edwards (1984) the amount of capital inflow during a given year, ΔK_t, is determined in the model:

$$\Delta K_t = \min \, [\theta \, (D_t^* - D_{t-1}), \overline{\Delta K_t}] \tag{12.5}$$

where D_t^* is the desired level of foreign debt (which for simplicity is assumed to bear a positive and stable relationship with a growing level of real GNP) and D_{t-1} is the actual stock of foreign debt. The θ term is a one-period partial adjustment factor. The symbol $\overline{\Delta K_t}$ is the increase in foreign debt allowed by government regulations. Capital inflow will be the lower – or minimum – of $\theta(D_t^* - D_{t-1})$ and $\overline{\Delta K_t}$.

Assuming that capital-import controls have been binding for some time, a gap will have grown between the desired and actual levels of foreign debt as in each previous period $\theta(D_t^* - D_{t-1}) > \overline{\Delta K_t}$. When the capital account is liberalized, foreign capital borrowing will surge by the amount $\theta(D_t^* - D_{t-1})$. However, gradually the difference between the actual and desired foreign debt levels will narrow as foreign debt accumulates and, with a constant θ, capital inflow will decline from its temporarily 'over-shot' level to approach the long-run growth rate determined by the rate of growth of GNP.

An important effect of capital inflow overshooting is that it will cause the exchange rate to appreciate and also to overshoot. However, the sudden, large, appreciation can reasonably be expected to be followed by depreciation as the level of capital inflow begins to decline. Hence, on the basis of Edwards' model, the overvalued exchange rates which were observed in much of Latin America during the late 1970s and early 1980s were (in part at least) *equilibrium responses* to the political act of liberalization of foreign exchange markets.

Capital flight can be explained within this foreign indebtedness stock-adjustment model. Since the exchange rate can be expected to depreciate from the temporarily overshot level, some domestic wealth-holders – including foreign multinational corporations – will diversify into foreign assets, so sending capital abroad. This is capital flight and will occur if $C > (i_d - i_f)$, where C is the expected rate of currency depreciation and i_d and i_f are the domestic and foreign deposit rates of interest. It will be recalled from the discussion in chapter 11 that in a financially repressed country the domestic deposit rate of interest is likely to be very low.

As far as the growth of foreign indebtedness is concerned capital flight has two important implications. First, of lesser importance in relation to the debt 'crisis', capital flight will have the effect of reducing the extent of exchange rate overshooting during the early days after the capital account is liberalized. An advantage of this is that the adverse effect of real exchange rate appreciation on resource allocation – *into* the non-traded goods sector and *away from* the traded goods sector (so worsening the current account) – based upon a 'false', or, at least, a temporary, real exchange rate signal, is reduced.

Secondly, however, capital flight has the effect of worsening the debt service problem which has to be managed by a country's government. After all, the additional capital inflows have to be serviced and, at the time of liberalization in the Southern Cone, debt service ratios, as well as many other indicators of debt burden, moved markedly upwards. On top of this, as was mentioned earlier, the interest earned on residents' capital placed abroad is unlikely to become available to a government to service the growing foreign debt. In these circumstances it is a country's gross debt rather than its net debt which is a debt service burden upon government.

An additional interesting point is that capital flight can also take the form of currency substitution in the domestic economy. It was reported that some \$3–\$5 billion in the form of currency circulated freely in Argentine in 1984 (Morgan Guaranty, 1985). The US dollar bill was apparently viewed as superior to the peso as a medium of exchange, store of value, standard of value and means of deferred payment owing to the very high and unstable rates of inflation being recorded in Argentina at the time. The irony, of course, is that Argentine residents, because of their government's failure to issue a stable domestic currency, substituted dollar bills for pesos and paid interest to the US for the privilege of doing so.

The 'Lenders' Trap'

If so many Latin American and other ldcs built up debt service obligations to levels which obviously threatened their creditworthiness, why did the international banks continue to make loans to them on a large scale? Once having made loans to a client state, banks can become locked in even if there is a threat that the client cannot service the debt. For the banks the choice is stark: either lend more money so that the service payments on the old loans can be made (in effect capitalizing the interest payments), or, declare the borrower to be insolvent and prepare to write off the loan.

New lending will be the chosen alternative so long as the expected benefit from doing so exceeds the expected cost. Following Cline (1984) the expected benefit of new lending is:

$$E(B) = (P_0 - P_1) \cdot D \qquad (12.6)$$

where P_0 and P_1 are respectively the probabilities of default before and after the new loan is made and D is the oustanding debt prior to the new loan. The expected cost of new lending is:

$$E(C) = P_1 \cdot L \qquad (12.7)$$

where L is the dollar value of the new loan. Net benefit of the new loan expressed as a percentage of outstanding debt is:

$$N(B) = E(B) - E(C) = P_0 - P_1 \left[1 + \frac{L}{D} \right] \cdot 100 \qquad (12.8)[2]$$

Hence, whether to make new loans depends upon the 'before' and 'after' probability of default and the size of the new loan relative to debt outstanding. A bank will make a new loan in circumstances where P_0 is high and L/D is small but the new loan is expected to bring about a marked reduction in the probability of default. For example, it was the world's largest debtor, Mexico, who precipitated the debt crisis by suspending debt service in mid-1982, yet the banking community rushed in with new loans. This was not surprising: Cline assessed that at that time in Mexico's case P_0 was 'substantial' while P_1 was low and the required new loans amounted to only 7 per cent of outstanding debt.[3]

Nineteenth and Twentieth Century Debt Management Arrangements

In chapter 10 it is argued that the Eurocurrency banks have played the role of financial intermediaries between debtor and creditor countries, so providing a system for managing international debt. This banking-organized debt management system is quite different to that developed in the last century when borrowers issued bonds rather than raising bank loans as a means of borrowing medium- and long-term funds from foreigners.

In the nineteenth century, and particularly in the inter-war period, bond prices would be written down if interest payments were delayed. Or, if the debt was threatened with repudiation the loss would be shared by many thousands of creditors. The international debt management system today is quite different as the immediate creditors are a group of relatively few banks. Debt repudiation, or even delay of interest payments, could bankrupt some of these banks and have serious implications for the wider international financial system. Nor is it entirely clear that a 'lender of last resort' could be arranged quickly enough through a central bank to head off a crisis, a major obstacle here being the difficulty of identifying the responsible central bank authority. The international bank threatened with bankruptcy could, for example, be the foreign subsidiary in London of a German bank intermediating loans largely denominated in US dollars. No precedent has yet been set to determine which of the three possible central banks – the Bank of England, the Bundesbank and even the Federal Reserve should act as lender of last resort.

Solving the Debt Crisis: Some Proposals

Several proposals to 'solve' the debt crisis were made soon after it came to a head in the late summer of 1982 but no general agreement has ever been reached as to the best single approach with which to deal with it. The reason for this was that there was (and is) a wide range of viewpoints as to the nature of debt problem that had actually developed during the 1970s and 1980s. The arguments were between those who claimed that the debt problem was a liquidity crisis, those who claimed that it was a question of long-term solvency and those who argued that it was an exchange rate or monetary-role crisis.

Those who claimed that it was a liquidity crisis – a temporary shortage of foreign funds with which to service international debts – were quite sanguine in that they saw negligible risk of sovereign default. Debtor countries could not afford to lose their creditworthiness and be cut off from foreign bank loans. They argued primarily for enhanced public funding of Third World debt service obligations and were confident that world trade would soon pick up – as it in fact did in 1984 and 1985. The principal credit channel that the liquidity 'school' wanted enlarged – and it was subsequently arranged – was through the IMF by an enlargement of up to $100 billion of the members' quotas. US Secretary of the Treasury Donald Regan (1983) also proposed (but without result) that an additional public fund be set up to be used to deal with threats to the stability of the international debt-management system. US Trade Secretary Baker's scheme (1985) to lend an additional $20 billion to debtor nations derives from this view.

A major difficulty with the 'enlarged-public-funds' viewpoint was that it was seen as 'bailing out the banks'. The banks were able to privatize the gains from international banking but the associated risks of default, or even delayed service payments, were to be socialized. Another viewpoint was that there was no point in a bailout which increased world debt when the problem was already too much indebtedness.

Those who felt that the debt problem was one of long-term solvency saw the prospects for long-term economic growth in the OECD area – and, hence, Third World exports – as poor. They suggested that, instead of merely increasing debt outstanding and postponing debt repayments, the existing loans should be consolidated and stretched out at lower interest rates. One of the main proponents of this idea was Kenen (1983) who proposed the setting up of an international organization that could sell bonds guaranteed by the member countries mainly the industrial nations. The organization would purchase developing country debt from the banks at $0.90 on the dollar. In exchange the banks would get long-term bonds due in ten to 20 years and lower interest rates. For example, Mexico had a $60 billion debt to commercial banks with an average maturity of five years and average interest rate of 14 per cent. The new organization would exchange with the banks $54 billion of ten to 20 year bonds for the debt at an average interest rate of 12 per cent. In effect the organization would act as a broker, paying the banks as it got paid by the debtor country, keeping the $6 billion as a reserve against default. The key feature of the scheme was the write-down of the value of the creditors' assets (the loans) in recognition of the near-impossibility of the debtors servicing the debt on the original terms. One of the main barriers to implementation of this proposal as Kenen said, was to induce the borrowers, the guarantor nations, the IMF and thousands of international banks 'to sit down and settle this thing. If they could, it would be a good trick'.

The third view taken of the debt problem was that it was (and is) an exchange rate or monetary system role crisis (Mundell, 1983). The fundamental point was that the flexible exchange rate system was seen as having ended money's role as a predictable measure of value. As a result, proper valuation of long-term trade and contracts had been destroyed, because it depended so much on the stability of currency exchange rates. Mundell felt that money was the central feature of civilization and its health depended upon the predictability of its value. He argued that

> today, in 1983, the US does not have a gold standard, or a Keynesian commodity standard, or a Friedman paper standard. It has a Volcker [Chairman of the US Federal Reserve Bank] standard. But who can predict the future value of the pound, the dollar or the yen on the basis of a Thatcher standard, a Volcker standard or a Naskasone standard?

The lack of a stable unit of international value meant that monetary discipline was negligible, debtors were encouraged to borrow as they thought that repayment would always be made in depreciated currency, as a consequence of world inflation. And, as Hogan and Pearce (1982) so cogently argued, the lack of monetary discipline has meant that for years together the same group of countries has been able to run current account deficits and accumulate debts while surplus countries were also not disciplined – either by an effective IMF or by an automatic adjustment mechanism. Instead, they preferred to place surplus funds with the international banking system, whose loans were being made to countries of deteriorating creditworthiness. See chapter 10 for a discussion of the Euro-currency system and chapter 11 on the IMF and Third World debt.

Notes

1 Equation 12.1 is easily derived as, by definition, aggregate national expenditure on goods and services is:

$$D = C + I + G + (X - M)$$

and the disposition of aggregate national income is:

$$Y = C + S + T + R_F$$

In short run flow equilibrium D and Y are set equal to each other and equation 12.1 is derived by rearrangement.

2 Equation 12.8 is obtained by rearranging:

$$N(B) = ([(P_0 - P_1)D - P_1L]/D)100.$$

3 For example if $P_0 = 80$ per cent, $P_1 = 40$ per cent and $L/D = 7$ per cent, net benefit expressed as a fraction of outstanding loans would be 34.2 per cent.

13 The European Monetary System

Introduction

As the global dollar standard system deteriorated in the late 1960s, and world inflation took off in the 1970s, nations found it necessary to make some sort of institutional response to improve international monetary relations. In 1971 the immediate reaction was a collective realignment of exchange rates, at the Smithsonian Institute in the December of that year. However, tensions within the newly established parity grid were too great and by 1973 many member countries adopted floating exchange rates. The members of the European Economic Community (EEC), while adopting floating exchange rates against non-EEC member currencies, also tried to create a 'zone of monetary stability' in Europe through various devices which concentrated upon narrowing exchange rate fluctuations between the members' currencies. From 1972 onwards the EEC members operated the so-called currency 'snake' of limited bands of exchange rate fluctuation, and in 1979 a more ambitious attempt at European monetary co-operation was sought when the European Monetary System (EMS) was created.

As is shown later in this chapter, the goal of European monetary union was not only the EEC's response to the instabilities of the deteriorating international monetary system but also lay deep within the political ideals of the EEC itself. Although not stated as an outright objective in the Treaty of Rome (1957) which created the EEC, monetary union would be an important step in the creation of a 'United States of Europe'. At the very least, failure of the EMS idea would mean that the EEC lost momentum towards the ultimate goal of European political and economic unity. Moreover, in the international monetary sphere, the EEC members would either have to continue to look towards the USA to provide stable world monetary conditions, as they did in the 1960s, or they would separately have to create a stable monetary environment. Separability, if it could be achieved at all, would probably have to be achieved through floating exchange rates (arrangements which have lost rather than gained favour in the last decade) or through erecting barriers to international money and capital flows which would sit uneasily with the goal of political and economic integration in Europe.

At the very minimum, monetary union requires that countries irrevocably fix exchange rates between national currencies and play by the 'rules of the game' by allowing the balance of international payments to govern changes in national money supplies. Unless the latter rule is followed, national inflation rates might differ and exchange rate adjustments would eventually be required. The adoption of a common currency (the 'Europa' has been suggested) would by political act irrevocably fix exchange rates between the Europa and each national currency. Then, changes in national money supplies would be governed by the size of balance of international payments disequilibria and exchange rate adjustments would never arise. In the case either of irrevocably fixed exchange rates or of a common currency, independent national monetary policy, including interest rate policy, would be ruled out. National central banks as they currently operate would cease to exist. However, a central bank for the currency area as a whole would be required if the area wanted to operate an independent monetary policy. The EMS provides for this through the creation of a European Monetary Fund (EMF).

This chapter continues with a discussion of the institutional, political and economic background to European monetary unification as it has developed into this decade. In separate sections the origins, objectives and institutional features of the EMS are discussed in turn. Then the anticipated economic benefits (macroeconomic and microeconomic) as well as political constraints are analysed. Finally, the efficiency of the EMS in bringing about greater monetary harmony in the EEC during its first five or six years of operation is examined.

The Origins of the European Monetary System

The EMS became effective in March 1979 and was represented by some observers at that time as being a major step on the road to monetary integration in Europe. In fact, so far the EMS is much less than this, but its adoption does show that the ideal of European political, economic and financial integration is still alive a generation or more after the Treaty of Rome was signed.

The Treaty of Rome recognized (in Articles 103–9) that increasing economic interdependence in the EEC required the co-ordination of national economic policies. This was to be brought about by a reduction in and, ultimately, removal of, tariff barriers and other controls on intra-EEC trade and capital movements. However, monetary union was *not* stated in the Treaty of Rome to be an objective. In fact, the idea of monetary union was taken up only in February 1969 at the Hague Summit of Heads of Government and was spelled out in detail in the Werner Report of October 1970. In the meantime the co-ordination of the EEC members' economic policies was delegated by the EEC Commission to three committees – the Committee on Short-Term Economic Trends (created in 1960), the Medium-Term Economic Policy Committee (1964) and the Budgetary Committee. These were later to be amalgamated into the Economic Policy Committee.

The Werner Report set the objective of complete economic and monetary union in the EEC by 1980. The political implications of transferring decision-making powers over matters of economic policy from the national to the Community level were made quite explicit in the report. EEC fiscal policy would have to be the responsibility of a new body, the Centre for Economic Policy, and a standing conference of Central Bank Governors would be needed to manage monetary policy. According to the Werner Report EEC exchange rates would initially be pegged against each other within a band of ±1.2 per cent, that is, narrower than ±2.25 per cent allowed by the then existing IMF rules. This proposal was the origin of the EEC's currency 'snake'. The need for convergence of national economic policies in order to facilitate economic and financial integration was explicitly recognized in the Report. Provisions were also made for financial compensation in cases of regional economic imbalances and unemployment which might arise when members lost direct control over national monetary and fiscal policies.

As it turned out, the currency snake and a European Monetary Compensation Fund (EMCF) were the only monetary institutions to be originated by the Werner Report. The original membership of the currency snake, which became operational in April 1972, was the six EEC countries (West Germany, France, Holland, Belgium, Luxembourg and Italy) plus the UK, Denmark, Norway and Sweden. Henceforth these countries were to intervene in the foreign exchange markets so as to reduce deviations in their exchange rates against the other snake currencies to ±1.125 per cent of the par value. These rates of exchange with all other currencies were permitted to vary by up to ±4.5 per cent as allowed by the December 1971 Smithsonian agreements. It was the snake's rules of narrower bands for exchange rate variation between the members' currencies than was allowed with the US dollar that led to the notion of the 'snake in the tunnel'. The members' exchange rates were confined to the narrower band of fluctuation but this band could move within the wider band relative to the dollar. The 'tunnel' was abandoned in 1973 when the EEC members moved on to a generalized float against the dollar.

The EMCF was an integral part of the snake system – created in April 1973 with $1.8 billion of EEC monetary support credits. The credits were to be extended to member countries in balance of payments deficit. Apart from being a credit giving organization, the EMCF was planned eventually to become the financial focus of EEC monetary policy. This was in line with the Werner Report's proposals for a common EEC monetary policy. However, neither the steps by which the EMCF would achieve its supra-national role, nor even a timetable were laid down. In any event, under the Brussels agreements of December 1978 on the new European Monetary System, the EMCF was to be replaced two years after the initiation of the System by the European Monetary Fund. Even now this has not happened. More importantly, by the mid-1970s, widespread currency turbulence had ruled out any real possibility of the EEC members narrowing the bands in which their exchange rates could fluctuate.

At most, the snake-EMCF system was a limited first step on the path to full economic and monetary integration. In fact, during the 1970s both institutions were destined to be of only marginal importance within the context of the wider international monetary system. The funding of the EMCF was quite inadequate as member countries experiencing pressure on their exchange rates were unable to raise an adequate quantity of intervention funds from the EMCF. Moreover, the UK was soon to leave the snake – in June 1972 – after a substantial loss of foreign exchange reserves. France also dropped out in January 1974, rejoining in 1975 only to leave again in 1976. Ultimately, the membership of the snake was reduced to that of West Germany and certain small economies closely linked with that dominant economy. In effect, the snake became a Deutschmark zone.

The Bremen Proposals

Currency instability together with the unsatisfactory nature of the snake-EMCF led the Chairman of the EEC Commission, Britain's Roy Jenkins, to reopen the question of European monetary integration in Florence in late 1977. The idea was enthusiastically championed by

President Valery Giscard d'Estaing of France and Chancellor Helmut Schmidt of West Germany. EEC Heads of Government also considered the subject in April 1978 at their Copenhagen summit. They met again three months later in Bremen where the new proposals for an EMS took on a definite form and were supported by the Community's members.

The Brussels Summit (December 1978)

Between the Bremen and Brussels summits intensive negotiations on the EMS were conducted at the intergovernmental level. But the agreed scheme was, in fact, little different from that originally envisaged by the West Germans and French and broadly agreed to by the other EEC members at the earlier Bremen Summit. Three countries – the UK, Italy and Ireland – initially declined to accept the EMS arrangements. However, within two weeks both Italy and Ireland agreed to join, in the latter's case following an improved offer of aid (i.e. subsidized interest rates on outstanding drawings from the EMCF). The UK gave as its reason for indefinitely postponing acceptance of the agreed terms the deflationary effect that might follow from tying sterling to the strong Deutschmark. However, although not a full member, the UK is not excluded from participating in either the EMS's credit arrangements or in any further negotiations on the development of the EMS.

Operation of the EMS

The main technical details of the EMS agreed at Brussels were as follows.

Exchange Rates

A parity grid system was adopted with an exchange rate band of ±2.25 per cent of declared par values. Currency market intervention is in the currencies of the participatory countries. Importantly, adjustments to par values are subject to mutual international agreement.

The European Currency Unit

The ECU is a basket of nine currencies, in proportions as set out in column 1 of table 13.1. Given the contents of the ECU basket, which were decided upon according to each country's importance in EEC

Table 13.1 Calculation of Deutschmark Exchange Rate with the ECU

	Amount of each currency per ECU	Cross rate[a] DM per . . .	DM cost of 1 ECU
	(1)	(2)	(3)
Deutschmark	0.828	1.00	0.828
Sterling	0.0885	3.905	0.346
French franc	1.15	0.324	0.373
Italian lira	109.00	0.00162	0.177
Dutch guilder	0.286	0.887	0.254
Belgium franc	3.66	0.0488	0.179
Danish crown	0.217	0.274	0.059
Irish pound	0.00759	3.076	0.023
Luxembourg franc	0.14	0.049	0.007
			2.246

[a] As reported in *The Financial Times*, 22 February 1984.
Given that 1 ECU = DM 2.246, then 1 DM = ECU 0.445.

trade, the value of a currency measured against the ECU depends upon its exchange rate with each currency component of the ECU. For example, column 2 of table 13.1 shows the cost in Deutschmarks of a single unit of each of the other eight currencies. Column 3 then shows that to purchase the £0.0885 contained in the ECU would cost DM 0.346 and the Deutschmark cost is shown for each of the other currency components. When the Deutschmark cost of each of the currency components is added, on 22 February 1984, the cost (or exchange rate) of 1 ECU was DM 2.246. Similar calculations would be done by computer for all the constituent currencies.

The ECU is used in a very limited way to settle 'intervention debts' between member central banks. The ECU is far from being a true 'ultimate' reserve asset and as yet does not exist as a separate entity. In fact, the EMCF, which runs the ECU accounts, only *borrows* the gold and foreign exchange which back the ECU from member countries on a revolving three month basis. Moreover, even when settlement of credits drawn falls due, the creditor country has to take only up to 50 per cent of the oustanding repayment in ECUs.

The Divergence Indicator

While the EMS is basically a parity grid system – like the snake – national currency–ECU exchange rates are used as a divergence indicator (what *The Economist* called the 'rattlesnake'!). This feature of the EMS resulted from a compromise between those who favoured the parity grid system and those who favoured the so-called 'basket system'. In the discussions prior to the Brussels Summit, countries with weak currencies, such as the UK and Italy, were in favour of the basket system because diverging currencies, for example, the strong Deutschmark, could be clearly identified. In a parity grid system just who is responsible for a divergence is ambiguous because simultaneously if one currency falls to its lower intervention limit another currency will reach its opposite limit in the exchange rate band. Weak currency countries feared that they would be obliged to adjust to a disequilibrium exchange rate even though they were not necessarily responsible for the exchange rate-divergences from central rates. Since the Deutschmark has to a limited extent become an alternative to the dollar as a reserve currency, weakness in the dollar is usually associated with strength in the Deutschmark against the dollar *and* other currencies. Under such circumstances West Germany has shown itself able to sterilize for prolonged periods the effects of currency inflow upon the Deutschmark's exchange rate. Under these circumstances adjustment would be forced upon weak currency countries because their foreign exchange reserves are not unlimited while the West Germans could resist for much longer the pressures to adjust upwards the exchange rate. The divergence indicator arrangements are meant to prevent this state of affairs arising. If any currency reaches 75 per cent or more of its parity value *against the ECU*, it is singled out as the diverging currency and is expected to take adjustment measures. However, because of the German stand on the divergence issue, adjustment, when the indicator is triggered, is 'presumptive' rather than automatic.

The European Monetary Fund

It was envisaged that the EMF would replace the EMCF in 1981, but its birth is still awaited. In the first instance, the main function of the EMF would be to run the ECU credit system and to oversee the exchange rate system. These are modest enough functions, taking over as they do from the EMCF. Where controversy over the EMF is strong, however, is over the far more ambitious plans to turn it into a central bank, with powers to create money that only national central banks currently enjoy. Indeed, in some of the more ambitious plans for European currency integration the EMF would become Europe's only central bank and individual member countries would lose their independent powers of money creation.

Credit Facilities

These take the following forms:

1 Very short-term unconditional credit for up to 45 days after the month of intervention with no limit on the amount of drawings. This feature of the EMS has its origins in the European Payments Union (1950) where multilateral payments imbalances were financed by automatic credit from the surplus countries.
2 14 billion ECU's of short-term credit.
3 11 billion ECU's of medium-term credit.

Objectives

The objectives of European monetary union (EMU) are several and lie in the fields of both economics and politics. The economic objectives are probably the more straightforward and will be considered with reference to the worldwide currency instability of the 1970s and to the theory of the optimal currency area (discussed in the next section). The political objectives behind EMU are closely bound up with those of the EEC itself – the creation of a 'United States of Europe'. An understanding of the political setting is essential because it helps to explain two important matters: first, why the Werner Report failed to institute anything more than very limited steps – the snake and the EMCF – towards EMU; and, secondly, the clearly limited scope of the EMS when measured against the goal of full EMU, and the slow progress towards the second stage – the creation of the European Monetary Fund with powers of a central bank.

Political Background

According to one influential view, the high-watermark in the history of the 'European movement' was the year 1953 (Swann, 1978, p. 22). In the Council of Europe Winston Churchill had called for a 'United States of Europe' and this goal was enthusiastically supported by many leading European politicians such as Jean Monnet, Paul-Henri Spaak and Robert Schuman. Moreover, the impetus for European unity given by the desire to avoid another European conflagration had achieved the creation of an important supra-national European institution: the European Coal and Steel Community (ECSC, 1951). The enthusiasm for European unity carried over to the visionary idea of a European Defence Community (EDC) and ideas were seriously floated for European political integration with the trappings of European democracy – a European Parliament and a European Court. However, neither the British nor, especially, the French were willing to submit sovereignty to the European ideal and the EDC Treaty never became effective.

The Treaty of Rome which created the EEC, when viewed against the background of the earlier failure of the so-called 'European movement' was an attempt to create European political unity by other means. The means were to be gradual economic integration, which would of necessity bring in its wake political integration. This process can be characterized as 'supranationalism through economic enmeshment'. Thus, as more and more economic decisions had to be taken at the European level, political decision-making itself would become more and more integrated.

Against this background it is not at all difficult to understand why European monetary unification has made so little effective headway. Perhaps more than any other single economic measure, currency unification would most diminish the sovereign powers of the EEC members. For management of money, credit and the exchange rate is of central importance in the armoury of national economic management.

Moreover, the reasons for the limited scope of the EMS as it was instituted in 1979 compared with the objectives of the Werner Report can also be appreciated: if full monetary unification was not possible in one gulp, then perhaps it could be achieved in steps – the enmeshment process in the monetary sphere. The first stage of the EMS involves no more the snake-EMCF system of narrower exchange rate bands and limited medium-term credits for the financing of intra-European payments deficits. However, the second stage, whose timetable had to be postponed, could take monetary unification a step further through the creation of a European proto-central bank, the EMF. But even on this most important issue, the conferences at Bremen and Brussels left entirely vague what exactly the functions of the EMF would be. Indeed, a conference of leading international monetary economists and monetary officials could only, even months after the EMS came into operation, tentatively and inconclusively consider no more than 'The EMF: Topics for Discussion' (Padoa-Schioppa, 1980).

The World Economic Background

Notwithstanding the political limitations, however, in the 1970s and 1980s the need for some measure of European monetary unification was almost certainly stronger than at any other time in the post-war period. Chapter 10 on the dollar standard explained the crucial role played by the USA in the post-war international monetary system. Essentially it fell to the USA to provide the monetary stability required for non-inflationary economic growth in both America and Europe. However, successive US administrations found this to be an increasingly difficult thing to achieve. It was argued in chapter 9 that the USA's failure to provide a stable monetary basis led to the world-wide inflation of the 1970s and beyond, the period that was characterized as 'the dollar standard on the booze'.

The desire of the Europeans in the late-1970s to create 'a zone of monetary stability' (quoted from the Bremen communiqué) through the creation of the EMS should be measured against this American failure as well as the latent desire on the part of the European Commission to continue with the process of enmeshment. Thus, the Werner Report of 1970 should be understood in a more nearly European context, while the origination of the EMS nearly a decade later is not only European in context but also grew out of the faltering international financial environment. The EMS was not created as a challenge to the established order (the dollar system) but as a response to the deterioration of that order. Indeed, the Americans welcomed the creation of the EMS, partly because it might contribute to the strength of Western Europe as a political and economic entity and partly because successive administrations have sought a reduced international role for the dollar.

A deeper understanding of the economic motives for and effects of monetary unification can be gained from a consideration of the concept of *the optimal currency area*. Attention is now turned to this matter.

Theory: The Optimum Currency Area

A fuller understanding of the range of economic costs and benefits that monetary union can bring can be gained from an examination of the theory of the optimum currency area. This theory, or rather, set of contributions to the understanding of the currency area phenomenon, can be used to show (a) why at this level of analysis the EEC finds appealing the idea of fixed exchange rates among its members; and (b) why there is great reluctance to embrace fully the concept of monetary union. That is, the benefits of monetary union found under point (a) are not obviously greater than the costs which would be found under point (b). Nor would benefits and costs necessarily be spread equally between the partners in the monetary union, i.e. monetary union may not be Pareto optimal (create a net benefit while harming no one member) even at the level of nation states, and almost certainly will not be at the level of national regions.

The first contribution to the theory of the optimal currency area was that of Mundell (1961) who argued that a pair or group of countries should fix the exchange rate between themselves only if labour mobility between them was high. Otherwise, countries with high unemployment should be allowed to devalue their exchange rates in order to maintain competitiveness and contain unemployment levels. Since labour mobility even between two regions in a given country is always far from perfect (compare for example Ohio's high and Massachussetts' low unemployment rates in the mid-1980s), Mundell's insight has been found to be most useful when considering the benefits of *breaking up* an existing currency area rather than the reverse. For instance, if it has the freedom to do so, might Ohio be able to cut its high unemployment rates by withdrawing from the Federal Reserve monetary union and devaluing the 'Ohio-dollar' relative to the US-dollar? A provocative thought, but not terribly useful in the American context. However, in cases where monetary disentanglement is a (distant) possibility – say, the break-up of the UK as desired by the Scottish Nationalists – then Mundell's ideas do have relevance if only they could be understood by the electorate. Mundell ruled out the absurdity of very small currency areas down to the level of the small town or village, arguing that the optimum currency area could not be too small, because first, when nearly all goods were 'internationally' traded, the lack of a fixed exchange rate would mean that the 'national' price level was unstable in the face of exchange rate variations, so reducing the usefulness of money and distorting the pattern of consumption, investment and saving; secondly, the proliferation of foreign exchange dealers and transactions would impose a real economic cost; and thirdly, thin foreign exchange markets are likely to be unstable in character.

The discussion of the optimal currency area concept was taken further by McKinnon (1963) who argued that an *open economy should adopt a regime of fixed exchange rates*. 'Openness' here is measured in terms of a high ratio of internationally traded goods (exports plus imports) in gross domestic product. The argument is quite simple: if the share of *non-tradeables* in GDP is low, that sector will not be able easily to absorb the effects of resources reallocation between itself and the traded goods sector that were induced by exchange rate fluctuations. In other words, a relatively small non-traded goods sector would have both its output and its price levels destabilized by variations in the exchange rate and that would be harmful to economic efficiency. A numerical example will make the point clearer. If non-tradeables constituted 40 per cent of GDP, a ten per cent fall in demand for and production of tradeables caused by a change in the exchange rate would require a 15 per cent (6/40 x 100) rise in the output of non-tradeables if the level of real GDP was to remain unchanged. This is a hefty adjustment in the non-tradeables sector and is caused as a secondary effect of a change in the exchange rate. Fixing the exchange rate under such circumstances would avoid, in the short term at least, such resource reallocation signals. If the exchange rate fluctuation had been caused by temporary factors which were later reversed, the fixing of the exchange rate would have meant that resource reallocation in the non-traded goods sector could have been avoided entirely, and this is beneficial. However, if the change in the exchange rate had been caused by fundamental factors, the fixing of the exchange rate could remain viable in the long term only if the resource reallocations in the non-traded goods sector were in fact made. But the speed of adjustment could be slowed down and dislocation costs reduced.

In a near-closed economy floating or adjustable exchange rates do not suffer from the same objection because the large non-traded goods sector can quite easily absorb the secondary 'shocks' caused by exchange rate variations. Again a numerical example is illustrative. A ten per cent fall in demand for tradeables (caused by an appreciation of the exchange rate), when the tradeables sector makes up only ten per cent of GDP, requires, for real GDP to be stabilized, only a 1.1 per cent (1/90 x 100) rise in the output of non-tradeables. This is an adjustment which can be achieved with relatively little disruption.

McKinnon's argument can be used to make out a case for European monetary integration, at least in the form of fixed exchange rates between the members. For each of the 11 EEC members intra-EEC trade as a percentage of total foreign trade and as a percentage of GDP is high (the Community averages were respectively 51 per cent and 13 per cent in 1981). Fixed exchange rates between the EEC members would reduce foreign exchange risk on a large proportion of the members' trade and could, therefore, be a further inducement to specialization in production among the members. Secondly, given monetary union, intra-EEC trade would be treated as internal or 'domestic' trade, so that the share of non-internationally traded goods in GDP would rise sharply. Thus, balance of payments adjustment between the EEC and the rest of the world could be affected by exchange rate adjustments, perhaps floating exchange rates. Indeed, European monetary integration would probably lead to the creation of three currency blocks – those of the dollar area, yen area and 'Europa' area (if that was the name given to the currency of Europe), each block with more or less fixed exchange rates between members of the group and floating exchange rates with the other two blocs.

Other economists have put forward theoretical arguments of the optimal currency area type. Kenen (1969) argued that countries with *diversified* export structures (such as the EEC) should try to reap the benefits of fixed exchange rates, because demand fluctuations at the microeconomic level for one exported product or service are more likely to be offset by an opposite fluctuation in demand for another product or service than is the case with countries with narrow export bases. Ingram (1969) and Scitovsky (1967) have appealed to a financial integration criterion of the optimal currency area. When financial integration between two or more countries is complete, balance of payments deficits can be easily financed without large and economically dislocative exchange rate or interest rate changes. So such countries would be free to practise a regime of floating exchange rates because the exchange rate is most likely to be stable and predictable. But when financial integration is far from complete, the authorities should fix exchange rates because the exchange rate might be unstable.

It is possible to use the degree of financial integration argument in support of the case for fixed exchange rates in the EEC. Some European money and capital markets tend to be integrated with American rather than other European capital markets so that there can be no assurance that intra-EEC capital flows would be stabilizing of exchange rates. Indeed the progress towards financial integration has been deadlocked since 1962 and the degree of financial integration has declined since then (Commission of the EEC, 1982). In fact, the government-managed intra-European credit facilities which have been in existence since the European Payments Union was created in 1950 right through to the EMCF arrangements of the early 1970s and the three-tier credit system of the EMS are an explicit expression of the official belief that private capital market flows are not necessarily always sufficiently stabilizing of European exchange rate movements.

The models of Mundell, McKinnon, Kenen, Ingram, and Scitovsky have been described as 'single criterion cases' (Ishiyama, 1975) and as such may be regarded as overly restrictive in their judgement of what is and what is not an optimal currency area. These contributors do point out just where exchange rate variation to correct balance of payments disequilibria is ineffective, unnecessary, or economically destabilizing; however, little is said about the positive benefits of monetary integration. A preferable approach would be to lay down in an explicit fashion the list of benefits and costs likely to be associated with the creation of a currency area (Ishiyama, 1975).

Four main benefits of a common currency can be listed:

1 As mentioned above, increased allocative efficiency and integration of production and trade will occur to some degree because, by eliminating exchange risk on intra-currency area trade, a common currency tends to improve the functions of money as a medium of exchange, store of value and unit of account. Thus, at the margin, economic specialization and integration will be increased.
2 The elimination of intra-currency area speculative capital flows will, to the extent that these flows were important, relieve the authorities of some frustration of their monetary control.
3 The members' pooling of foreign exchange reserves would lead to an economy in their desired level since trade imbalances within the area can be financed in local currencies (in Europe, ultimately the ECU) rather than dollars; and, for the currency area as a whole, random net trade imbalances with the rest of the world are likely to be smaller than the aggregate of the members' individual temporary imbalances.
4 Risk pooling will occur as risks are spread over a larger geographical space – a poor harvest or a strike in one area may be offset by a good harvest or overtime working in another area – the flow of foreign exchange reserves for the group of countries as a whole being stable.

The costs of a common currency are especially worrisome for a national government since these costs are likely to be obvious to the electorate while the benefits are much less so. An important cost of monetary integration is the loss of autonomy of monetary policy – to alter domestic interest rates or the aggregate money supply, or the exchange rate. Countries which persistently tend to have higher rates of inflation than the Community's average (Italy, Denmark), perhaps because of the existence of strong cost-push factors, would be condemned to decreasing levels of competitiveness and rising unemployment if the exchange rate was irrevocably fixed at a given level. Secondly, national control might also be lost over the stance (expansionary, contractionary) of fiscal policy if the currency area's overall fiscal stance became geared to the needs of external balance rather than the internal requirements of any single member. Finally, there is a strong presumption that backward economies, national or regional, within the currency area would suffer increasing rates of unemployment as the result of the combination of low labour mobility and high outward capital mobility.

The EMS: How Efficient Is It?

Measured against the goal of 'the creation of closer monetary cooperation leading to a zone of monetary stability in Europe' the EMS in its first five years or so was not particularly successful. However, there was one notable achievement – reduction in the degree of fluctuation in the *nominal* exchange rates of the EMS members. Nor could it have been expected that the EMS would have had an immediate success in harmonizing the economies of these countries given that it came into operation at a time of worldwide economic and monetary instability that was unprecedented in the post-war period. But it remained true that, into the mid-1980s at least, monetary divergences between the EMS members remained wide – particularly in terms of rates of inflation and movements in real exchange rates. These two factors were responsible for tension in the structure of nominal EMS exchange rates and the appearance, after 1980, of frequent changes in EMS central (par) exchange rates. The evidence supporting these points follows.

Inspection of graphs of the EMS members' exchange rates relative to the Deutschmark shows that in the first few years after the formation of the EMS in March 1979 their nominal exchange rates tended to move over time more closely together than in the preceding three years (BIS *Annual Reports*). This remained true in the fourth year (1982–3), although wider divergences between them began to appear. The impression of reduced nominal exchange rate variability is supported by figure 13.1 which shows the variability of nominal *effective* exchange rates for the EMS group of currencies together with that of the dollar, yen and sterling. It is clear that EMS nominal effective exchange rates were less variable than were those of the other three currencies, although there is an impression of increasing variability of EMS currency exchange rates throughout the first four years. Moreover, by 1982 the variability of effective exchange rates was somewhat higher than in some of the years prior to the creation of the EMS (e.g. 1976 and 1977). Where the EMS has had more definite success is in reducing the volatility of daily exchange rate movements: the Bank for International Settlements reported that in the EMS's first four years, the Deutschmark/French franc exchange rate movement was only 0.16 per cent while against

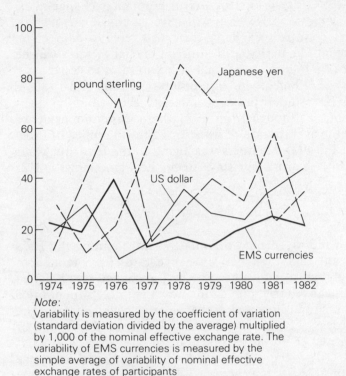

Note:
Variability is measured by the coefficient of variation (standard deviation divided by the average) multiplied by 1,000 of the nominal effective exchange rate. The variability of EMS currencies is measured by the simple average of variability of nominal effective exchange rates of participants

Source: IMF Survey, 29 June 1983, p. 186.

Figure 13.1   Variability of nominal effective exchange rates

both the dollar and the yen the Deutshmark fluctuated by a daily average of 0.53 per cent (BIS, 1983, p. 146).

Inflation Rates

Unless greater stability of nominal exchange rates is accompanied by a convergence of national inflation rates, real exchange rates cannot converge and are likely even to diverge from one another. Persistent divergence of real exchange rates breaks with the purchasing power parity condition and will eventually become a serious problem for fixed (or adjustable peg) exchange rate regimes. The country with the overvalued exchange rate will become less competitive both in foreign and home markets and unless the real exchange rate divergence is corrected, prolonged balance of payments disequilibria will cause tension in the parity grid structure of nominal exchange rates. Then, either the domestic price level will have to adjust downwards or else the deficit country's exchange rate will have to depreciate. Frequent adjustments in parity grid nominal exchange rates can be taken as evidence of a failure of national inflation rates to converge.

The evidence on EMS members' inflation rates to the mid-1980s is not encouraging. Consumer price movements showed only slight signs of convergence, although from 1981 there was some evidence of a reduction in the average rate of inflation. The variability of inflation rates among the EMS members was higher in the first four years (1979–82 inclusive) than at any time since the demonetization of gold in 1971.

Real Exchange Rates

The persistently wide divergence of inflation rates among the EMS members has meant that their real exchange rates have tended to move apart rather than to converge. The real exchange rate is calculated as the nominal exchange rate divided by a country's retail price index. Figure 13.2 shows how real exchange rates have behaved. The extent of this process of divergence is a measure of the degree of failure of the EMS to create in its first four or five years 'a zone of monetary stability'. It is the continuation of diverging real exchange rates that is responsible for the increased frequency of realignments

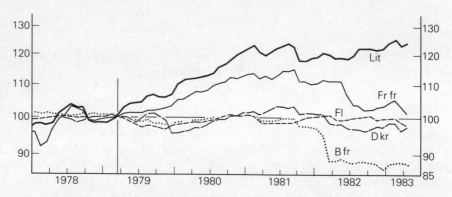

Source: Bank for International Settlements, *Annual Report 1983*,
        (Vol. 53), p. 145.

Note: Nominal exchange rate with the DM in index form divided
      by the index of consumer prices

Figure 13.2   Real exchange rates with the Deutschmark

of central rates between the EMS members. In fact there were seven such realignments between 1981 and 1983, and a further one in 1986.

Thus in its first four or five years the EMS contributed little to the convergence of monetary conditions in Europe, especially as measured by the behaviour of real exchange rates. However, this is not surprising given the background of world economic and financial instability and the lack of political will in Europe to proceed rapidly with the process of 'enmeshment'.

References

Agarwala, R. (1984), *Price Distortions and Growth*, World Bank Staff Working Paper, No. 575).

Ainley, M. (1985), 'Supplementing the Fund's lending capacity', *Finance and Development*, June.

Alexander, S. S. (1952), Effects of a Devaluation on a Trade Balance, *IMF Staff Papers*, 263-78.

Aliber, R. Z. (1973), *National Preferences and the Scope for International Monetary Reform* (Princeton Essays in International Finance, No. 101, November).

Allen, P. R. and Kenen, P. B. (1978), *The Balance of Payments, Exchange Rates and Economic Policy* (A Survey and Synthesis of Recent Developments), Centre of Planning and Economic Research, Athens.

Angell, J. W. (1926), *The Theory of International Prices*, Cambridge, Mass., Harvard University Press.

Argy, V. (1981), *The Postwar International Money Crisis*, London, Allen and Unwin.

Artis, M. J. and Currie, D. A. (1981), 'Monetary Targets and the Exchange Rate: A Case for Conditional Targets', in W. Eltis and P. Sinclair, *The Money Supply and the Exchange Rate*, Oxford.

Artus, J. R. (1976), 'Exchange Rate Stability and Managed Floating: The Experience of the Federal Republic of Germany', *IMF Staff Papers*, 312-33.

Artus, J. R. and Young, J. H. (1979), 'Fixed and Flexible Exchange Rates: A Renewal of the Debate', *IMF Staff Papers*.

Aubrey, H. G. (1969), *Behind the Veil of International Money* (Princeton Essays in International Finance, No. 71, January).

Backus, D. (1984), 'Empirical Models of the Exchange Rate: Separating the Wheat from the Chaff', *Canadian Journal of Economics*, 17, 824-46.

Baillie, R. T., Lippens, R. E. and McMahon, D. C. (1983), 'Testing Rational Expectations and Efficiency in the Foreign Exchange Market', *Econometrica*, 51, 553-64.

Balassa, B. (1964), 'The Purchasing Power Parity Doctrine: A Reappraisal', *Journal of Political Economy*, Vol. 72, pp. 584-96.

Balassa, B. (1978), 'Export Incentives and Economic Performance in Developing Countries', *Weltwirschaftliches Archiv*, Band 114, 24-60.

Balassa, B. (1982), *Adjustment Incentives and Development Strategies in Sub-Sahara Africa, 1973-78*, World Bank, Development Research Department, Report No. DRD41 (November).

Bank for International Settlements (1982, 1983, 1984), *Annual Report.*

Barclays Bank, *Barclay's Review* (various years).

Barro, R. J. (1974), 'Are Government Bonds Net Wealth?', *Journal of Political Economy*, 82, 1095-117.

Baumol, W. J. (1957), 'Speculation, Profitability and Stability', *Review of Economics and Statistics*, 263-71.

Bean, D. (1976), 'International Reserve Flows and Money Market Equilibrium, The Japanese Case', in H. G. Johnson and J. A. Frenkel (eds), *The Monetary Approach to the Balance of Payments*, London, Allen and Unwin.

Begg, D. K. H. (1982), *The Rational Expectations Revolution in Macroeconomics*, Oxford, Philip Allan.

Bernstein, E. M. (1982), 'The Future of the Dollar and Other Reserve Assets', in J. S. Dreyer, G. Haberler and T. D. Willett (eds), *The International Monetary System*, American Enterprise Institute for Public Policy Research.

Bhagwati, J. N. and Desai, P. (1970), *India: Planning for Industrialization*, (Oxford, Oxford University Press).

Bhandhari, J. S., Driskell, R. and Frenkel, J. A. (1984), 'Capital Mobility and Exchange Rate Overshooting', *European Economic Review*, 24, 309-20.

Bilson, J. F. O. (1978), 'Rational Expectations and the Exchange Rate' in H. G. Johnson and J. Frenkel (eds), *The Economics of Exchange Rates*, Addison-Wesley.

Bilson, J. F. O. (1981), 'The "Speculative Efficiency" Hypothesis', *Journal of Business*, 54, 435-51.

Bilson, J. F. O. and Frenkel, J. A. (1979), *Dynamic Adjustment and the Demand for International Reserves*, National Bureau of Economic Research Working Paper No. 407.

Bisignano, J. and Hoover, K. (1983), 'Some Suggested Improvements to a Simple Portfolio Balance Model of Exchange Rate Determination with Special Reference to the US Dollar/Canadian Dollar Rate', *Weltwirtschaftliches Archiv*, 19-38.

Black, J. (1959), 'Savings and Investment Approach to Devaluation', *Economic Journal.*

Black, S. W. (1976), *Exchange Policies for Less Developed Countries in a World of Floating Rates*, (Princeton Essays in International Finance, No. 119).

Blanchard, O. (1982), 'Credibility and Gradualism', unpublished manuscript, Harvard University.

Bomhoff, E. S. and Korteweg, P. (1983), 'Exchange Rate Variability and Monetary Policy under Rational Expectations: Some Euro-American Experiences 1973-1979', *Journal of Monetary Economics*, 11, 169-206.

Boyer, R. (1977), 'Devaluation and Portfolio Balance', *American Economic Review*, 276-300.

Branson, W. H. (1968), *Financial Capital Flows in the US Balance of Payments*, Amsterdam, North-Holland.

Branson, W. H. (1969), 'The Minimum Covered Interest Differential Needed for International Arbitrage Activity', *Journal of Political Economy*, 77, 1028-35.

Branson, W. H. (1975a), 'Stocks and Flows in International Monetary Analysis', in A. Ando et al. (eds), *International Aspects of Stabilization Policies*, Federal Reserve Bank of Boston, 27–50.

Branson, W. H. (1975b), 'Monetarist and Keynesian Models of the Transmission of Inflation', *American Economic Review*, 65, 115–19.

Branson, W. H. (1977), 'Asset Markets and Relative Prices in Exchange Rate Determination', *Sozial Wissenschaftliche Annalen*, Band 1.

Branson, W. H. (1983), 'Macroeconomic Determinants of Real Exchange Risk', in R. J. Herring (ed.), *Managing Foreign Exchange Risk*, Cambridge.

Branson, W. H., Haltunen, H. and Masson, P. (1977), 'Exchange Rates in the Short Run', *European Economic Review*, 10, 395–402.

Branson, W. H. and Haltunen, H. (1979), 'Asset Market Determination of Exchange Rates: Initial Empirical and Policy Results', in J. P. Martin and A. Smith (eds), *Trade and Payments Adjustment under Flexible Exchange Rates*, London, Macmillan.

Brasse, V. (1983), 'The Inaccuracy of Exchange Rate Forecasting Devices in the UK', C.U.B.S. *Economic Review.*

Brett, E. A. (1983), *International Money and Capitalist Crises*, London, Heinemann.

Brittain, B. (1981), 'International Currency Substitution and the Apparent Instability of Velocity in Some Western European Economies and in the United States', *Journal of Money Credit and Banking*, 13, 135–55.

Brunner, K. and Meltzer, A. H. (1982), *Economic Policy in a World of Change*, Carnegie-Rochester Conference Series on Public Policy, Vol. 17, Amsterdam, North-Holland.

Buiter, W. H. and Tobin, J. (1974), 'Debt Neutrality: A Brief Review of Doctrine and Evidence', in G. M. Von Furstenberg, ed., *Social Security versus Private Savings*, Cambridge.

Cairncross, A. and Eichengreen, B. (1983), *Sterling in Decline*, Oxford, Blackwell.

Carr, J. and Darby, M. (1981), 'The Role of Money Supply Shocks in the Short Run Demand for Money', *Journal of Monetary Economics*, 8, 183–99.

Carli, G. (1971), 'Eurodollars: A Paper Pyramid?', *Banca Nazionale del Lavoro Quarterly Review*, June, 95–109.

Caves, R. E. (1982), *Multinational Enterprise and Economic Analysis*, Cambridge, UK, Cambridge University Press.

Caves, D. and Feige, E. (1980), 'Efficient Foreign Exchange Markets and the Monetary Approach to Exchange Rate Determination', *American Economic Review*, 70, 1, 120–34.

Clements, K. (1981), 'The Monetary Approach to Exchange Rate Determination', *Weltwirtschaftliches Archiv*, 20–9.

Cline, W. R. (1983), 'Economic Stabilization in Developing Countries: Theory and Stylized Facts', in Williamson (1983), 175–208.

Cline, W. R. (1984), *International Debt: Systematic Risk and Policy Response*, Cambridge, Mass., MIT Press.

Commission of the EEC (1982), *Bulletin of the European Communities*, No. 4, Vol. 16.

Connolly, M. and Taylor, D. (1976), 'Testing the Monetary Approach to

Devaluation in Developing Countries', *Journal of Political Economy*, 84, 849–59.

Cooper, R. N. (1982), 'The Gold Standard: Historical Facts and Future Prospects', *Brookings Papers on Economic Activity*, No. 1, 1–56.

Cooper, R. N. and Lawrence, R. S. (1975), 'The 1972–73 Commodity Room', *Brookings Papers on Economic Activity*, No. 3, 671–715.

Coppock, D. J. (1980), 'Some Thoughts on the Monetary Approach to the Balance of Payments Theory', *The Manchester School*, 186–208.

Cosandier, P. A. and Laing, B. R. (1981), 'Interest Rate Parity Tests: Switzerland and Some Major Western Countries', *Journal of Banking and Finance*, 5, 187–200.

Crockett, A. (1977), *International Money*, Sunbury, Middlesex, Nelson.

Cross, R. and Laidler, D. E. W. (1976), 'Inflation, Excess Demand and Expectations in Fixed Exchange Rate Open Economies: Some Preliminary Empirical Results', in M. Parkin and G. Zis (eds), *Inflation in the World Economy*, Manchester University Press.

Cumby, R. E. and Obstfeld, M. (1981), 'Exchange Rate Expectations and Nominal Interest Rates: A Test of the Fisher Hypothesis', *Journal of Finance*, 36, 697–703.

Currie, D. A. (1976), 'Some Criticisms of the Monetary Analysis of Balance of Payments Correction', *Economic Journal*, 86.

Dale, W. B. (1983), 'Financing and Adjustment of Payments Imbalances', in Williamson (1983), 3–16.

Darby, M. R. (1983), 'Sterilization and Monetary Control: Concepts, Issues and a Reduced-Form Test', in M. R. Darby and J. R. Lothian (eds), *The International Transmission of Inflation*, University of Chicago.

Darby, M. R. and Lotihan, J. R. (1983), *The International Transmission of Inflation*, Chicago University Press.

Despres, E., Kindleberger, C. P. and Salant, W. S. (1966), 'The Dollar and World Liquidity – A Minority View', *The Economist*, 5 February 1966.

de Grauwe (1983), 'What Are the Scope and Limits of Fruitful Intervention Monetary Cooperation in the 1980s?' in Furstenberg (1983), 375–408.

de Vries, M. G. (1985), 'The IMF: 40 Years of Challenge and Change', *Finance and Development*, September 1985.

de Vries, R. and Porzecanski, A. C. (1983), 'Comments', in J. Williamson (ed.), *IMF Conditionality*, 1983.

Donovan, D. J. (1981), 'Real Responses Associated with Exchange Rate Action in Selected Upper Credit Tranche Stabilization Programmes', *IMF Staff Papers*, Vol. 28, 698–727.

Dooley, M. and Isard, P. (1974), 'The Portfolio Balance Model of Exchange Rates', *International Finance Discussion Papers*, 141.

Dooley, M. P. and Isard, P. (1980), 'Capital Controls, Political Risk and Deviations from Interest Rate Parity', *Journal of Political Economy*, 88, 370–84.

Dornbusch, R. (1973), 'Devaluation, Money and Non-Traded Goods', *American Economic Review*, 63, 871–80.

Dornbusch, R. (1976), 'Expectations and Exchange Rate Dynamics, *Journal of Political Economy*, 84, 1161–76.

Dornbusch, R. (1976), 'Exchange Rate Expectations and Monetary Policy', *Journal of International Economics.*

Dornbusch, R. (1980a), 'Evidence to the Treasury and Civil Service Committee', *Memoranda on Monetary Policy*, HC770, London, HMSO.

Dornbusch, R. (1980b, 'Exchange Rate Economics: Where Do We Stand?', *Brookings Papers on Economic Activity*, 1, 143-94.

Dornbusch, R. (1982), 'Flexible Exchange Rates and Interdependence', *IMF Staff Papers*, 30, 3-30.

Dornbusch, R. (1983), 'Comments' in G. M. Furstenberg (ed.), *International Money and Credit: The Policy Roles.*

Dornbusch, R. (1984), 'External Debt, Budget Deficits and Disequilibrium Exchange Rates', *NBER*, Working Paper, 1336.

Dornbusch, R. and Fischer, S. (1980), 'Exchange Rates and the Current Account', *American Economic Review*, 70, 960-71.

Driskell, R. A. and Sheffrin, S. M. (1981), 'On the Mark: Comment', *American Economic Review*, 71, 1068-74.

Duck, N., Parkin, M., Rose, D. and Zis, G. (1976), 'The Determination of the Rate of Change of Wages and Prices in the Fixed Exchange Rate Economy, 1956-71', in J. M. Parkin and G. Zis (eds), *Inflation in the World Economy*, Manchester University Press.

Dufey, G. and Giddy, I. H. (1978), *The International Money Market*, Englewood Cliffs, NJ, Prentice-Hall.

Edwards, S. (1982), 'Exchange Rates, Market Efficiency and New Information', *Economic Letters*, 9, 377-82.

Edwards, S. (1983), 'Exchange Rates and "News": A Multi-Currency Approach', *Journal of International Money and Finance*, 3, 211-24.

Edwards, S. (1984), 'The Order of Liberalization of the External Sector in Developing Countries', *Essays in International Finance*, No. 154, Princeton University.

Edwards, S. (1985), 'Stabilization and Liberalization: Chile 1973-1983', *Economic Development and Cultural Change*, Vol. 33, No. 2, January, 223-54.

Einzig, P. (1970), *A Textbook of Foreign Exchange*, London, Macmillan.

Fama, E. F. (1970), 'Efficient Capital Markets: A Review of Theory and Empirical Work', *Journal of Finance*, 25, 383-417.

Federal Reserve Bank of New York, *Quarterly Review*, Summer 1980, Vol. 5, No. 2.

Feige, E. L. and Pierce, D. K. (1976), 'Economically Rational Expectations: Are Innovations in the Rate of Inflation Independent of Innovations in Measures of Monetary and Fiscal Policy?', *Journal of Political Economy*, 84, 499-522.

Fleming, J. M. (1962), 'Domestic Financial Policies under Fixed and Floating Exchange Rates, *IMF Staff Papers*, 369-79.

Flood, R. P. and Marion, N. P. (1980), 'The Transmission of Disturbances under Alternative Exchange Rate Regimes with Optimal Indexing', *NBER*, Working Paper No. 500.

Flood, R. and Garber, P. (1982), 'Collapsing Exchange Rate Regimes', manuscript, *Board of Governors of the Federal Reserve.*

Frankel, J. A. (1979a), 'On the Mark: A Theory of Floating Exchange Rates Based on Real Interest Differences', *American Economic Review*, 69, 610–22.

Frankel, J. A. (1979b), 'Tests of Rational Expectations in the Foreign Exchange Market', *Southern Economic Journal*, 1083–101.

Frankel, J. A. (1981), 'On the Mark: Comment', *American Economic Review*, 71, 1075–82.

Frankel, J. A. (1982), 'A Test of Perfect Substitutability in the Forward Exchange Market', *Southern Economic Journal*, 406–16.

Frankel, J. A. (1983), 'Monetary and Portfolio Balance Models of Exchange Rate Determination', in J. Bhandari and B. Putnam (eds), *Economic Interdependence and Flexible Exchange Rates*, MIT Press.

Fratianni, M. and Wakeman, L. M. (1982), 'The Law of One Price in the Eurocurrency Market', *Journal of International Money and Finance*, 1, 307–23.

Frenkel, J. A. and Levich, R. M. (1975), 'Covered Interest Arbitrage: Unexploited Profits?', *Journal of Political Economy*, 83, 325–38.

Frenkel, J. A. (1976), 'International Reserves: Pegged Exchange Rates and Managed Float' in K. Brunner and A. Meltzer, (eds), *Public Policies in Open Economies*, Carnegie-Rochester Conference Series Vol. 9.

Frenkel, J. A. and Levich, R. M. (1977), 'Transaction Costs and Interest Arbitrage: Tranquil versus Turbulent Periods', *Journal of Political Economy*, 85, 1209–24.

Frenkel, J. A. (1978), 'Purchasing Power Parity Doctrinal Perspectives and Evidence from the 1920s', *Journal of International Economics*, 8, 169–91.

Frenkel, J. A. (1980), 'The Demand for International Reserves under Pegged and Flexible Exchange Rate Regimes' in *The Functioning of Floating Exchange Rates*, D. Bigman and T. Taya (eds), Ballinger Publishing Co.

Frenkel, J. A. (1981a), 'The Collapse of Purchasing Power Parity During the 1970s', *European Economic Review*, 16, 145–65.

Frenkel, J. A. (1981b), 'Flexible Exchange Rates, Prices and the Role of the "News": Lessons from the 1970s', *Journal of Political Economy*, 89, 665–704.

Frenkel, J. A. and Razin, A. (1980), 'Stochastic Prices and Tests of Efficiency of Foreign Exchange Markets', *Economic Letters*, 6, 165–70.

Frenkel, J. A. and Musa, M. (1980), 'The Efficiency of Foreign Exchange Markets and Measures of Turbulence', *American Economic Review*, Papers and Proceedings, 374–81.

Frenkel, J. A. and Rodriguez, L. (1981), 'Exchange Rate Dynamics and the Overshooting Hypothesis', *IMF Staff Papers*, 1–30.

Friedman, B. (1979), 'Optimal Expectations and the Extreme Information Assumptions of Rational Expectations Macromodels', *Journal of Monetary Economics*, 5, 23–41.

Friedman, M. (1953), 'The Case for Flexible Exchange Rates', in *Essays in Positive Economics*, University of Chicago, 157–203.

Friedman, M. (1969), 'The Eurodollar Market: Some First Principles', *Morgan Guaranty Survey*, October, 4–14.

Furstenberg, G. M. (1983), *International Money and Credit: The Policy Roles*, IMF, Washington DC.

Genberg, H. (1976), 'Aspects of the Monetary Approach to Balance of Payments Theory: An Empirical Study of Sweden', in H. G. Johnson and J. A. Frankel (eds), *The Monetary Approach to the Balance of Payments*, London, Allen and Unwin.

Genberg, H. (1977), 'The Concept and Measurement of the World Price Level and Rate of Inflation', *Journal of Monetary Economics*, 3, 231-52.

Genberg, H. (1978), 'Purchasing Power Parity Under Fixed and Flexible Exchange Rates', *Journal of International Economics*, 8, 247-76.

Genberg, H. and Kierzkowski, H. (1979), 'Impact and Long Run Effects of Economic Disturbances in a Dynamic Model of Exchange Rate Determination', *Weltwirtschaftliches Archiv*, 605-27.

Girton, L. and Roper, D. (1981), 'Theory and Implications of Currency Substitution', *Journal of Money Credit and Banking*, 13, 12-30.

Glahe, F. R. (1977), *Macroeconomics*, New York, Harcourt, Brace, Jovanovich.

Gold, J. (1978), 'The Second Amendment of the Fund's Articles of Agreement: A General View, 1', *Finance and Development*, March.

Goldstein, H. N. and Mikesell, R. F. (1975), 'Rules for a Floating Rate Regime', (Princeton Essays in International Finance, No. 109).

Goldstein, H. N. and Haynes, S. E. (1984), 'A Critical Appraisal of McKinnon's World Money Supply Hypothesis', *American Economic Review*, 74, 217-24.

Grassman, S. and Lundberg, E. (1981), *The World Economic Order*, London, Macmillan.

Gray, M. R., Ward, R. and Zis, G. (1976), 'The World Demand for Money Function: Some Preliminary Results', in M. Parkin and G. Zis (eds), *Inflation in the World Economy*, Manchester University Press.

Green, R. H. (1983), 'Political-Economic Adjustment and IMF Conditionality: Tanzania 1974-81', in Williamson (1983), 347-80.

Grossman, S. J. and Stiglitz, J. E. (1980), 'Information and Competitive Price Systems', *American Economic Review*, 66, 246-53.

Grubel, H. G. (1981), *International Economics*, revised edition, Homewood, Illinois, Irwin.

Guitian, M. (1976), 'The Balance of Payments as a Monetary Phenomenon, Empirical Evidence, Spain 1955-71', in J. A. Frenkel and H. G. Johnson, *The Monetary Approach to the Balance of Payments*, London, Allen and Unwin.

Guitian, M. (1981), 'Fund Conditionality and the International Adjustment Process', *Finance and Development*, Vol. 18, No. 2, June, 14-17.

Gweke, J. and Feige, E. (1979), 'Some Joint Tests of Markets for Forward Exchange', *Review of Economics and Statistics*, 334-41.

Haberler, G. (1949), 'The market for foreign exchange and the stability of the balance of payments', *Kyklos*, Vol. 3, 193-218.

Haberler, G. (1972), 'Prospects for the Dollar Standard', *Lloyds Bank Review*, No. 105, July, 1-17.

Hacche, G. and Townend, J. (1981), 'Exchange Rates and Monetary Policy: Modelling Sterling's Effective Exchange Rate' in W. Eltis and P. Sinclair (ed), *The Money Supply and the Exchange Rate*, Oxford.

Hakkio, C. S. (1981), 'Expectations and the Forward Exchange Rate', *Inter-

national Economic Review, 22, 663-787.

Hallwood, C. P. and Sinclair, S. W. (1981), *Oil, Debt and Development: OPEC in the Third World*, London, Allen and Unwin.

Halm, G. N. (1968), *International Financial Intermediation: Deficits Benign and Malignant* (Princeton Essays in International Finance, No. 68), June.

Hansen, L. P. and Hodrick, R. J. (1980), 'Forward Exchange Rates as Optimal Predictors of Future Spot Rates: An Economic Analysis', *Journal of Political Economy*, 88, 829-53.

Hartley, D. (1984), 'Rational Expectations and the Foreign Exchange Market', in J. Frenkel (ed), *Exchange Rates and International Macroeconomics*, NBER.

Hausman, J. A. (1978), 'Specification Tests in Econometrics', *Econometrica*, 46, 1251-72.

Havrylyshyn, O. and Alikhani, I. (1983), 'Is There a Case for Export Optimism?', *Finance and Development*, Vol. 20, No. 2, June, 9-12.

Haynes, S. E. and Stone, J. A. (1981), 'On the Mark: Comment', *American Economic Review*, 71, 1060-7.

Heller, H. R. (1976), 'International Reserves and Worldwide Inflation', *IMF Staff Papers*, 61-87.

Hewson, J. and Sakakibara, E. (1975a), *The Eurocurrency Markets and their Implications*, Lexington, Mass., Lexington Books.

Hewson, J. and Sakakibara, E. (1975b), 'Eurodollar Deposit Multiplier: A Portfolio Approach', *IMF Staff Papers*, July.

Hewson, J. (1976), 'Credit Creation in the Eurocurrency Markets – Is There a Case for Control?', in W. Kasper (ed), *International Money – Experiments and Experience*, Department of Economics, Australian National University, Canberra.

Hodrick, R. J. (1978), 'An Empirical Analysis of the Monetary Approach to the Determination of the Exchange Rate', in H. G. Johnson and J. Frenkel (eds), *The Economics of Exchange Rates*, Addison-Wesley.

Hoffman, D. L. and Schlagenhauf, D. E. (1983), 'Rational Expectations and Monetary Models of Exchange Rate Determination: An Empirical Examination', *Journal of Monetary Economics*, 11, 247-60.

Hogan, W. P. and Pearce, I. F. (1982), *The Incredible Eurodollar*, London, George Allen and Unwin.

Hood, W. C. (1983), 'International Money Credit and the SDR', *Finance and Development*, September.

Hooper, P. and Morton, J. (1983), 'Fluctuations in the Dollar: A Model of Nominal and Real Exchange Rate Determination', *Journal of International Money and Finance*, 1, 39-56.

Houthakker, H. S. and Magee, S. P. (1969), 'Income and Price Elasticities in World Trade', *Review of Economics and Statistics*.

Hughes, H. (1977), 'The External Debt of Developing Countries', *Finance and Development*, Vol. 14, No. 4, December.

Hume, D. (1752), 'Of the Balance of Trade', Essay V, Part II of *Essays, Moral Political and Literary*.

IMF (1970a), *International Reserves: Needs and Availability*, Washington, D.C.

IMF (1970b), 'The Role of Exchange Rates in the Adjustment of International Payments', *Report of the IMF Executive Directors*.

IMF (1983a), *IMF Survey*, 27 June.

IMF (1983b), *IMF Survey*, 7 November.

IMF (1983c), *Interest Rate Policies in Developing Countries*, Occasional Paper No. 22, Washington, D.C., October.

Ingram, J. C. (1969), 'Comment: The Optimum Currency Area Problem', in A. Mundell and A. K. Swoboda, *Monetary Problems in the International Economy*, University of Chicago Press, 95-100.

Isard, P. (1977), 'How Far Can We Push the Law of One Price?', *American Economic Review*, 67, 942-8.

Isard, P. (1978), *Exchange Rate Determination: A Survey of Popular Views and Recent Models* (Princeton Studies in International Finance, No. 42).

Ishiyama, Y. (1975), 'The Theory of Optimum Currency Areas: A Survey', *IMF Staff Papers*, Vol. 22, 344-83.

Johnson, H. G. (1961), *International Trade and Economic Growth: Studies in Pure Theory*, Chapter VI, London, Allen and Unwin.

Johnson, H. G. (1970), 'The Case for Flexible Exchange Rates, 1969' in G. N. Hack (ed.), *Approaches to Greater Flexibility of Exchange Rates*, Princeton University Press.

Johnson, H. G. (1976), 'Elasticity, Absorption, Keynesian Multiplier, Keynesian Policy and Monetary Approaches to Devaluation Theory: A Simple Geometric Exposition', *American Economic Review*.

Johnson, H. G. (1977), 'The Monetary Approach to the Balance of Payments: A Non-Technical Guide', *Journal of International Economics*, 7, 251-68.

Johnson, O. and Salop, J. (1980), 'Distributional Aspects of Stabilization Programmes in Developing Countries', *IMF Staff Papers*, March, 1-23.

Jones, M. (1983), 'International Liquidity: A Welfare Analysis', *Quarterly Journal of Economics*.

Kaldor, N. (1970), 'The New Monetarism', *Lloyds Bank Review*, July, 1-18.

Kenen, P. B. (1969), 'The Theory of Optimum Currency Areas: An Eclectic View' in R. A. Mundel and A. K. Swoboda, *Monetary Problems of the International Economy*, University of Chicago Press, 41-60.

Kenen, P. B. (1983), quoted in 'Foreign Debt Difficulties Prompt Proposals for Drastic Restructuring', *The Wall Street Journal*, 8 February.

Kincaid, G. R. (1983), 'Korea's Major Adjustment Effort', *Finance and Development*, Vol. 20, No. 4, December, 20-23.

Kindleberger, C. P. (1965), *Balance of Payments Deficits and the International Market for Liquidity* (Princeton Essays in International Finance, No. 46).

King, D. T., Putnam, B. H. and Wilford, D. S. (1977), 'A Currency Portfolio Approach to Exchange Rate Determination: Exchange Rate Stability and the Independence of Monetary Policy', in B. W. Putnam and D. S. Wilford (eds), *The Monetary Approach to International Adjustment*, New York, Praeger.

Klopstock, F. H. (1968), *The Eurodollar Market: Some Unresolved Issues*, (Princeton Essays in International Finance, No. 65), March.

Kouri, P. J. K. and Porter, M. G. (1974), 'International Capital Flows and Portfolio Equilibrium', *Journal of Political Economy*, 82, 443-67.

Kravis, I. B. (1970), 'Trade as a Handmaiden of Growth: Similarities Between Nineteenth and Twentieth Centuries', *The Economic Journal*, Vol. 80, No. 320, December, 850–72.

Kravis, I. B. (1978), *International Comparisons of Real Product and Purchasing Power*, Baltimore, John Hopkins University Press.

Krueger, A. O. (1978), *Foreign Trade Regimes and Economic Development: Liberalization Attempts and Consequences*, Cambridge, Mass., Ballinger, for NBER.

Krugman, P. R. (1978), 'Purchasing Power Parity and Exchange Rates: Another Look at the Evidence', *Journal of International Economics*, 8, 397–407.

Laidler, D. E. W. and Parkin, J. M. (1975), 'Inflation: A Survey', *Economic Journal*, 85, 741–809.

Laidler, D. E. W. (1976), *The Demand for Money*, International Text Book.

Laidler, D. E. W. and Nobay, A. R. (1976), 'International Aspects of "Inflation": A Survey', in E. Claassen and P. Salin (eds), *Recent Issues in International Monetary Economics.*

Laskar, D. M. (1983), 'Short-Run Independence of Monetary Policy under a Pegged-Exchange Rates System: An Econometric Approach', *Journal of International Money and Finance*, 1, 57–79.

Lee, B. E. (1973), 'The Eurodollar Multiplier', *Journal of Finance*, Vol. 28, September, 867–74.

Lerner, A. (1944), *The Economics of Control*, New York, Macmillan.

Levich, R. (1978), 'Further Results on the Efficiency of Markets for Foreign Exchange', in *Managed Exchange Rate Flexibility: The Recent Experience*, Federal Reserve Bank of Boston, 58–80.

Levich, R. (1979), 'On the Efficiency of Markets for Foreign Exchange', in R. Dornbusch and J. Frenkel (eds), *International Economic Policy Theory and Evidence*, John Hopkins, 246–67.

Levich, R. (1982), 'How the Rise of the Dollar Took Forecasters by Surprise', *Euromoney*, 98–111.

Liviatan, N. (1980), *Anti-Inflationary Monetary Policy and the Capital Import Tax* (Warwick Economic Research Paper, No. 171).

Lucas, R. E. (1977), 'Econometric Policy Evaluation: A Critique', in *The Phillips Curve and Labour Markets*, Carnegie-Rochester Conference Series on Public Policy, 1, 19–46.

Lutz, F. A. (1974), 'The Eurocurrency System', *Banca Nazionale del Lavoro Quarterly Review*, No. 110, September.

MacDonald, R. (1983), 'Some Tests of the Rational Expectations Hypothesis in the Foreign Exchange Market', *Scottish Journal of Political Economy*, 30, 235–50.

MacDonald, R. (1986), *Floating Exchange Rates: Theories and Evidence*, London, Allen and Unwin.

Machlup, F. (1971), 'The Magicians and their Rabbits', *Morgan Guaranty Survey*, May, 3–13.

Magee, S. P. (1976), 'The Empirical Evidence on the Monetary Approach to the Balance of Payments and Exchange Rates', American Economic Association, *Papers and Proceedings*, 66, 163–70.

Magee, S. P. and Rao, R. K. S. (1980), 'Vehicle and Non-Vehicle Currencies in International Trade', *American Economic Review, Papers and Proceedings*, May 1980.

Makin, J. H. (1972), 'Demand and Supply Functions for Stocks of Eurodollar Deposits: An Empirical Study', *The Review of Economics and Statistics*, No. 54, November, 381-91.

Marston, R. C. (1976), 'Interest Arbitrage in the Euro-Currency Markets', *European Economic Review*, 7, 1-13.

Mayer, H. W. (1970), 'Some Theoretical Problems Relating to the Eurodollar Market', *Essays in International Finance*, No. 79, February.

McCormack, F. (1971), 'Covered Interest Arbitrage: Unexploited Profits? Comment', *Journal of Political Economy*, 87, 411-17.

McCulloch, J. H. (1975), 'Operational Aspects of the Siegel Paradox', *Quarterly Journal of Economics*, 98, 170-2.

McKinnon, R. I. (1963), 'Optimum Currency Areas', *American Economic Review*, Vol. 53, 717-25.

McKinnon, R. I. (1969), 'Portfolio Balance and International Payments Adjustment', in R. Mundell and A. K. Swoboda (eds), *Monetary Problems of the International Economy*, University of Chicago Press.

McKinnon, R. I. (1969), *Private and Official International Money: The Case for the Dollar* (Princeton Essays in International Finance, No. 74, April).

McKinnon, R. I. (1973), *Money and Capital in Economic Development*, Washington D.C., The Brookings Institution.

McKinnon, R. I. (1974), *A New Tripartite Monetary Agreement or a Limping Dollar Standard?* (Princeton Essays in International Finance, No. 106, October).

McKinnon, R. I. (1976), 'Floating Exchange Rates 1973-74: The Emperor's New Clothes', in K. Brunner and A. Meltzer (eds), *Institutional Arrangements and the Inflation Problem*, Amsterdam, North Holland.

McKinnon, R. I. (1979), *Money in International Exchange: The Convertible Currency System*, New York, Oxford, Oxford University Press.

McKinnon, R. I. (1981), 'Financial Repression and the Liberalization Problem within Less Developed Countries', in Grassman and Lundberg (eds), 365-86.

McKinnon, R. I. (1982), 'The Order of Economic Liberalization: Lessons from Chile and Argentina', in Brunner and Meltzer (1982), 159-86.

McKinnon, R. I. (1982), 'Currency Substitution and Instability in the World Dollar Standard', *American Economic Review*, 72, 329-33.

McKinnon, R. I. (1983), 'A Program for International Monetary Stability', Discussion Paper No. 3, Center for Economic Policy Research, Stanford University.

McKinnon, R. I. and Oates, W. (1966), *The Implications of International Economic Integration for Monetary, Fiscal and Exchange Rate Policy* (Princeton Studies in International Finance, No. 16).

McKinnon, R. I. and Tan, K-Y. (1983), 'Currency Substitution and Instability in the World Dollar Standard: A Reply', *American Economic Review*, 73, 474-6.

McKinnon, R. I. et al. (1984), 'International Influences on the US Economy:

Summary of an Exchange', *American Economic Review*, 74, 1132–4.

Meade, J. E. (1951), *The Balance of Payments*, Oxford University Press.

Meese, R. A. and Rogoff, K. (1984), 'Empirical Exchange Rate Models of the Seventies: Do They Fit Out of Sample?', *Journal of International Economics*, 14, 3–24.

Meiselman, D. I. (1976), 'Worldwide Inflation: A Monetarist's View', in P. M. Barman and D. G. Tuerck, *World Monetary Disorder*, New York, Praeger, 21–66.

Michaely, M. (1962), *Concentration in International Trade*, Amsterdam, North-Holland.

Mikesell, R. F. (1983), 'Appraising IMF Conditionality: Too Loose, Too Tight or Just Right?', in J. Williamson (1983).

Minford, P. and Peel, D. A. (1983), *Rational Expectations and the New Macroeconomics*, Oxford, Martin Robertson.

Morgan Guaranty (various issues), *World Financial Markets*.

Mundell, R. A. (1961), 'A Theory of Optimum Currency Areas', *American Economic Review*, Vol. 51, 657–65.

Mundell, R. A. (1962), 'The Appropriate Use of Monetary and Fiscal Policy', *IMF Staff Papers*.

Mundell, R. A. (1963), 'Capital Mobility and Stabilization Policy under Fixed and Flexible Exchange Rates', *Canadian Journal of Economics and Political Science*, 475–85.

Mundell, R. A. (1968), *International Economics*, New York, Macmillan.

Mundell, R. A. (1983), 'The Debt Crisis: Causes and Solutions', *The Wall Street Journal*, 31 January.

Mussa, M. (1976), 'The Exchange Rate, the Balance of Payments and Monetary and Fiscal Policy Under a Regime of Controlled Floating', *Scandinavian Journal of Economics*, 78, 229–48.

Mussa, M. (1979), 'Empirical Regularities in the Behaviour of Exchange Rates and Theories of the Foreign Exchange Market', in K. Brunner and A. H. Meltzer (eds), *Policies for Employment, Prices and Exchange Rates*, Carnegie-Dorchester Conference Series on Public Policy.

Mussa, M. (1981), 'The Role of Official Intervention', *Group of Thirty Occasional Papers*, No. 6.

Myhram, J. (1976), 'Experiences of Flexible Exchange Rates in Earlier Periods: Theories, Evidence and a New View', *The Scandinavian Journal of Economics*, 78, 2, 169–96.

Myint, H. (1964), *The Economics of Developing Countries*, London, Hutchinson University Press.

Myint, H. (1971), *Economic Theory and the Underdeveloped Countries*, New York, Oxford University Press.

Niehans, J. (1975), 'Some Doubts About the Efficiency of Monetary Policy Under Flexible Exchange Rates', *Journal of International Economics*.

Obstfeld, M. (1982), 'Can We Sterilize?, Theory and Evidence', *American Economic Review Papers and Proceedings*, 72, 45–50.

Officer, C. H. (1976), 'The Purchasing Power Parity Theory of Exchange Rates: A Review Article, *IMF Staff Papers*, XXIII, 1–60.

Padoa-Schioppa, T. (1980), 'The EMF: Topics for Discussion', *Banca Nazionale Del Lavoro Quarterly Review*, No. 134, September.

Paish, F. W. (1936), 'Banking Policy and the Balance of International Payments', *Economica*.

Parkin, M., Richards, L. and Zis, G. (1977), 'The Determination and Control of the World Money Supply under Fixed Exchange Rates 1961-1971, *The Manchester School*, 293-316.

Patinkin, D. (1965), *Money Interest and Prices*, New York, Harper Row.

Pattison, L. (1976), 'The International Transmission of Inflation', in M. Parkin and G. Zis (eds), *Inflation in the World Economy*, Manchester University Press.

Polak, J. J. (1957), 'Monetary Analysis of Income Formation and Payments Problems', *IMF Staff Papers*, Vol. 4, November, 1-50.

Putnam, B. H. and Woodbury, J. R. (1980), 'Exchange Rate Stability and Monetary Policy', *Review of Business and Economic Research*, 15, 1-10.

Rabin, A. A. and Yeager, L. B. (1982), *Monetary Approaches to the Balance of Payments and Exchange Rates* (Princeton Essays in International Finance, No. 148).

Radcliffe Committee (1959), *Report on the Working of the Monetary System*, Cmnd 827, London, HMSO.

Radcliffe, L., Warga, A. D. and Willett, I. D. (1984), 'Currency Substitution and Instability in the World Dollar Standard: Comment', *American Economic Review*, 74, 1129-31.

Regan, D. T. (1983), 'The United States and the World Debt Problem', *The Wall Street Journal*, 8 February.

Robinson, J. (1937), 'The Foreign Exchanges', *Essays on the Theory of Employment*.

Roper, D. (1975), 'The Role of Expected Value Analysis for Speculative Decisions in the Forward Currency Market', *Quarterly Journal of Economics*, 89, 157-69.

Ross, M. H. (1983), 'Currency Substitution and Instability in the World Dollar Standard: Comment', *American Economic Review*, 73, 473.

Ruff, G. (1967), *A Dollar-Reserve System as a Transitional Solution* (Princeton Essays in International Finance, No. 57, January).

Rugman, A. M. (1981), *Inside the Multinationals*, New York, Columbia University Press.

Salant, W. (1941), 'Foreign Trade Policy in the Business Cycle', *Public Policy*.

Scitovsky, T. (1967), 'The Theory of Balance of Payments Adjustment', *Journal of Political Economy*, Vol. 95, 523-31.

Servan-Schreiber, J. J. (1968), *The American Challenge*, Harmondsworth, Penguin. The French versions came out one year earlier.

Sharpley, J. (1983), 'Economic Management and IMF Conditionality in Jamaica', in Williamson (1983), 233-62.

Shaw, E. S. (1973), *Financial Deepening in Economic Development*, New York, Oxford University Press.

Siegel, J. (1972), 'Risk, Interest Rates and the Forward Exchange', *Quarterly Journal of Economics*, 86, 303-9.

Sinclair, S. W. (1978), *Urbanization and Labour Markets in Developing Countries*, London, Croom Helm; New York, St. Martin's Press.

Spinelli, F. (1983), 'Currency Substitution, Flexible Exchange Rates, and the Case for International Monetary Cooperation', *IMF Staff Papers*, 30, 755–83.

Stern, R. M. (1973), *The Balance of Payments: Theory and Economic Policy*, London, Macmillan.

Stockman, A. (1978), 'Risk, Information and Forward Exchange Rates' in H. G. Johnson and J. A. Frenkel (eds), *The Economics of Exchange Rates*, Addison-Wesley, 193–212.

Swan, T. (1955), 'Longer-run Problems of the Balance of Payments' in *Readings in International Economics*, American Economic Association, London, Allen and Unwin.

Swann, D. (1978), *The Economics of the Common Market*, 4th edn, Harmondsworth, Penguin.

Swoboda, A. K. (1968), *The Eurodollar Market: An Interpretation*, Essays in International Finance, No. 64, February.

Swoboda, A. K. (1976), 'Monetary Policy Under Fixed Exchange Rates: Effectiveness, the Speed of Adjustment, and Proper Use', in H. G. Johnson and J. A. Frenkel (eds), *The Monetary Approach to the Balance of Payments*, London, Allen and Unwin.

Taylor, L. (1983), *Structuralist Macroeconomics*, New York, Basic Books.

Tew, B. (1977, 1982), *The Evolution of the International Monetary System 1945–81*, London, Hutchinson, 1977.

Tinbergen, J. (1952), *On the Theory of Economic Policy*, Amsterdam, North-Holland.

Tobin, J. (1969), 'A General Equilibrium Approach to Monetary Theory', *Journal of Money Credit and Banking*, 1, 15–30.

Triffin, R. (1960), *Gold and the Dollar Crisis*, Yale University Press.

Tsiang, S. C. (1961), 'The Role of Money in Trade-Balance Stability: Synthesis of the Elasticity and Absorption Approaches', *American Economic Review*, 912–36.

Vaubel, R. (1980), 'International Shifts in the Demand for Money, their Effects on Exchange Rates and Price Levels and their Implications for the Pre-announcements of Monetary Expansion', *Weltwirtschaftliches Archiv*, 116, 1–44.

Westphal, L. E. (1978), 'The Republic of Korea's Experience with Export-Led Industrial Development', *World Development*, Vol. 6, March.

Whitman, M. (1975), 'Global Monetarism and the Monetary Approach to the Balance of Payments', *Brookings Papers on Economic Activity*, 3, 491–536.

Williamson, J. (1973), 'International Liquidity: A Survey', *Economic Journal*.

Williamson, J. (1976), 'Exchange Rate Flexibility and Reserve Use', *Scandinavian Journal of Economics*, 78, 327–39.

Williamson, J. (1977), *The Failure of World Monetary Reform 1971–74*, Nelson.

Williamson, J. (1983), *IMF Conditionality*, Cambridge, Mass., London, Tokyo, MIT Press.

Yeager, L. B. (1958), 'A Rehabilitation of Purchasing Power Parity', *Journal of Political Economy*, LXVI, 516–30.

Zecher, J. R. (1976), 'Monetary Equilibrium and International Reserve Flows in Australia' in J. A. Frenkel and H. G. Johnson (eds), *The Monetary Approach to the Balance of Payments*, London, Allen and Unwin.

Zulu, J. B. and Nsouli, S. M. (1984), 'Adjustment Programmes in Africa', *Finance and Development*, Vol. 21, No. 1, March, 5-9.

Index